# A HISTORY OF PAGAN EUROPE

# A HISTORY
# OF PAGAN EUROPE

*Prudence Jones and
Nigel Pennick*

London and New York

First published 1995
by Routledge
11 New Fetter Lane, London EC4P 4EE

Simultaneously published in the USA and Canada
by Routledge
29 West 35th Street, New York, NY 10001

Reprinted 1995

First published in paperback 1997

© 1995 Prudence Jones and Nigel Pennick

Typeset in Garamond by Florencetype Ltd, Stoodleigh, Devon

Printed and bound in Great Britain by
Biddles Ltd, Guildford and King's Lynn

*British Library Cataloguing in Publication Data*
A catalogue record for this book is available from the British Library.

*Library of Congress Cataloguing in Publication Data*
Jones, Prudence.
A history of pagan Europe/Prudence Jones and Nigel Pennick.
p. cm.
Includes bibliographical references and index.
1. Europe–Religion. 2. Paganism–History. 3. Mythology,
European. 4. Goddess religion. I. Pennick, Nigel. II. Title.
BL689.J66 1995
291'.094–dc20   94–21101

ISBN 0–415–09136–5 (hbk)
ISBN 0–415–15804–4 (pbk)

# CONTENTS

# ILLUSTRATIONS

## MAPS

## PLATES

# PREFACE AND
# ACKNOWLEDGEMENTS

This book has been in the making for twenty years, since one of the authors lived in Canada, a European culture made intangibly different by the absence of encrusted layers of European history. Part of the reason for this intangible difference is made clear in the present volume. The European Pagan heritage is one that is generally overlooked, but here we bring it to light.

Over the years many people have helped with ideas and research. For the present volume, two people in particular have given of their time and expertise and our manuscript would be much the poorer without them. One is Mr Phil Line, who kindly offered his considerable knowledge of Finnic and Baltic religion in reading our chapters 9 and 10. The other, and principal helper, is Dr Ronald Hutton, who valiantly read through the whole manuscript, making many observations on matters of fact, restraining any impulse to comment on points of interpretation, but keeping us up to date with current scholarship on the subject. Any errors that remain are ours and not theirs.

We are acutely aware that worthwhile research is impossible without easy access to literary sources and commentaries. The open bookstacks of the Cambridge University Library are a blessing to the serious investigator, and its friendly and help-ful staff turn research into a pleasure.

All references are credited in the footnotes, but we are grateful to the following for permission to reprint longer passages of copyright material:

Viking Penguin, Inc., Laurence Pollinger Ltd and the Estate of Frieda Lawrence Ravagli for the quotation from D.H. Lawrence on p. 2; Thomas Kinsella for the quotation from his edition of *The Táin* on p. 91; Chatto & Windus for the quota-tions from the *Orkneyinga Saga* on p. 150; Basil Blackwell Ltd and Harper Collins USA for the quotation from J.M. Wallace-Hadrill's *The Barbarian West* on p. 152; and Macmillan Ltd for the quotation from Eric Christiansen's translation of the *Galician-Livonian Chronicle* on p. 172. All attempts at tracing the copyright holder of the quotations from John Holland Smith's *Death of Classical Paganism* in chapter 4 have been unsuccessful, but we are grateful to Cassell plc, present owners of the Geoffrey Chapman imprint, for their help in the matter.

Prudence Jones
Nigel Pennick
Lammas 1994

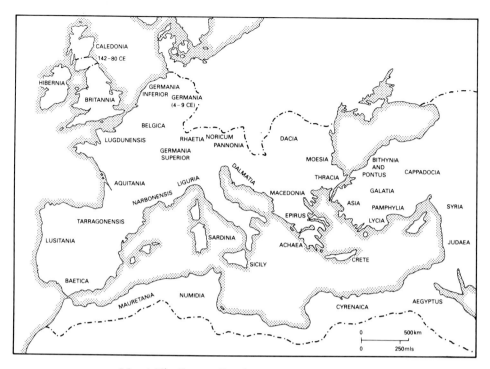

*Map 1* The Roman Empire at its maximum extent
(dates in brackets denote short-term occupations).

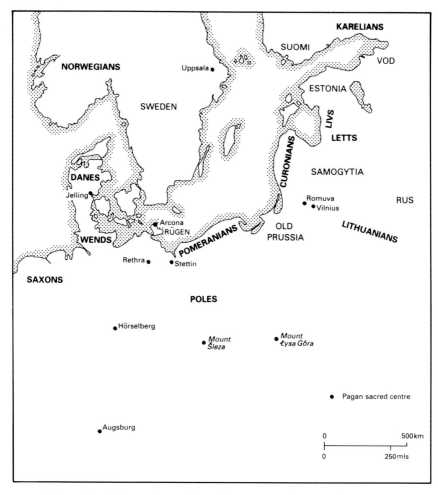

*Map 2* The Baltic and East–Central Europe, tenth to twelfth century.

# 1

# INTRODUCTION: PAGANISM OLD AND NEW

In this book we describe the hidden history of Europe, the persistence of its native religion in various forms from ancient times right up to the present day. Most people today are more familiar with native traditions from outside Europe than with their own spiritual heritage. The Native American tradition, the tribal religions of Africa, the sophistication of Hindu belief and practice and the more recently revived Japanese tradition, Shinto, are widely acknowledged as the authentic native animistic traditions of their respective areas. In marked contrast, the European native tradition, from the massive civilisations of Greece and Rome to the barely documented tribal systems of the Picts, the Finns and others on the northern margins of the continent, has been seen as having been obliterated totally. This tradition is presented as having been superseded first by Christianity and Islam and, more recently, by post-Christian humanism. In this book we argue that, on the contrary, it has continued to exist and even to flourish more or less openly up to the present day, when it is undergoing a new restoration.

But first to define our terms. The word 'pagan' (small 'p') is often used pejoratively to mean simply 'uncivilised', or even 'un-Christian' (the two generally being assumed to be identical), in the same way that 'heathen' is used. Its literal meaning is 'rural', 'from the countryside (*pagus*)'. As a religious designation it was used first by early Christians in the Roman Empire to describe followers of the other (non-Jewish) religions, not, as was once thought, because it was mainly country bumpkins rather than sophisticated urban freethinkers who followed the Old Ways, but because Roman soldiers of the time used the word *paganus*, contemptuously, for civilians or non-combatants. The early Christians, thinking of themselves as 'soldiers of Christ', looked down on those who did not follow their religion as mere stay-at-homes, *pagani*. This usage does not seem to have lasted long outside the Christian community. By the fourth century, 'Pagan' had returned closer to its root meaning and was being used non-polemically to describe anyone who worshipped the spirit of a given locality or *pagus*.[1]

The name stuck long after its origin had been forgotten, and developed a new overlay of usage, referring to the great Classical civilisations of Greece

1

and Rome, Persia, Carthage, etc. Early Christian writers composed diatribes 'against the Pagans', by which they meant philosophers and theologians such as Plato, Porphyry, Plutarch, Celsus and other predecessors or contemporaries. Much later, when Classical literature resurfaced in the European Renaissance, the literati of the time composed essays on Pagan philosophy, and by the nineteenth century the use of the word as a near-synonym for 'Classical' had become established. At the beginning of the twentieth century, D.H. Lawrence's literary group 'The Pagans' drew its inspiration from Greece and what he later called its 'big, old Pagan vision, before the *idea* and the concept of personality made everything so small and tight as it is now'.[2]

Lawrence's terminology has overtones of more recent contemporary usage, where 'Pagan' is employed once more in its root meaning to describe a Nature-venerating religion which endeavours to set human life in harmony with the great cycles embodied in the rhythms of the seasons. In what follows we adhere broadly to this convention, using the word 'Paganism' (capital 'P') to refer to Nature-venerating indigenous spiritual traditions generally, and in particular to that of Europe, which has been specifically reaffirmed by its contemporary adherents under that name. Pagan religions, in this sense, have the following characteristics in common:

- They are polytheistic, recognising a plurality of divine beings, which may or may not be avatars or other aspects of an underlying unity/duality/trinity etc.
- They view Nature as a theophany, a manifestation of divinity, not as a 'fallen' creation of the latter.
- They recognise the female divine principle, called the Goddess (with a capital 'G', to distinguish her from the many particular goddesses), as well as, or instead of, the male divine principle, the God. (Throughout this book we use the word 'god' exclusively to refer to male divinities, not to the divine source or godhead itself.)

In this sense all native animistic religions worldwide are Pagan, fulfilling all three characteristics. A religion such as Hinduism is Pagan, but Judaism, Islam and Christianity are obviously not, since they all deny the Goddess as well as one or both of the other characteristics. Buddhism, which grew out of the native Hindu tradition, is a highly abstract belief system, dealing with that which is beyond time and manifestation rather than with the interventions of deities in the world. In its pure form it retains little in common with its Pagan parent. All three characteristics listed above are, however, shared by modern Paganism in its various forms with the ancient religions of the peoples of Europe, as this book will show.

In recent years many people of European origin have been drawing on the ancient indigenous tradition as the basis of a new religion for the twenty-first century. This new religion, called neo-Paganism or simply Paganism, is most broadly a form of Nature-mysticism. It is a belief which views the Earth and all material things as a theophany, an outpouring of the divine presence, which itself is usually personified in the figure of the Great Goddess and her consort, the God or masculine principle of Nature. Between them, these two principles are thought to encompass all existence and all development. In some ways this is a new religion for the New Age. Modern thought is represented in these two basic divinities whose influence is complementary rather than hierarchical or antagonistic. Present-day Pagans tend to see all gods and goddesses as being personifications of these two, in contrast to the situation in antiquity, when the many gods and goddesses of the time were usually thought of as truly independent entities. In its most widely publicised form, neo-Paganism is a theology of polarity, rather than the polytheism of ancient European culture.

But modern Paganism is also an outgrowth from the old European tradition. It has reclaimed the latter's sacred sites, festivals and deities from obscurity and reinterpreted them in a form which is intended to be a living continuation of their original function. Followers of specific paths within it such as Druidry, Wicca and Ásatrú aim to live a contemporary form of those older religions which are described or hinted at in ancient writings, as in Iceland, where Ásatrú is a legally established religion, drawing its guidelines directly from the Old Norse sagas and shaping their outlook into a form which is continuous with the past but appropriate for the twentieth century. At the opposite extreme, many neo-Pagans, in Anglo-Saxon countries in particular, follow no structured path but adhere to a generally Nature-venerating, polytheistic, Goddess-centred outlook which is of a piece with the general religious attitude chronicled here.

Why has Paganism arisen again in modern Europe and America? We deal with the historical process in the final chapter, but the underlying impetus seems to have been first, the search for a religion which venerated the Goddess and so gave women as well as men the dignity of beings who bear the 'lineaments of divinity'. This has been thought necessary by women whose political emancipation has not been paralleled by an equivalent development in their religious status. (Even in Pagan, polytheistic Hinduism the cult of Kali, the Great Mother, is one of the most rapidly growing popular religions at the present time.[3]) Secondly, in Europe and America a greater respect for the Earth has come into prominence. The ecological 'green' movement has gone hand in hand with a willingness to pay attention to the intrinsic pattern of the physical world, its rhythm and its 'spirit of place'. This has led to a renewed recognition of the value of understanding traditional skills and beliefs and their underlying philosophy, which is generally Pagan. And finally, the influence of Pagan philosophies from the Orient has gone hand in hand with this development, providing a sophisticated rationale for practices which might in former times have been dismissed as superstitious and unfounded. The Pagan resurgence thus seems to be part of a general process of putting humanity, long seen by both the monotheistic religions and by secular materialism in abstraction from its surroundings, back into a more general context. This context is both physical, by reference to the material world understood as an essential part of life, and chronological, as shown in the search for modern continuity with ancient philosophies. The ancient religions are often not well known outside their areas of academic specialisation, and the evidence for their continuation is often misunderstood or misrepresented as 'accident' or 'superstition'. It is the evidence for such continuity which this book investigates.

The area of our study covers the whole of Europe, beginning with Greece and the eastern Mediterranean, home of the earliest written records; continuing west by way of Rome and its Empire; then through the so-called 'Celtic fringe' of France, Britain and parts of the Low Countries; then to what are now Germany and Scandinavia; and finally to eastern and central Europe, the Baltic states and Russia, which (apart from Russia and the South Slav states) emerged most recently into historical record. Europe in this sense is a geographical entity divided roughly into north and south by the Alps, and into east and west by the Prague meridian. After the Holy Roman Empire in the west and the Byzantine Empire in the east defined Christendom between them, Europe became a cultural unity, and its native religious tradition disappeared area by area into relative obscurity. This vital, yet half-hidden, European tradition is what we put on record here.

The centuries covered run from the dawn of recorded history to the present day: different timescales in different areas. The process of interpreting Stone-age remains is too extensive and currently too embattled to be capable of fair handling in the context of this book. It is enough to describe what people believed and what they did, at what times and in what places. In this lies a fascinating story, and we shall begin with the earliest records.

# 2

# THE GREEKS AND THE EASTERN MEDITERRANEAN

The earliest written records in Europe come from Crete. This civilisation, flourishing without a break from about 2800 to the beginning of the 300-year-long Dark Age in about 1100 BCE, provides a unique link between archaeology and written history. From later Greek legend (written down after 800 BCE) we hear that Crete was well populated and prosperous, that its navy ruled the seas, and that one of its kings, Minos, exacted tribute of seven boys and seven girls every seven years from Athens. These victims were said to be sacrificed to the Minotaur, a monster half man, half bull, which lived at the centre of a labyrinth built by the great technician Daedalus.[1] The Greeks spoke of the main deity of the island as Poseidon, their own god of the sea, earthquakes and storms, and of his cult animal as the bull. Archaeology shows evidence of high culture and prosperity, of a lack of fortifications indicating protection by the sea rather than by a garrison. It shows an extensive bull-cult, and in the deciphered Cretan writings (the so-called Linear B script, dating from around 1500 BCE) Poseidon himself is named. His name means simply 'Lord'.

However, Poseidon is never depicted, at least in human form, in the art of the Cretans themselves. The only anthropomorphic divinity which is pictured throughout Cretan iconography is, in fact, a goddess, or several goddesses, which in style resemble one from nearby Asia Minor who was later known as the Great Mother. This goddess was worshipped continuously in Asia Minor from the seventh millennium before our era until the fall of the Roman Empire.[2] Her worship was brought to Athens and later to Rome. Nevertheless, the Cretan inscriptions do not name a Great Mother. They mention various goddesses, some known from Greek times, such as Hera and Athene, and others who are unknown from later writings.

At this time many peoples in the Near East, an area with which Crete had trading links, worshipped goddesses similar to the later Great Mother, each accompanied by a male consort who was named but never portrayed, a sky-god of lightning and storms. Examples are the Syrian Atargatis and Ramman, and, of course, the Canaanite Asherah and Baal, against whose worship the Israelite prophets of the rival god Jahweh campaigned.[3] A double axe like that of the Near Eastern sky-gods also appears in Cretan art, but in Crete it is almost always found in the hands of a woman, a goddess, presumably, or her priestess. Its Cretan name is *labrys*, and it apparently gave its name to the labyrinth, home of the monstrous Minotaur, half man, half bull. In ninth-century Canaan, Asherah, represented not by a human image but by a tree or a pillar, had a bull as her cult animal, the bull that is criticised by the prophets of Jaweh in the Old Testament as the golden calf. It is heir to a long tradition of bull images reaching back to Çatal Hüyük in the seventh millennium BCE, which itself no doubt had another legacy in the bull-cult of Egypt, likewise an active participant in the political and trading network of the eastern Mediterranean. It is against this background of deity-forms and sacred images that the bull horns, bull sacrifices and bull-god of legendary Crete must be seen.

The Greek goddess Hera's epithet, 'ox-eyed', may also recall the Cretan goddess and her contemporaries in the Near East. Her original cult image at Samos was a plank, and at Argos a pillar, later decorated with garlands and jewels, but in its original form recalling the wooden pillar of Asherah. The oldest temples in Greek culture (dating from about 800 BCE) were built to house cult images of this goddess, which may be because she was the most important deity of the time, or perhaps because her image was thought of as most in need of protection.[4] As late as the first century of our era, Lucian, describing the worship of the Great Mother Atargatis in Syria, calls the goddess Hera, and her consort, the sky-god Ramman, he calls Zeus. Such persistent accounts and images of the Queen of the Immortals, her pillar, her ox and her consort, the aniconic god of storms and (in Greece and Asia) lightning or (in Crete) sea and earthquakes, are difficult to ignore. This storm-god – Baal, Ramman, Poseidon, Zeus – is no boyish son of the Great Mother, he is not Tammuz or Attis, but an independent principle, worshipped in his own right alongside the goddess and sometimes described as her brother (as Zeus is of Hera, and Baal is of Ana't). In using gender to symbolise a complementary duality the early culture of Greece, through Crete, appears to be continuous with that of the Near East.

Many sanctuaries in later Greek culture centred on a sacred tree, and the Cretan icons reveal a similar practice. The single tree, fenced or walled off, with or without an altar beside it, is a universal feature of European sacred culture, and indeed it appears throughout Eurasia and Africa. In Minoan Crete the icons show people dancing in the walled-off area around a single fig or olive tree. Sometimes a goddess appears hovering in the air above the dancers, perhaps seen by them in a visionary state brought on by their activity. Once more, Greek legend (e.g. the *Iliad* XVIII.591) tells how King Minos built a dancing-floor for his daughter Ariadne. Some of the early tombs also have what appear to be dancing-floors next to them. Were the dances a solemn celebration of the ritual event, as in later Greek choral practice? Or did the dancers dance themselves into ecstasy in order to see

*Plate 2.1* Cretan seal showing female figures, perhaps goddesses or priestesses, with the familiar symbol of the double axe and the Sun and Moon. The waning Moon and shield-bearing warrior (a god?) on the left may indicate death and diminishment; the Sun and the berries or grapes on the right may indicate life and abundance, 1500 BCE.

their deities, as did the later Greek worshippers of Dionysos? We do not know.

Another Cretan goddess we know of (from the *Odyssey* XIX.188) is Eileithyia, whose cave is found at Amnisos near Knossos. In this cave are found shards of pottery dating from neolithic to Roman times. Eileithyia was the Greek goddess of childbirth and her cave is a remarkable site. At the entrance is a rock formation similar to a recumbent belly with a noticeable navel. At the back is what appears to be a seated figure, and near it is a pool of mineral water, a healing spring. In the middle of the cave is a stalagmite which unmistakably resembles a female figure, although the top of it (the head) has been broken off. It is surrounded by a low wall, with a stone block in front which may have served as an altar. The goddess-like stalagmite was worn smooth by constant touching. Here is a Goddess site at which worship seems to have been continuous throughout human habitation in the area.[5]

The deities were also worshipped on mountain tops, where we have the only archaeological evidence of sacrifice by fire. The charred remains both of votive terracottas and of animals have been found, but otherwise there is no evidence, literary or pictorial, of what was done there or which deities were worshipped. In the cities, however, many houses had a sanctuary or temple room, with a low altar on which stood the well-known figurines of bare-breasted women – goddesses? – in flounced skirts, often holding snakes or other animals such as cats. There were temples, too, and the Linear B inscriptions mention priestesses (but only in one case a priest). No trace has been found, however, of the sort of lifesize or larger cult statues which existed in later Greek temples. We can speculate once more about the pillar-goddess of the Near East. Plato, in the *Critias* (IX c), describes the sacred pillar, made of orichalcum, in the temple of Poseidon in Atlantis, on which bulls were sacrificed and which was lustrated with their blood afterwards. However, no such pillar has been found on Crete.[6]

In Crete, then, we see the population, protected by the sea and their fleet, pursuing an artistic, creative celebration of the forces of Nature, expressed through dance and through athletic rituals such as bull-leaping. Since the majority of Crete's inhabitants did not have to be perpetually ready for war, and since, according to Greek legend, a king of the island, Minos, instituted the first laws in the world, a ceremonial culture emerged. The icons of that culture did not depict Poseidon, the raging storm-god, but an impressive, even inspirational goddess (or goddesses) whose names are unknown.

But Cretan culture was not simply an outpost of Middle Eastern Goddess-worship. On the mainland of Greece, a civilisation grew up which from the second millennium intermingled with it. This was initially characterised, in the third millennium, by walled settlements with large central buildings. In contrast to the Cretans, who mostly sacrificed by gifts to their deities, placed on the altar and left whole, the mainland settlements show traces of animal sacrifice by fire. The few statues which have been found include ithyphallic male figures, and masks,[7] both of which are used worldwide as symbols of defence, warnings of the reality which the settlement walls embodied. On the mainland, all settlements had to be ready to defend themselves in hand-to-hand combat, and warriors had a high status. This early culture matured by the middle of the second millennium BCE into the Mycenean civilisation which is the subject of the *Iliad*.

In Mycenae itself, the contents of the shaft-graves dating from the seventeenth and sixteenth centuries make it clear that this was a warrior society, not simply a self-protective community which fortified its settlements. The tall, strong skeletons and the large quantities of weapons contained in the graves argue for a warrior elite whose members were given sumptuous burials. The style of Mycenean artwork, seal-stones, frescoes and metalwork is Minoan, but the scenes depicted are scenes of warfare and of hunting, not the dances and rituals of Minoan art. Beginning with the Cretan earthquake of 1730 BCE, which flattened the buildings of early Minoan culture, the Mycenean and Minoan communities became more strongly interconnected, perhaps through trading, perhaps through conquest, perhaps through migration. Cretan colonies sprang up on the other Aegean islands, but the Myceneans ruled the mainland of Greece from their citadel cities, and after the eruption of Mount Thera (Santorini) around 1500 they conquered Crete itself and became the undisputed rulers of the whole Mediterranean.

The Myceneans spoke Greek, an Indo-European language, and probably introduced it to the islands if not to the mainland. Linear B, the script which appears on Crete after their conquest, as well as in Pylos, Thebes and Mycenae, is a form of Greek. It gives us invaluable information about the deities worshipped at the time. There are references to Zeus (Diwija) and Hera, Athene (Atana), Poseidon (Posedaon), Paeon (Pajawo – the Greek form is an epithet of Apollo) and to Dionysos (Diwonusojo), who never became an Olympian and who had previously been assumed to be a new god, imported from Thessaly or from Asia Minor. As Crete was reported to be, the Greek ports which traded with Crete are indubitably sites of Poseidon worship.[8] We do not know, however, whether the Cretans also worshipped these other deities who later became the Olympians, or whether the Myceneans brought them with them from the mainland.

## THE GREEKS

After the fall of the Myceneans around 1150, history is silent for nearly four hundred years until the poems of Hesiod and of Homer were committed to writing and fixed the names and natures of the Olympian deities. The names of these twelve deities and the stories of their family squabbles as told by Homer and the other poets have become common knowledge in European culture. Scholars once assumed that this was all there was to Greek religion: the imposition of a model of the patriarchal extended family upon the more 'primitive' indigenous cults of a conquered land. In fact, the dichotomy is not so simple.

There was no one clear conquest. The sixth-century historian Herodotus claims that another Greek-speaking people, the Dorians, invaded Mycenean land from the north-west of Greece and took over almost all the peninsula (except Attica). The gods and goddesses in the ensuing Greek literature, beginning with the poems attributed to Homer and to Hesiod, were said to live on Mount Olympus, a peak in the north of Thessaly, near Macedonia. Under economic as well as military pressure, many of the previous inhabitants, now calling themselves Ionians, dispersed eastward to Asia Minor and the Aegean islands, southward to Libya, Egypt and Ethiopia, and westward to found such colonies as Gades (Cadiz) in what is now Spain, Massilia (Marseilles) in France, and the extensive Italian settlements of Magna Graecia. In Italy, the Greek colony later shaped early Roman culture.

The distinction between the old deities and those of the newcomers is not clear cut. As we have seen, several of the deities of Olympus, long thought to have been introduced by the Dorian invaders, were known in Minoan-Mycenean Crete as early as 1500 BCE. On the mainland, the new Greeks took over many of the old sanctuaries dating back to pre-Mycenean times.

They erected fire altars and later temples to house the divine images. The cults set up by the conquerors, immigrants and traders became continuous with the existing cults based on the personified spirit of place. In Athens, for example, the ruling family had traced its descent to a snake-ancestor, Erechtheus, whose tomb stood on the Acropolis. An oracle spoke and also allowed sacrifices to be made to Poseidon in the temple of Erechtheus. Poseidon, as we have already seen, was already worshipped in the Aegean and was not a new deity imported by the Dorians. As a gift to the city he gave a salt-water spring which gushed from the rocks of the citadel.[9] Later Poseidon is said to have 'quarrelled' with the goddess Athene over which one of them was to become the guardian deity of the enlarged city. Now Athene, under her byname, Pallas, may have been the goddess of the earlier ruling clan, the Pallantidae, and so the quarrel would have been a human quarrel of succession. In a vote between the two deities, Athene won. Her gift to the city was the olive tree. A sacred spring and a sacred tree: these totems are typical of indigenous religion the world over, they embody the spirit of place. Early icons of Athene show her with a cloak fringed by snakes, with snakes in her hands, perhaps in continuity with the local ancestor-cult, perhaps in continuity with the snake-goddesses of Crete. In the contest with Poseidon, interestingly, she won because of the women's votes, which outnumbered the men's and as a result of which the Athenian women supposedly lost their voting rights and citizenship. This story reads like a justification for the change in women's status, which again suggests that Athene presided over an earlier state of social organisation. Perhaps among the Pallantidae women did have full citizenship. Athene's name also indicates that she was the personification of Athens, itself the citadel of the state of Attica. Yet both she and Poseidon are fitted by Hesiod and by Homer, writing in the eighth century, into the genealogy of Olympus.

Similar stories can be told from cities all over Greece and the Aegean. Pagan religions always interact creatively with their neighbours, their deities developing or being assimilated under such influence. Yet something new came into Greek religious culture at the time of the Dorian migrations. A mobile, nomadic lifestyle produced a religion which valued abstraction and self-reliance at least as much as clan obligations and affiliation with the spirit of place. Like the god of the Israelites by contrast with the gods and goddesses of the settled Canaanites, the deities of the incoming Dorians stayed with their people wherever they were, and gave them help in dire need. Unlike the One God of the Israelites, however, the various Olympian deities favoured particular individuals and had an affinity with such individuals' characters, thus emphasising the distinguishing traits of personality which had affiliated the person with that deity in the first place.

Thus in the *Hippolytos* of Euripides the chaste and self-contained hero worships the virgin huntress, patroness of wild untamed things, Artemis. Artemis is, of course, the tutelary deity of Hippolytos' mother, the queen of the Amazons. However, his worship of Artemis proves to be excessive, and for his insulting indifference to the goddess of love and enjoyment, Aphrodite, he is cursed. Interestingly, Hippolytos dies through the intervention of the god of the place, Poseidon, rather than through Aphrodite's direct intervention. The abstract, internationalised deities Artemis and Aphrodite (themselves originally local goddesses from elsewhere) battle it out through the medium of the spirit of place. Poseidon was, of course, an earlier 'portable' god from the international Minoan-Mycenaean seafaring culture, being the patron of many cities around the Aegean including Athens, as we have seen. In this tale, however (his followers having presumably settled in Athens some time ago), he is presented as the 'father' of Theseus the king, i.e. the latter's mythical ancestor and justification of his kingship according to the ancient tenets of ancestor-worship – soon to be challenged, as we have already seen, by Pallas Athene and her followers, hearkening back to an even older ancestor clan.

Like the Myceneans, the Dorian Greeks offered burnt sacrifices to their deities as well as what were said to be the older 'bloodless' and 'wineless' offerings of milk, wool, oil and honey. Athenaeus (I.46) tells us how gluttonously the heroes of Homer ate meat by contrast with the fruit, fish and vegetable diet of the coastal people, and this distinction is embodied in the different foods brought to sacrifice. Only about half of the Mycenean deities were recognised by the new culture, perhaps because writing effectively died out during the Dark Age, or perhaps because their worship seemed irrelevant to the new ways. Two new deities, Apollo and Aphrodite, are named by Homer and have cult sites going back to the eighth century and the twelfth century respectively. They again were originally local deities, both of them apparently introduced from the Near East via Cyprus. The culture of the eastern Mediterranean was one large interrelated continuum. Its deities interacted, many of its religious practices remained constant, but the cultural attitude to them changed.

The Greeks, like the Myceneans, lived in fortified hilltop cities. The acropolis, the citadel of each settlement, seems originally to have been simply a fortified burgh which was a refuge for the inhabitants of the surrounding villages.[10] An Athenian called Hipparchos is said to have instituted stone pillars in about 520 to mark the halfway point between each of the Attic villages and the Acropolis at Athens. Normally the temple, home of the city's protective deities, was housed in the acropolis, but many exceptions occur. In particular the temples of Hera at Argos, Samos and Olympia, and that of Aphrodite at Paphos, are well outside the Greek cities, a pattern which argues for continuity with pre-Mycenean times. The Greek cities stood on the same fortified hilltops as those of the Myceneans before them, but these sanctuaries of goddesses had been sited independently.

## SACRIFICE AND SANCTIFICATION

The basic site for the honouring of a deity was the open-air altar. Early sanctuaries had included the hearth-house, a roofed building with a circular hearth inside it, as found at a few places (Dreros and Pinias) on Crete and at the oracle of Apollo at Delphi. The domestic hearth remained sacred, dedicated to Hestia, and the head of the household would make ritual offerings at it as part of domestic life. Plutarch, in his *Quaestiones Graecae* 296 F, describes how in Argos the hearth of a house in which someone has died is ritually extinguished and then, after the prescribed period of mourning, is rekindled, with a sacrifice, by fire from the state hearth. At some time during the Dark Age, however, the hearth-house was superseded by the raised altar in the open, around which all the celebrants stood while the sacrifice was offered.

At the mountain-top sanctuaries in Crete, dating from before 1700 BCE, there are deposits of layers of ash with animal bones as well as terracotta votive objects and occasional metal objects. There is no way of knowing whether the presumed burnt sacrifices at these places were of the nature of a ritual meal with the gods in the later Greek fashion, or were a holocaust, as were the rituals of Artemis at Patrae in Greek times, described by Pausanias (VII.18.12), where the altar was encircled by green logs of wood with an earthen ramp leading up to it, up which the virgin priestess would advance in a car drawn by deer:

*Plate 2.2* The Lady of the Wild Things, painting on a Boeotian amphora, 750–700 BCE. Female figures, thought to be goddesses, flanked by wolves or lions, were depicted in Greece, Asia Minor, Crete and the Aegean islands throughout the prehistoric and archaic periods.

12

They throw animals onto the altar, including edible birds and all kinds of victims, wild boar, deer and gazelles, and some bring wolf and bear cubs, others fully grown animals . . . I saw there a bear and other beasts that had been thrown on, struggling to escape the first rush of the flames and escaping by brute force. But those who threw them on put them back on the fire. I cannot recall anyone being harmed by the wild beasts.

A similar story is repeated at the beginning of the Common Era by Lucian in his quasi-antique account of the worship of Atargatis ('Hera') in Syria (*De Dea Syria* 49):

Of all the festivals, the greatest that I know of is held at the beginning of spring. Some people call it the Pyre, and others the Torch. At this feast the sacrificing is done as follows. Having cut down large trees and set them up in the courtyard, they also bring goats and sheep and other herd animals and hang them from the trees. They also bring birds and garments and artefacts of gold and silver. When all is prepared, they bear the victims round the trees and set fire to them and then all are consumed.

Here the Asiatic sacrifice is a ceremonial dedication of total combustion which anticipates Adam of Bremen's account, over 1,000 years later, of the festival at Uppsala in Sweden. We do not know whether the mountain-top bonfires in Minoan Crete followed the same pattern, but the bulk of sacrifices among the later Greeks did not. Both Pausanias (IV.32.6) and Lucian also say that all kinds of tame animals were kept in the court of the sanctuary. This recalls the sacred animals and birds kept in Egyptian and northern European temple-complexes. Birds and fish are present in Roman-age depictions of the temple of Aphrodite at Kouklia (Old Paphos), Cyprus, and there were sacred horses kept in the fanes of the Prussians and Lithuanians.

The deities which Homer calls the Olympians – Zeus, Hera, Athene, Artemis, Apollo, Hermes, Poseidon, Aphrodite, Ares, Demeter, Hestia, Hephaistos – were honoured mainly with sacrifices which were of the nature of a ritual meal: 'more a feast for the honoured lord', as Lucian observes in the second century of our era. One thousand years before, Homer described Odysseus telling Telemachus to 'Sacrifice the best of the pigs so that we can eat soon' (*Odyssey* XXIV.215). The formula had not changed. In a time far distant from modern deep freezes and supermarkets, when the store cupboard was the grazing herd and a beast had to be killed whenever meat was to be eaten, the ritual slaughter of an animal before the altar, its ceremonial roasting or boiling and the offering of certain parts – conveniently the inedible ones – to the presiding deity, was at times merely the sanctification of a feast. On most occasions, however, it was indeed an offering which caused some financial hardship to the supplicant. But the slaughter would always be followed by a roast meal, even if several of the choice cuts were handed over to the temple-priest. The Olympian 'fragrant' burnt sacrifice, unlike the holocaust of the Anatolians, was not an orgy of destruction but a convivial meal. Greek society, despite its cult of individual prowess, had a strong sense of community and of public duty.

Other sacrifices were, however, holocausts. Sometimes a small animal such as a piglet or a cock would be burnt before the main sacrifice[11] and in the cult of the ancestors and of the underworld deities total combustion was common. The ancestors in particular demanded blood sacrifice: the blood of the sacrificed animal would be poured into a trench dug beside the tomb towards the west, which was the direction of endings in sacred cosmology[12]. As in many societies today, the ancestors were seen as continuing the vengeful motives of the living from beyond the grave, and were thought to need placating. In modern Rajasthan many villagers fear the *bhootha*, the unquiet spirit which may haunt burial grounds and secluded places, ready to possess and injure unsuspecting humans. Here the spirit can be exorcised by the local *bhopa* (the shaman or mantis, as the Greeks would have called him), and if its identity is known it can be placated. Sometimes family spirits remain benevolently active towards the living and will have a shrine built for them. Local heroes and heroines – people who have saved the community in some case of need – are also venerated in modern Rajasthan, and some of these give oracles. The family and community spirits are presented with offerings of perfume, strong liquor, tobacco and sweets, as in the 'fireless and bloodless' sacrifice of the Greeks. However, the local protector god, Bhairon (who complements the local mother goddess, Mata), has two forms. His bright form, Gora Bhairon, is worshipped with gifts of sweetmeats, but his dark form, Kala Bhairon, demands liquor and animal sacrifices. This recalls the two forms of sacrifice in ancient Greece: bloodless offerings of first-fruits for the earth-deities, but blood sacrifice and holocaust for the ancestors and the spirits of the Underworld.[13]

The local shrines of modern Rajasthan are, like the historical Greek shrines of ancestors, those of local heroes and heroines and of local deities, essentially independent of the central Hindu pantheon. In Greece local deities were however sometimes given the names of Olympian equivalents, perhaps as a justification of their continuance. One example is Zeus Meilichios, who seems to have absorbed the attributes of an ancestral snake-cult from the area and to have functioned as an avenger of blood-guilt.[14]

The 'pure' bloodless and fireless sacrifices which were offered at various altars and sanctuaries even to gods who were elsewhere served by burnt offerings, were thought by the later Greeks themselves to be the practice of an earlier, simpler world.[15] When fruit and honeycombs and wool were laid on the altar of the Black Demeter in Arcadia, and olive oil poured over, or when wheat and barley and cakes were offered without fire to Apollo the Sire in Delos, both the celebrants themselves and their later commentators saw the conservative retention of practices from before the discovery of fermentation, before the invasion of meat-eating immigrants from the plains of Middle Europe, i.e. from the third millennium BCE. Certainly in Minoan Crete, as we have seen, burnt sacrifices were far and away the exception in all but the mountain-top sanctuaries, whereas for the Myceneans and for the Dorian Greeks they were the rule.

Libation, the pouring of drink into the ground or onto a special libation-table or onto an altar for the use of the presiding deity, can perhaps be seen in the context of the fireless sacrifice of milk, oil and honey, perhaps also in the context of sharing a meal with the gods, since the first cup of an evening's drinking-party was always poured as a libation, and since in other contexts a deity was asked to accept the libation and enter into companionship with the human being who was pouring it. At blood sacrifices, too, the blood from the slaughtered animal had to spill onto the altar. Plato tells us in the *Critias* that in ancient Atlantis (which may have been Minoan Crete) the blood from bulls sacrificed in the temple was made to gush over the pillar on which was inscribed the laws which governed the island, given by Poseidon to its founders.

The emphasis that comes through the main practice of sacrifice is one of social responsibility: of sharing what one has with other people and with the originators of all bounty, the Immortals. The ceremonial pouring of liquids in addition sanctifies a place, whether the ground itself, its altar or its omphalos. The other kind of sacrifice is a re-sanctification, the redressing of a wrong, an alternative to the punishment which the Fates would otherwise inflict. We invoke this kind of retributive justice even today when we swear an oath by some sacred object, inviting the divine powers to strike us down if we perjure ourselves. The ancient Greek when swearing an oath simply stood on the dismembered carcass of his sacrificial animal and dedicated himself to the same sort of destruction as the victim if he broke his word. Such ceremonies have a powerful psychological effect, just as the ancestors – our parents and family – have imprinted us strongly with their thoughts, both conscious and unconscious. Perhaps the ancient ceremonies of riddance were effective in 'dis-spelling' such internalised curses. Aeschylus, of course, tells us in his *Oresteia* (458 BCE) how the Athenians eventually replaced the burden of blood-guilt, which no riddance had lifted from Orestes and which drove him fruitlessly from place to place, by the rule of law, in which the lawful punisher is absolved from revenge, the criminal is purified by punishment, and so the cycle of vendetta is broken. The old rituals were thus capable of modification.

## THE SITE AND THE GODDESS

As we have seen, the sanctuary itself could be marked by a built altar, by a sacred tree, by a spring (as at several of the oracle sites – see below), or by a stone called the omphalos, or navel. We have already seen the navel-stone

*Plate 2.3* The *Oresteia*. Vase from Magna Graeca showing the judgement of Athene on Orestes, 350–340 BCE. © British Museum.

at the Cave of Eileithyia on Crete, but the classic Greek omphalos was a much more elaborate object. It was a dome-shaped stone about one metre high, often elaborately carved, and was the regular site of libations and other offerings. The original omphalos at Delphi, which still exists, was an unworked stone bearing the inscription *Ge*, probably an aniconic image of the earth-goddess Ge-Themis (Gaia). Vase paintings show omphaloi draped with fillets – knotted strands – of wool, which were the routine form of sacrifice of first-fruits of sheeprearing, but which later became the adornment of the sacrificial victim and, indeed, of the seer or anybody else 'given up' to the will of the Immortals. The omphalos is often shown on vase paintings with a gigantic female figure arising from the earth beside it. It is an attribute of the earth-goddess. Sometimes the figure is called Ge (Earth),

16

sometimes Pandora (All-giving) or Aneisidora (Giver of Earth's Bounty), and sometimes Meter (Mother).

In many sanctuaries before sacrificing to other deities a preliminary sacrifice had to be made to Earth. Aeschylus, in the *Eumenides*, has the priestess at Apollo's shrine at Delphi begin her address with the words:

> First in my prayer before all other gods
> I call on Earth, primeval prophetess.

The next lines explain Apollo's rulership of the sanctuary as a gift from the goddess:

> Next Themis on her mother's oracular seat
> Sat, so men say. Third by unforced consent
> Another Titan, daughter too of Earth,
> Phoebe. She gave it as a birthday gift
> To Phoebus, and giving called it by her name.

In the *Choephori* 127, Aeschylus adds:

> Yea, summon Earth, who brings all things to life
> And rears and takes again into her womb.

The Athenians also called the dead 'Demeter's people'. We know that in the myth of the rape of Persephone it is Demeter's daughter, not Demeter herself, who becomes Queen of the Underworld, but popular culture preserved or conflated the identity of the two. The underworld goddess was thus the dark Earth, bringer of fruitfulness as well as ruler and holder of the dead. Aneisidora too was a bountiful earth/underworld goddess, mentioned by Aristophanes (*The Birds* 971, and schol. ad loc.) both as a goddess to whom white-fleeced lambs were sacrificed, and as the Earth, bestowing all things necessary for life. She was connected with Pandora, who has come down to us mainly in the death-dealing aspect of the Underworld. Her positive aspect appears, however, when in the first century of our era the sage Apollonius of Tyana, helping a man who wanted a dowry for his daughter, prayed successfully to Pandora.

A more differentiated theme, the marriage of heaven and Earth, appears in the cult of Zeus at Dodona. His priestesses declaim:

> Zeus was, Zeus is, Zeus will be: O great Zeus!
> Earth sends up fruits: so praise we Earth the Mother.

Zeus is described in an ancient children's rhyme from Athens as the bringer of rain. At the Eleusinian Mysteries, sacred to Demeter and her daughter, the worshippers at the conclusion of the ceremonies would look up to heaven and cry 'Rain!' then to Earth and cry 'Be fruitful!'. At Olympia, the sanctuary of Hera and Zeus, a cleft in the ground was sacred to Earth and a libation was poured into this before any other sacrifices.[16]

*Plate 2.4* The goddess of the Underworld: Persephone enthroned.

There seems, then, to have been a basic and apparently ancient veneration of the Earth itself, which continued alongside the newer cults and which was differentiated into the cults of particular goddesses such as Demeter and Kore (Persephone), Pandora and Aneisidora. The symbol of the Earth was the cleft, the underground chamber or megaron (at Eleusis), and the omphalos, all representations of the female anatomy. It is worth pointing out, however, that not all goddesses are earth-goddesses. The earth-goddesses in Greece were quite specific underworld deities of prosperity and destruction. In the same way, not all gods are sky-gods.

## ORACLES

The Greek goddesses and gods spoke through their followers by means of trance and inspiration. At one time it was thought that Classical religion was a matter of outward observance only, of going to the festivals and performing the prescribed sacrifices,[17] but this is manifestly false. Gods and goddesses appeared to individual people in dreams and on shamanistic flights of inner vision; they appeared to whole armies and crowds in visions; and from earliest times there were established oracles at permanent sanctuaries, staffed by professional seers, as we have seen is still the case in a modern Pagan country like India. The deities in the ancient world also were active in people's inner lives. The shrine of Zeus at Dodona, in the heartland of the mythical Dorians and styling itself the oldest oracle, was a tree sanctuary of the classic sort. It was founded in an ancient oak forest around the eighth century BCE by an Egyptian missionary priestess from Thebes.[18] In a clearing stood a single oak tree which she had identified as sacred. At its foot was an intermittent spring, and in its branches lived three doves (according to Hesiod) or three priestesses called doves, who entered a state of ecstasy and prophesied without remembering what they said.[19] We have already seen dancers receiving a vision of a goddess at the Cretan tree-shrines, so this practice is familiar.

Oracles sometimes grew up around springs. At the oracle of Apollo in Miletus the priestess sat with her feet in the waters of the spring and breathed its vapours in order to go into trance. At the same god's oracle in Klaros the priest drank the water and so became entranced. At Delphi the priestess bathed in the spring before prophesying. The Oracle of the Dead at Ephyra had two rivers, called Acheron (Sorrow) and Kokytos (Lamentation) after two of the rivers of Hades. A blood sacrifice at a local ancestor shrine, for example Odysseus' sacrifice at the grave of Teiresias described in the *Odyssey* XI.23 ff., could also attract the spirits of the dead so that they could be consulted. Here it was not the seer but the spirits who were entranced by the liquid, and so in this case it could be that the two procedures are entirely unconnected.

At Miletus Apollo's prophetess sat on an *axon* beside the sacred spring. An *axon* is literally an axle, but the word was used at the time to refer to the axis of the heavens. Thus the prophetess sat, symbolically, at the centre of the world. Similarly, at Delphi the seeress sat on a tripod beside the omphalos, in the sunken area at the end of the temple interior. The omphalos too was seen as the centre of the world, as Plato tells us ('Apollo sits in the centre on the navel of the earth'),[20] but unlike the *axon* at Miletus, which was open to the sky and presumably pointed to the Pole Star, the omphalos was placed in an underworld setting. Delphi, according to Aeschylus (see above), was originally a shrine of the earth-goddess, and so the tradition of prophecy must have continued in the time-honoured manner, by reference to the Underworld, not to the axis of the heavens. The tradition of seership by consulting the underworld spirits at the centre of the universe was carried on by the Etruscans (see chapter 3), who are thought to have migrated to Italy from the eastern Mediterranean and laid the foundations of Roman culture.

The tree, by contrast, is an image of the celestial axis: the pole of the heavens marked by the North Star, around which the constellations appear to revolve. The trees which marked certain shrines – the oak of Zeus at Dodona, the willow of Hera at Samos, the olive of Athene at Athens – are likely to have been seen as the local axis, linking the mundane world with the celestial world, just as the omphalos linked the mundane world with the hidden riches and terrors of the Underworld. It is just as appropriate to see the Cretan goddess appearing from above to the dancers at her tree-shrine as it is to see Demeter arising from the Earth at her omphalos. The model of the celestial, mundane and nether worlds linked by the cosmic axis and extended to the plane of the ecliptic is one which had been developed in detail, both symbolically and mathematically, by the Mesopotamians and the Egyptians. When we come to the northern tradition we will see its image as the tree developed to an unprecedented extent. Meanwhile, it seems that the same symbolism was alive in ancient Greece. Prophecy, for the Greeks, became objective by being integrated with the co-ordinates of the cosmos itself. The true seer was the one who sat at the centre of the visible world.

## TEMPLES AND IMAGES

The scholiast of Aristophanes states that the olive tree was Athene's temple and her image before the times of built temples and images.[21] Each deity had her or his own holy tree, e.g. Zeus, the oak; Aphrodite, the myrtle; Hera, the willow; and Dionysos, the vine. Sacred trees were often considered more holy than the altars associated with them.[22] According to tradition, the Greeks started religion by fencing off groves of trees. Pausanias asserts (X.5.9) that the first temple of Apollo at Delphi was a hut made of laurel trees. No temple was dedicated unless there was a holy tree associated with it.[23] Hera's tree at Samos was incorporated into the altar itself. In a relief of Amphion and Zethos in the Palazzo Spada in Rome, an image of Artemis stands before a sacred tree at the centre of a temple.

Temple buildings came after the open-air altars at Greek sanctuaries. The oak tree of Zeus at Dodona was replaced by a temple only in the fourth century. The oldest temples which have been found so far are all dedicated to Hera, from the ninth-century Heraion on Samos with its tenth-century altar, through Argos to Olympia, where her temple predates that of Zeus.[24] This might mean that Hera was the most important deity in the Dark Age, or it might mean simply that her image was the first to be thought of as being in need of shelter. The temples were used to house the images of the deities, and are patterned after the Mycenean megaron or throne room. The original cult image of Hera at Samos was, according to Phoronis (fr. 4), simply a plank. In Argos it was a pillar. These were later decorated with pectorals and chains of fruit. We see the same simple iconography on vase paintings showing the worship of the 'womanish' Dionysos (but not in the worship of other deities). Here the cult image is a plank with a mask hung on it and a robe and woollen fillets draped over it. This may be another aspect of tree-worship, since stone pillars, the other obvious image-bearers, do not seem to have been used in this role. (But for images of Hermes, see below.)

Votive offerings brought to the sacred place were left there after the ceremonies. Animal skins, skulls, bones, horns and antlers, eggs, garlands of flowers, sheaves of corn, flowers and fruit, ropes, nets, tools and weapons are all recorded. These are the fabric of the ornament reproduced in stone on temples: almost every design component of the Classical temple derives from one or other of these elements.[25] Fully developed temples preserved and revered the original sacred objects. The original rock where rites were celebrated was left exposed (as can be seen today at the Dome of the Rock mosque in Jerusalem and the chapel in the Christian monastery of Mont-Sainte Odile, Alsace, France, both built on the sites of earlier Pagan sanctuaries). Temples were erected around stones that contained sacred virtue. The most famed of these is the aniconic image of Aphrodite, a baetyl (a meteorite which still exists in the Cyprus Museum, Nicosia) revered in the shrine at Paphos, Cyprus.

Certain deities, in particular Zeus and Poseidon, were never depicted by images during the Archaic period (c.800–c.530 BCE). Zeus was the daytime sky, its rain and its lightning. We have already seen this symbolism expressed in verse and ritual. So Zeus, like Ge, the Earth, and Poseidon, spontaneous natural force, was thought of as an abstract principle, without an image. Similarly, the primary image of Aphrodite was aniconic. It was the *baetylos* mentioned above, a black meteoric stone kept in her temple at Kouklia (Old Paphos), Cyprus, which dated from around 1200 BCE, predating Greek temples of Hera. Hermes, on the other hand, appears from earliest times as one of several sorts of boundary-marker. The earliest herms are cairns, piles of stones as used all over the world to mark boundaries and way-stations. From the sixth century on we find the characteristic stone pillar, which was reputedly instituted by Hipparchos of Athens in the year 520 to mark the halfway points between the Attic villages and the agora at Athens. Walter Burkert has convincingly observed[26] that ithyphallic male figures such as Hermes in Greece and Frey in Scandinavia are probably apotropaic figures, warning interlopers, like the baboons who sit in the same attitude guarding

*Plate 2.5* Roman coins with representations of the temple of Aphrodite at Kouklia (Old Paphos), Cyprus, showing sacred fence, enclosure with offerings, aniconic image of the goddess, crescent and star symbols on the roof. The modern aniconic image at Costarainera (1992) (plate 3.2) reflects the archaic Aphrodite. Nigel Pennick.

their band, that fit adult males are at hand to defend the territory. Also, in the case of Priapus, the phallus is invoked for the fertility as well as the protection of horticulture.

Until the fifth century Hermes was always depicted (on vase paintings and elsewhere) as an adult male with a beard. The winged boy who appears in later art is an expression of his rulership of adolescence. Hermes is the god of intermediate states, and so serves to establish boundaries as well as to cross them. Similarly, in modern Rajasthan, there is a god of boundaries, an aspect of Bhairon, 'the powerful male principle'.[27] He protects the Indian village against intruders and is an aniconic presence in the no-man's-land around it. Visitors usually make an offering to him when they cross this no-man's-land. In Greece, local versions of Hermes could also have additional attributes. Pausanias (VII.22.2) saw an image of Hermes, the Market god, at Pharae in Achaea. This was a smallish square pillar surmounted by a bearded head. In front of it was a stone hearth with bronze lamps clamped to it with lead. Beside it was an oracle: the enquirer would arrive at evening, burn incense on the hearth, light the lamps, lay a coin on the altar to the right of the image and whisper his question into the ear of the image. Then the enquirer would stop up his ears and leave the market place. After a while, the enquirer would uncover his ears and take whatever word was first heard for an oracle.

## LATER DEVELOPMENTS

The deities of Olympus, then, were assimilated to and usually descended from a host of local gods and goddesses who had practical functions in the everyday life of their human communities. The Greek genius for storytelling and classification was overlaid onto religious practices which were concerned with the veneration of the spirits of place, the ancestors and other more abstract beings. The Classical period, dating from the realistic, non-symbolic style of Athenian red-figure vase painting which began c.535 BCE, saw a systematic development of speculative thought. The law became more impersonal, and so did the deities, as in the conversion of the Furies to the Kindly Ones and their installation in a temple, a change fancifully clothed with great antiquity by Aeschylus in his *Oresteia*. Thales' discovery of the method of predicting eclipses (585 BCE) had no doubt already contributed to humanity's sense of objective distance from the natural world. People in the eastern Mediterranean began to work out how to anticipate, rather than simply to react. (The transcendental religions, such as Buddhism and Zoroastrianism, date from this time.) Tremendous advances in astronomy were made, the laws of mathematics and of reasoning itself were investigated, and eventually Athens acquired its own school of philosophy with the advent of Socrates (d. 399) and his pupil Plato (428–347).

Socrates was put to death for corrupting the youth of Athens by teaching them to question the traditions which everyone had held unthinkingly, or at least not questioned so effectively, until then. But the demon of free thought (Socrates' *daimon*, his inspiring spirit) was out of the bag. The western intellectual tradition follows in a direct line from the methods of reasoning developed in the eastern Mediterranean during the sixth to the fourth centuries BCE and crystallised so notably in the schools at Athens. The contemporaries of Socrates thought that the intellect offended the divine powers, and so they found him guilty of corruption. In the long run, however, his school of thought produced a mystical philosophy, Neo-platonism, which coexisted with and (in the eyes of its adherents) even justified the Pagan religions of the time as well as the later monotheisms, and it has persisted to the present day. The methods of reasoning developed by Socrates, his contemporaries and his predecessors, as well as the parallel discoveries in mathematics and in astronomy, have been even more influential, but do not concern us here.

Plato's pupil Aristotle was tutor to the young Alexander of Macedon (356–323), who, as Alexander the Great, later conquered not only mainland Greece but its old enemy the Persian Empire, and much of Asia besides, thus introducing Greek philosophers and priests to Babylonians, Zoroastrians and Brahmins. Alexander's short reign had the result of binding together what became known as the Hellenistic cultural sphere. This not only had a common Greek language and administrative system in its various independent countries, but also a syncretistic religion, developed by Ptolemy I of Egypt in around 331. Based on the Nile cult of Isis and Osiris, this religion included Greek elements and was, in the normal Pagan fashion, hospitable to other local cults. Isis was a mistress of magic and a saviour goddess (*soteria*), who initiated human beings into the mysteries of everlasting life. Her cult generally eclipsed that of her consort, who was the judge of the dead in the Underworld, but in theory the two were worshipped together, and in whatever fashion their cult was widely followed throughout the Hellenistic and later Roman Empires.

Alexander set up his new Hellenistic states on the democratic pattern of ancient Athens, with magistrates, a council and a popular assembly. But each city also had a king, and these kings rapidly became the focus of a ruler-cult. The monarch and his consort were worshipped as deities in their lifetime, rather than being posthumously heroised as demigods. The existing protective divinities of the city-state concerned did, however, retain their own cult. So for example at Teos in Ionia, statues of the conquering king and his queen were placed in the temple alongside that of the city's god, Dionysos, and every year an offering of first-fruits was placed beside the statue of the king in the council chamber. The cult of the monarch, which was perhaps introduced from Oriental sources, or perhaps grew up in the wake of Alexander's own claim to be the divinely begotten son of Zeus, was generally thought to preserve the wellbeing of the kingdom itself.[28] It introduced a new element

*Plate 2.6* Goddess building a trophy, fourth century BCE. The tradition of commemorating notable events and dedicating them to a divinity is an integral part of the Pagan tradition. The assembling of trophies was practised also by the Celts, and in modern times by European nation-states. © British Museum.

into Mediterranean Paganism. During the third century, the Greek colonies in the western Mediterranean were gradually invaded by the rising power of Rome, and so it is to this area that we now turn.

# 3

# ROME AND THE WESTERN MEDITERRANEAN

## THE ETRUSCANS

In the eighth century, the time when Greek society was emerging after the post-Mycenean Dark Age, an elaborate civilisation grew up in western and central Italy. For three hundred years the Etruscans dominated the western Mediterranean. They mined copper, made weapons, utensils and jewellery, developed agriculture, practised engineering, including agricultural irrigation, and traded with the Greeks, Carthaginians, Phoenicians and other members of the international community of the time. Overland, their merchants travelled to Gaul, Germany and the Baltic, trading wine and copper for amber and salt. It is thought that they introduced the two-wheeled war chariot to the Celts of central Europe. Around 545 BCE their formidable navy joined that of the Carthaginians to limit Greek power in the western Mediterranean. Their engineering and organisational skills produced the city of Rome in the late seventh century, and two if not three of Rome's early kings were Etruscan.[1]

The Etruscans were experts in divination and the mantic arts, and as the frescoes from their tombs show, their culture included the arts of music, dancing, banquets, athletics and writing. The sixth century, the period of the last three semi-legendary Roman kings, marks the height of Etruscan power. Afterwards, the Etruscan cities, civilised but disorganised, fell before the single-minded militarism of Republican Rome. History was rewritten by the victors, and the remnants of Etruscan civilisation can now only be glimpsed from archaeology, from reports by the ancient historians, and from a few inscriptions which have been only partly deciphered. The twelve-volume history of this people, written by the Emperor Claudius in the first century CE, is lost.

Scholarly opinion is divided about where the Etruscans originated. Most ancient commentators thought that they arrived in Italy from the eastern Mediterranean, but Dionysius of Halicarnassus, in the first century BCE, thought that they were native Italians who had learned quickly from foreign traders and invaders, particularly the Greeks in the south of Italy. Modern archaeological evidence is inconclusive. Etruscan artwork, however, was Greek or Phoenician in style, their hydraulic engineering was typical of that of Egypt and the Fertile Crescent rather than of anything in Italy beforehand or contemporaneously, and their political organisation is more reminiscent of the centralised theocratic kingdoms of the Middle East than of the loosely organised Greek city-states, in which no one would have seen a king as an incarnate god. Each Etruscan city was independent, but in the original Etruscan settlement area, modern Tuscany, the main cities formed a League of Twelve. This centred on a common shrine at Tarquinii, where there was a pan-Etruscan gathering and sacrifice once a year.

The earliest Etruscan remains date from around 750 BCE. During the seventh century, Etruscan cities grew up in north and central Italy as farming, trading, mining and manufacturing centres. Their complex urban civilisation contrasted starkly with the simple village settlements of the native (Villanovan) culture. During the sixth century, the Etruscans expanded north into the Po Valley and south into Campania, also colonising parts of Latium, including Rome, between about 625 and 509. Etruscan trade extended north as far as the Black Sea and the Baltic, and their naval alliance with Carthage around 545 gave them mastery over the western Mediterranean. In the late sixth century, many Etruscan cities replaced the kingship by an oligarchy, and during the next two centuries Etruria gradually lost her power, through naval defeats in the Mediterranean, through Celtic incursions into the Po Valley and the Apennines, and through the expansionist tendencies of Republican Rome. Nevertheless, Etruscan cultural influence remained active in central Italy until as late as the fifth century CE, when, under attack by Alaric the Goth, the Christian city of Rome accepted the offer of some Etruscan visitors to perform a ritual to bring a thunderstorm which would turn back the invader. But the ritual had to be performed in public, with the whole Senate attending, and this the Pope would not allow, so the plan was abandoned.[2]

The earliest Etruscan remains are elaborate stone tombs dating from about 750 BCE, square and later cupola-shaped, in marked contrast to the simple urn burials and trench-graves which continued around them. The cult of the dead remained important throughout Etruscan culture, as in many Pagan societies, and the frescoes in the tombs show a wealth of divine beings which awaited the soul beyond death. The remains of the dead were elaborately honoured and they were housed in elaborate necropolises, but we do not know whether this amounted to an actual cult of the ancestors, including Greek-style hero-shrines and appeasement rituals, or whether the dead were thought of merely as subjects of the underworld deities.

The latter is more likely, for Etruscan religion was not simply a religion of practice and precedent, in the more usual Pagan style, but also a revealed religion, whose sacred writings gave detailed instructions for the practice of ceremonies and concerning the nature of the divine powers. In a field near Marta belonging to a farmer called Tarchon, so Cicero tells us,[3] a child mysteriously arose from a newly ploughed furrow. Tarchon summoned the priests, to whom the child (calling himself Tages, son of Genius, son of

Tinia, the chief god) dictated the sacred doctrine, upon finishing which he fell down dead. Following the instructions given by Tages, Tarchon founded a sacred city on the spot. It was called Tarquinii, and was to become the holy city of the League of Twelve. The doctrine of Tages was preserved in sacred books, which like many Etruscan *sacra* were divided into three groups. These were the books of divination (by entrails), the books of interpretation of omens (especially lightning) and the books of rituals. These last were themselves divided into three: the books of the allotment of time, the books on the afterlife, and the rules for interpretation, expiation and placation of spirits.

Etruscan priests and augurs were professionals trained for many years in their colleges, reminiscent of the learned Babylonian *baru*-priests. (Interestingly, the Etruscan word *maru* similarly means a priest or magistrate rather than the part-time priests and priestesses of the Hellenic world, or even of their full-time but untrained seers and seeresses.[4]) It appears that, for the Etruscans, all science had a sacred function (there was little or no 'secular' study, by contrast with Greece), and equally that the sacred world was carefully analysed and measured by means of precise divination to an extent which we moderns, and even the Romans, who coexisted with the Etruscans for some centuries, would call superstitious. The elaborate Etruscan techniques of divination were rejected on those grounds by many Romans (e.g. Cicero, Cato), who preferred to obtain a simple yes–no sign of approval from the gods, rather than the detailed prediction and analysis which Etruscan methods offered them.

The king of each city was also the high priest, the *lucumo*. The style of his diadem, his sceptre, his purple robe, his *lituus* or staff of office, and his ivory throne were adopted by the Roman magistrates, later by the emperors, and eventually by the Roman Catholic Pope and cardinals. The king's symbols of executive power, the *fasces*, or rods for scourging, and the double-headed axe, were also adopted by the Romans (but using a single-headed axe) and restored in the twentieth century by the Fascist dictator Mussolini.

The *lucumo* and his deputies were responsible for carrying out the public ceremonies of Etruscan religion, but they were advised by a college of scholars who are now chiefly remembered for their skill in divination, the *haruspices*. However, the *haruspices* were also astronomers, mathematicians and engineers. Even after Etruscan political power had been crushed by Rome, a college of *haruspices* was maintained in that city as part of the administrative establishment. It was a *haruspex* who warned Caesar against the Ides of March. The sacred offices of the *lucumones* were carried out after the overthrow of the Etruscan kings in Rome by a ceremonial 'king', the *rex sacrorum*.

The layout of the Etruscan cities and countryside conformed to sacred measure. It was foursquare, oriented to the cardinal points of the compass. Four roads (or, more usually, three, omitting the northern quarter) ran out from a central point to the four gates, one in the middle of each city wall. This layout probably dates from the Bronze Age, since a bronze plough was used in the ceremony of drawing the city boundaries, but it may have developed from an indigenous original, since the same foursquare pattern is also visible in the settlements of the north Italian lake dwellers of the Bronze Age, the *terramaricoli*. The Etruscan version may, however, come from a Middle Eastern sacred pattern reflecting the perceived layout of the cosmos, the annual path of the Sun quartered by the solstices and equinoxes, with which we are familiar from Mesopotamian sacred astronomy,[5] since the Etruscans are known to have quartered the sky as well as the Earth for purposes of divination. Varro describes the quartered pattern of an Etruscan settlement, and tells us that it is exactly reproduced in the ancient citadel of Rome, the ancient *Roma quadrata* on the Palatine. The Romans believed that they had inherited their pattern of city planning from the Etruscans, and the Roman foursquare city with its central shaft sealed by a stone (not an omphalos as in Greece), its three gates and its three roads survives in the modern streetplans of Turin, of Timgad in Algeria (founded by Trajan in 100 CE) and of Colchester in England, founded by the Tyrrhenophile Emperor Claudius in 49 CE. According to Polybius, Roman military camps, too, were laid out as specified in the *disciplina etrusca*, and Roman fields were also designed as grids of a specified size oriented to the cardinal points. The Romans acknowledged that their concern with land law was derived from that of the Etruscans. The outward form of Etruscan land discipline has persisted into the modern age, for the same foursquare, cardinal-oriented pattern was adhered to, in both town and country planning, by the founders of the modern USA. But in ancient Etruria, naturally enough, the purpose of the foursquare planning and its attendant ceremonial was not simply ease of organisation, but the thoroughgoing magical protection of the settlement and its inhabitants from all threats originating in the unseen world.

The earliest known temples date from about 600 BCE, and so may have been preceded, as in other cultures from Greece to (as we shall see) Norway, by open-air altars enclosed by a wall. One such altar still exists at Marzabotto. The typical Etruscan temple, however, was almost square, slightly deeper than it was wide, with an elaborately colonnaded front, plain sides and back (unlike the Greek temples, which were open, with columns, to all four sides), and inside it had three compartments, or *cellae*, for a triad of deities. Sometimes there was only one *cella*, with a wing on either side. The walls and roof were usually made of wood rather than stone, with overhanging eaves decorated with brightly painted terracotta images. In front of the temple stood an altar, and the whole precinct was enclosed by a wall.

Some of the Etruscan deities seem to have been specific to their culture, but many were borrowed from Greece. Three important Etruscan deities were Tinia, the god of boundaries and land law (claimed as ancestor by the legendary Tages), Uni, the goddess of dominion, who carried a sceptre, and Menrva, goddess of the skilled intellect, patroness of craft workers. The name 'Tinia' is Etruscan, but the Romans identified this god with Jupiter, their version of the Indo-European sky-god. Tinia was said to have instituted the sacred land law. Uni is an Italic goddess, sharing her name and nature with the Roman Juno, and Menrva is another Italic deity, known in Rome as Minerva. These three deities filled the three *cellae* in the central temple of the Roman Republic, the Temple of Jupiter, supposedly vowed by the Etruscan king Tarquinius Priscus in around 600, built on the Capitoline Hill at the foundation of the Republic in 509, and surviving until its wooden superstructure burnt down in 83 BCE.

According to Varro,[6] the Etruscans' chief god was not Tinia but Voltumna or Veltune, whose shrine was near Volsinii, at which the members of the original League of Twelve met annually to conduct the traditional ceremonies, including games and a fair, and to settle matters of law and policy. This celebration fell into disuse in the days of Etruria's decline, but was later revived, probably by the Emperor Claudius, and it continued into the fourth century CE, the reign of the Christian Emperor Constantine. The goddess Nortia, called Arthrpa after the Greek Atropos, also had a temple at Volsinii. In its wall the highest-ranking Etruscan official would hammer one nail at each annual festival. The accumulation of these nails, one per year, showed the passing of the aeons, and when the wall was covered it was thought that the lifetime of the Etruscan civilisation would be over. There was a goddess of implacable fate, called Vanth, who in the frescoes seems modelled on the Greek Artemis, with short skirt and hunting boots. The god of death was Mantus, after whom some ancient authors said the city of Mantua was named, and the god of the Underworld was Aita. After death, it was thought, souls were met in the Underworld by Charun, a monstrous figure with wings and a beaked nose, who brandished a mallet, and other winged deities were met in the infernal regions. Such terrors were not absorbed into Roman religion as such, but they did become part of its public pageantry. The Roman gladiatorial games, first recorded in 264 BCE, may have descended from the Etruscan funeral custom of staging a fight to the death between three pairs of warriors, and certainly the dead bodies of the losers in the Roman spectacle would be dragged out of the circus by an attendant gruesomely dressed as Charun.

Etruscan society seems to have acknowledged a fatalism which was not shared by the other cultures of the northern Mediterranean. Individuals did not always fight against death and endings, but by contrast saw themselves as powerless to oppose these. During the Roman seige of Veii, Livy tells us, the soldiers tricked a soothsayer into revealing the secret of the defences: that if ever the Alban Lake beside the city was drained, Veii would fall. When he discovered the trick, far from dissembling his error, the expert lamented the fact that the gods had led him to reveal the prophecy, and went on to give detailed instructions for draining the lake. The idea that everything had its fixed term has already been mentioned in relation to the temple at Volsinii, where the nails driven into the wall every year predicted the lifespan of Etruscan civilisation. We learn from Censorinus, writing in 238 CE,[7] that the civilisation was in fact thought to have a lifetime of ten *saecula* of unknown length. Portents, to be interpreted by the *haruspices*, would announce the end of each *saeculum*. The fifth *saeculum* began in 568 BCE, when Etruria was at the height of its power. Previous *saecula* had been one hundred years long, which takes us back to 968, a time before there was any evidence of Etruscan culture anywhere. The sixth *saeculum* began in 445, the seventh in 326 and the eighth in 207. In 88, when Etruscan political power had long been eclipsed by that of Rome, the *haruspices* announced the beginning of the ninth *saeculum*, and at the death of Caesar, when, as Shakespeare has it, 'the sheeted dead / Did squeak and gibber in the streets', Vulcatius the *haruspex* proclaimed the beginning of the tenth *saeculum*, which ended at the death of Claudius in 54 CE, when a comet, and lightning which struck the tomb of the dead emperor's father, provided the necessary portents.

*Plate 3.1* Medieval wall-painting of the black Sibyl of Europe in the Madonna shrine at Piani, Liguria, Italy. The sibylline tradition, important in Roman Paganism, was absorbed into Christian mythology. © 1992 Rosemarie Kirschmann.

## THE TRANSITION TO ROME

Near the mouth of the Tiber, on the opposite bank from the Etruscan Veii, was a ford surrounded by swamps, and on the hills above this a group of villages amalgamated to form a township. The tradition recorded by Livy would have it that Rome was founded in 753 BCE by Romulus, a descendant of Aeneas of Troy, himself the son of the goddess Aphrodite. Rome calculated its calendar from that date (*ab urbe condita* – AUC), and, at the time of Livy (the last years BCE), the imperial ruling family of Rome, the Julians, took their own divine ancestress, a local goddess called Venus, assimilated long before to the Greek Aphrodite, as the city's protectress. But archaeology shows that before about 625 BCE only a collection of wattle and daub huts existed on the site of the future city. If Romulus ever existed, he was the tribal chief of a group of villagers. Early images show the older tradition of Romulus being suckled by a wolf, the animal of Rome's original protector, Mars. The city itself was probably called after the Etruscan name of the Tiber, Rumlua. The three kings who are said by Livy to have followed Romulus – Numa Pompilius, Tullus Hostilius and Ancus Marcius – would similarly have been local chiefs, not kings on the sophisticated scale of the urban Etruscans. Each of these kings is said to have reigned thirty-five years, which brings us to 613 BCE and the reign of the Etruscan Lucius Tarquinius Priscus. As his Latin name shows, the Romans remembered him as the venerable priest-king (Roman *lucumo* for Etruscan *lauchme*) from Tarquinii (the shrine of Voltumnus, central city of the Etruscan League). Archaeology confirms that it was in the last quarter of the seventh century that the flood-plain of the Tiber was settled, presumably by Etruscan engineers who drained the swamps around the Tiber ford. Typical Etruscan potsherds bear witness to their presence, and Etruscan engineering skill was thenceforth devoted to the establishment of the new city.

The huts in the valley were demolished at the beginning of the sixth century and an open space, the Forum, built. Roads were laid out in the grid plan of the Etruscan discipline, houses made of stone and brick with tiled roofs were built, the foundations of the later Temple of Jupiter on the Capitoline Hill were laid, and, finally, the Circus Maximus was built, all before about 575 BCE. The *pagus* (countryside) was now an *urbs* (city) in the eastern Mediterranean style, like the cities of Etruria itself.

The next king of Rome, Servius Tullius, was said by Roman tradition to have reigned from 578 to 535 and to have been a Latin of humble birth. Etruscan tradition, however, identified him with the leader of a faction among the Etruscan nobility who deposed the first Tarquin. Independent evidence is slight on either count. Servius is credited with instituting the first known democratic system of government in the city, which did not, however, last beyond his lifetime. This included property bands of taxation and the principle of an armed citizenry, grouped into what the Romans later called *centuriae*. It was under Servius' rulership that the fortifications of Rome were extended by the Servian Wall to include all seven hills, and the temple of Diana, patroness of the Latin League, was built jointly by Romans and other Latin tribes. Rome had become head of the League. The last king, L. Tarquinius Superbus (534–510), restored the old patrician order and completed the temple on the Capitoline, built according to the Etruscan sacred measure. Tarquinius Superbus is also credited with the donation of the Sibylline Books of augury, offered to him at vast expense by a seeress, and (on the practical level) with the construction of the Cloaca Maxima, the main sewer, which is still operative today. By the end of his reign, Rome was a functioning city with craftsmen, temples, stone houses, mains drainage and a system of government which, however patrician, accustomed all the free inhabitants to civic responsibility and to organised corporate action.

After the overthrow of Tarquinius Superbus in 510, Etruscan names gradually disappeared from the lists of city dignitaries and Etruscan crafts-manship – jewellery, music, dance and banquets – disappeared from the newly constituted Republic of armed farmers. Simplicity and utility became the rule and luxury was frowned on, as the archaeological evidence and the romantic puritanism of later writers such as the elder Cato indicate. The localised religion of the Roman *pagus* (see next section) replaced the deities and ceremonies of Etruscan religion, but the Capitoline Triad of deities remained and was eventually to be reproduced in cities all over the later Empire. The Sibylline Books, which whether genuine or not were sanctified by antiquity, were used as a deciding authority in questions of religion, and the Etruscan augurs were consulted as acknowledged experts in matters of seership. As we have seen, the ceremonial regalia of the Etruscan kings, the sceptre, diadem, purple robe and ivory throne, were taken over for religious and ceremonial occasions by the new Republic, and have continued to this day, together with the *lituus*, or crooked staff of office, as the insignia of the Roman Catholic Papacy. It is even tempting to see the Etruscan demons, which had no part in Roman religion, surviving in the iconography of later Catholicism (though if Etruscan culture, like Christianity, originated in the Middle East, this shared origin would be enough to explain the coincidence).

The Etruscan cities failed to appreciate the Roman urge for the possession and control of territory, or at any rate they failed to respond effectively to the military threat which Rome soon posed. During the fourth and third centuries, Rome conquered first Veii, then Tarquinii, Vulci and Volsinii. Several tutelary deities were brought to Rome, so that the cities were spiri-tually as well as materially disempowered. Other Etruscan cities were shack-led by truces, and the Roman road network cut through Etruscan territory. The Greeks were pressing on Etruria from the sea, and the Celts overland from the north. During the third century the Etruscans made alliances against Rome with the Celts and with the Italic tribes, and then with Hannibal (225–203), but after the latter's defeat, Roman colonisation and control of Etruria, Campania and the Po Valley increased. During the events leading up to the civil war in Rome (83–82), Etruria again sided with the future loser, and Etruscan territory was promptly devastated by the victorious Sulla in 82. (We notice the ninth *saeculum* beginning in 88, the time of the Social War between Rome and her Italian client states, including Etruria.) By now the Etruscan cities were effectively Romanised and Rome had regained her Etruscan engineering skills, but curiously enough, Etruscan mantic skills (disastrous though these had obviously been in advising Etruscan generals from the fourth century on), were much in demand in Rome. They were seen as indigenous practices, by contrast with the 'depraved and foreign' (i.e. Oriental) mantic and religious cults which were flooding Roman popular culture through the city's new international links.

Etruscan culture was re-established in Rome by the Emperor Claudius (41–54 CE), a college of *haruspices* was reinstated, and the old League of Twelve became a League of Fifteen and resumed its celebrations at the shrine of Voltumnus near Volsinii. The Etruscan cities seem to have defined themselves as what we would call a cultural grouping rather than as what we (and the Romans) would call a properly political grouping, and it is in the cultural sphere that their achievements have persisted, from the foursquare layout of town and countryside through to the ceremonial practices of ancient Rome and of the Roman Catholic Church.


## REPUBLICAN ROME

The earliest written history which remains from Rome, the Greek prose work of Fabius Pictor, dates from around 202 BCE. Our picture of the early Republic (from 509), the Etruscan kings (supposedly from 613) and their predecessors (supposedly from 753), and of the tribal settlement before that, has to be pieced together from the sketchy accounts of contemporary Greek travellers, the imaginative accounts of later Roman apologists, and the evidence of epigraphy, anthropology and archaeology. Incomplete as this picture is, some of its outlines are still remarkably clear.

Rome's deities were originally guardians of the land. Both the fledgling city, reputedly laid out by Romulus in the mid-eighth century, and the farming localities or *pagi* of which it was the focus, were laid out in a foursquare pattern according, so Plutarch tells us, to the *disciplina etrusca*.[8] The *agrimensor*, or land-surveyor, would indicate the north–south and east–west orientations running from his position and use these to quarter a unit of land. In Classical times such units were twenty *actus* square: 2,400 Roman feet, with an area of one *centuria*: 200 *iugera*. The basic quartered square could be subdivided indefinitely, until each farmer had a square or a strip of land bordered by three or four identical ones. Each district with its various farmsteads was known as a *pagus*, and the spirits of the *pagi* were the original deities of ancient Rome.[9]

*Plate 3.2* 'Goddess' image in niche on a house at Costarainera, Liguria, Italy, 1992. Aniconic images such as this natural stone are a direct link with archaic representations of divinity. © 1992 Nigel Pennick.

Varro tells us that the early Romans worshipped their deities without images. Indeed, they seem to have worshipped them without personification of any kind. The basic Roman belief seems to have been in *numen* or supernatural power rather than in personified spirits.[10] An early ceremony for clearing a piece of ground for farming is addressed to 'Thee, whether god or goddess, to whom this place is sacred'. A sacred spot, *locum sacrum,* was one which had been ritually cleansed and ceremonially set aside for religious activities. There were also uncanny spots, *loca religiosa,* at which some portent such as a lightning strike had occurred. These were fenced off and set aside as numinous, as still happens more or less spontaneously nowadays, for example when flowers or children's toys or, notoriously in the case of a football crowd disaster in the 1980s, scarves and rosettes are left at the sites of accidents. Such modern shrines are ephemeral, but in earlier times memorial stones were laid. At Quy Fen in Cambridgeshire there is a stone commemorating the death of a local youth who was struck by lightning on the spot in the eighteenth century.

In Rome the spirits of the fields were known as Lares. They were not, as far as we know, given any personality or even an individual name. At each crossroads where four properties met was a shrine to the joint Lares, the *compitales.* Each of the four individual shrines looked out over its allotment, and fifteen feet in front of each one was a sacrificial altar. Ovid, in the *Fasti*

II.639ff., tells us that in December each locality would honour its various divinities at the crossroads. The farmers would celebrate at the shrine of the joint Lares. They would garland the boundary stone and sprinkle it with the blood of the animals sacrificed at their individual altars. (That is, the boundary stone would be honoured with gifts in the way already described from ancient Greece and modern India.) Fire had been brought from the family hearth by the mistress of the household, and a basket of produce was carried by one of the sons of the family and its contents tipped into the fire by one of his sisters. Then there would be feasting and jollity in the traditional Pagan way.

At first, there was a single *Lar familiaris*, but from the early first century BCE, there were two, represented as youthful, dancing images. In the houses of the poor, they were kept in a niche by the hearth, whilst in more prosperous households they had their own shrine, the *lararium*.[11] Their worship remained virtually unchanged through the regal, Republican and Imperial periods. In later times, the deity became known as *Monacello* (Little Monk) or *Aguriellu* (Little Augur), the *genius* of the household. Later, Christian images of the infant Jesus were direct continuations, in size, style and attributes, of Lares. The Isle of Capri is especially noted for them.[12]

In historical times the Lares were worshipped indoors (as *Lares familiares*), and were seen as the unseen masters of the household. Houses in Imperial times (after 27 BCE) contained shrines with statues of the family Lares, and the city itself had a shrine of the *Lares compitales*. The indoor *numina*, however, were originally the Penates, the rulers of the store cupboard or *penus*. Once again, these were known collectively and not given individual names. The table was never left empty, and at the main meal of the day, the midday *cena*, one of the sons of the family would get up and ceremoniously throw on the fire a piece of bread which had been baked according to an archaic recipe by the daughters of the family and placed on a small dish, a *patella*. As the flames blazed up to take it the boy would announce that the gods were favourable: *di propitii*. Vesta, the goddess of the hearth, is an Indo-European deity, identical with the Greek Hestia. Vesta was the flame in the hearth and was tended with all due reverence. The mistress of the household had to leave the hearth swept at the end of every evening.

The doorway (*ianus, ianua*) of the house, too, was sacred. Like Vesta, the flame on the hearth, it was itself a deity, the god Janus. As the transition point between the uncontrolled outer world and the safe territory indoors, the doorway was hedged about with taboos. When a new bride was brought to the household she had to smear the doorposts with wolf's fat and bind them about with woollen fillets, before being carried over the threshold. When a child was born to the household, the doorway became the object of a triple ritual. One person chopped at the threshold with an axe, another pounded it with a pestle, and a third swept it with a besom. These rituals were explained as protecting the household from ill luck: we would say, from ill luck being brought in. Outside the household were the ambivalent gods Mars, whose animal was the wolf, Faunus, the god of wild beasts generally, and Silvanus, the god of the woods. The Roman farmer would have been wise to propitiate these deities but extremely foolish to invite their influence indoors.

## URBAN RELIGION

Janus is, of course, better known as a god of the Roman state religion, which is thus revealed as the Romans' domestic religion carried out on a collective scale. Janus had no temple until 260 BCE but a huge freestanding double door, the *ianus geminus*, in the north-east corner of the Forum, through which the Roman armies marched out on their way to war. The door was left open when the Republic was at war and only closed in time of peace. On the opposite side of the Forum was the hearth of Vesta, and so the Forum reproduced the design of the individual house, with Janus as the taboo-ridden boundary between it and the outside world and Vesta as the sacred centre, the source of life within. Vesta's hearth was tended by the six Vestal Virgins, who were chosen at the age of ten from aristocratic families and who served for thirty years, carrying out elaborate forms of the archaic rituals which unmarried daughters had performed in the original homesteads of early Rome. By Republican times, in any full-length invocation of all the deities, the god Janus was to be addressed first and the goddess Vesta last. These two deities encompassed the extremes of existence, from the outermost to the innermost points of the Roman dominion, and their worship illustrates the fundamental Roman preoccupation with the possession and administration of territory.

From the early Republican calendar, which has been pieced together from the inscriptions on a series of tablets dating from Imperial times, we have the names of the thirty-three original deities of Rome. Twelve of these had permanent priests, individuals of aristocratic origin, i.e. descendants of the original founders of Rome, whose job it was to perform (later, to administer) the sacrifices and carry out the other rituals of their deity which were needed to ensure the peace between the divine world and the human world which the Romans sought to keep at all costs. This sacred peace, the *pax deorum*, was later embodied across the ever-expanding Republic as the *Pax Romana*, and finally, in Imperial times, found its expression in the *Pax Augusta*. Cicero, writing at the end of the Republic, stated bluntly: 'This whole empire is created and increased and maintained by the power of the gods.'[13]

Three of the sacrificing priesthoods were the major ones of Jupiter, Mars and Quirinus, and a fourth was the priesthood of Janus, which was administered by an official known as the *rex sacrorum*, the king of the sacred things, who oversaw the state celebrations. This official's wife, the *regina sacrorum*, sacrificed to Juno on the first of every month (see below), which was also sacred to Janus, the deity served by the *rex*. It may be that the *rex sacrorum* took over the functions once carried out by the Etruscan priest-king, but his name and function also remind us of the Mycenean office of *basileus*, the sacred king who was distinct from the secular king or *anax*, a distinction which goes back 1,000 years before Republican Rome. The headquarters of the Roman 'king' was known as the Regia, or Palace, a building which in fact dates from the beginning of the Republic (*c.*509), not from the time of the monarchy, and which, despite its name, is clearly designed as a temple, not a residence.

Jupiter's priest was the *flamen Dialis*, whose office was restricted by many taboos. He could not engage in such ordinary activities as riding a horse, seeing an army in battle array (a familiar sight in Rome), wearing a ring or knots on his clothing, or doing any secular work. Needless to say, in Republican times this office was not easy to fill. It has been suggested[14] that Jupiter was the original god of Alba Longa, the nearby city and head of the Latin League, which Rome is said to have conquered before the period of the Etruscan monarchy. Jupiter presided over the period of the full moon (which later became the Ides of each calendar month), over lightning and oak trees and hilltops. In Rome his earliest sanctuary was that of Jupiter Feretrius on the Capitoline Hill, where there was an oak tree on which Romulus was said to have hung the spoils of his battles, and where (so Dionysius of Halicarnassus tells us) there was in the first century BCE a small temple, fifteen feet wide, which contained a sacred stone used by the Fetiales, one of the guilds of priests, to sanctify oaths. These oaths were sworn 'by Jupiter the stone', indicating that the god was thought to be immanent in the object itself, just as Vesta was thought of as immanent in the hearth flame. The *flamen Dialis* also administered the archaic rite of aristocratic marriage, in which a cake made of *far*, a form of wheat, was solemnly broken and eaten by the bride and groom, perhaps as a sacrament to the marriage vows.

The priest of Mars must have been an important official in early Rome. In the archaic ritual of the homesteads, Mars was an outsider god whose animal was the wolf. He was invoked in the ancient boundary ritual of the farmsteads, preserved for us by Cato,[15] but in Rome he did not have a temple within the city boundary until the reign of Augustus, beginning in 27 BCE. The altar of Mars was of course in the Campus Martius, the army training ground outside the city, but his rites were also carried on by two colleges of twelve priests each within the city. These were called the Salii, or 'leapers'. Every year in March, the month named after the god, they collected the sacred weapons, or *ancilia*, which had been stored in the Regia over the winter, and performed a sacred dance, sung to archaic words, which invoked the fruitfulness of the fields and announced the start of the military campaigning season. A similar rite the following October involved a horserace and sacrifice, the singing of another hymn which ended the campaigning season, and the replacement of the ceremonial weapons in the Regia. Here, then, we see Mars as the god of youthful male vigour, perhaps symbolised by the growing shoots of vegetation, perhaps associated with the protection of the fields, but certainly presiding over warfare. In historical times, at the declaration of war, the consul responsible would go to the Regia and rattle the sacred weapons, shouting 'Mars, awake!'.

Mars was a god of central importance in Rome, probably the original protective deity of the city. His priest, as we have seen, was the second in importance after the priest of Jupiter, and his nature may indeed have been echoed by the last of the three major deities, the god Quirinus. Almost nothing is known about Quirinus. The hill named after him, the Quirinal, was the home of one of the two Martial guilds, the Salii. These were called simply the Salii of the Hill, by contrast with the Salii of the Palatine, whose home was the hill on which the original settlement of Rome was said to have been founded by Romulus. Thus it seems that the Quirinal Salii predated the Palatine Salii, and perhaps that the god Quirinus was the battle-god of the township on the Quirinal, whilst Mars served the same function in early Rome, the township on the Palatine. In formal orations the Roman people are also known as the 'Roman Quiritian' people, which again argues for an early identification of the two settlements under their two gods.

These were the major sacrificing priesthoods, administered by the principal *flamines* or 'flame-kindlers'. Among the remaining priesthoods, only one was for a deity whom the general public knows well, i.e. Ceres. The remainder were for long-forgotten and presumably ancient deities such as Furrina, Falacer, Portunus etc., whose origins were unknown even to the commentators of the later Republic. But even among the familiar deities who do not appear among the sacrificial priesthoods, their original functions, before their later assimilation to the Olympians of Greece, are not always what we would expect. There is no evidence, for example, that the deities came in married pairs. We certainly see pairs of deities, for example Saturn and Lua Mater, Mars and Nerio, but these seem to have been independent deities with related functions, not husband-wife teams. Juno, in particular, was not originally the wife of Jupiter, but a deity whose name meant 'youth' and who was thought to preserve the vigour and fertility of men and women from puberty until age forty-five (the end of junior status and of its associated liability for military service) for men, and presumably until the menopause for women. As a goddess of vigour and strength, Juno appears as the presiding deity of many towns and as a goddess of battle, in her chariot and with her spear.[16] As we have seen, she ruled over the beginning of each calendar (originally lunar) month: the Calends. She was a goddess of increase, and her many shrines in Rome and elsewhere in Italy identify her area of influence. Juno Rumina protected the city of Rome, Juno Populona the Roman people, Juno Lucina the sacred grove (*lucus*), etc. Each woman also had her individual Juno, her protective spirit of youthful vigour, just as a man also had his *genius* (from the same root as 'engender'), his power of procreation and of originality. In Imperial times the *genius* or *numen* of the emperor became the object of religious cult, and in all households from archaic times the *genius* of the *paterfamilias* was celebrated on the latter's birthday; but from the very beginning of the Republic we also see the king's Juno, Juno Regina, venerated in the temple on the Capitol.

Juno, then, has roots quite distinct from the Greek Hera. So, too, with the other deities. Venus, a goddess of fruit trees and market gardens, was the presiding deity of Ardea and Lavinium. She was later assimilated to the Greek Aphrodite, the legendary mother of Aeneas of Troy, and was claimed as the ancestress of Rome, which, according to this account, current in the Greek settlements of south Italy and popularised in Rome by Virgil in the first century BCE, had originally been founded by Aeneas. But the original Venus had never been worshipped as the guardian deity of Rome; on the contrary, as we have seen, Rome's guardian seems to have been Mars or Quirinus.

By contrast, Diana was assimilated early on to the Greek Artemis. Diana presided over several towns in Latium, in particular one which seems to have been an early shrine of the Latin League, Aricia. Her priest at Aricia was the notorious Rex Nemorensis (another priestly 'king', the King of the Grove). Each holder of this office had seized it by challenging and slaying the previous incumbent, and each was destined to be slain in his turn. During the early sixth century, under the traditional kingship of Servius Tullius, a temple to Diana was built outside the walls of Rome on the Aventine Hill, marking Rome's treaty with the towns of the Latin League. The statue in this temple was in fact a copy of the Artemis of Massilia (Marseilles), itself a copy of the great Artemis of Ephesus. Here the links between the Greek and Roman deities go back to early times. Servius Tullius was also credited with building the temple of Fortuna, who became notorious in Imperial times as the goddess of blind chance. She was, however, originally a goddess of plenty, ruling childbirth and later the fate of children. Fortuna had an oracle at Praeneste, which operated not through seership but through the drawing of lots. It is easy to see how, once her agricultural roots were forgotten, she could develop into the goddess of blind fate which she later became.[17]

The god of the winter sowing was Saturn. His name was derived by the Romans from *saeta*, seed, and he was associated with the legendary Golden Age of plenty, celebrated at the Saturnalia of the winter solstice. Modern research, however, sees his name as an Etruscan word of unknown meaning.[18] Saturn presided over many archaic ceremonies of cleansing and purification, and so it can be conjectured that this was his original function. His cult partner, Lua Mater, apparently derives her name from the verb for ritual purification or expiation, *luere*. The verb for the purification ceremonies over which Saturn presided, *lustrare*, gives us our modern word 'lustration'. It was

*Plate 3.3* Wire caducei, symbols of Mercury, from a sacred well at Finthen, Mainz, Germany, first century CE. Votive offerings for good luck at wells and fountains continue today, with coins as the usual sacrifices. Nigel Pennick.

only after the reforms of the Second Punic War (in 217 BCE) that Saturn became identified with the Greek Kronos, who also had a festival at midwinter. Lua was then replaced as his cult partner (in the new style, his wife) by Ops, who had originally been the cult partner of Consus. Both these last two deities are obscure, but Ops was apparently identified with the Greek Rhea and so was assigned to the Hellenised Kronos-Saturn.

These individual cults with their altars and temples seem to have been the oldest forms of worship in Republican, if not in regal, Rome. When the Romans moved into the city from the countryside, they continued worshipping individual deities who presided over places and functions, and seem to have made no attempt to relate them to one another, either through legend or through theology in the sense of a rational arrangement of functions. The individual cults of family and farmstead were generalised to national cults without losing their essential nature. We have seen the state doorway and the state hearth with their cults in the Forum. In addition, the perambulation of the farm boundaries was echoed by the perambulation of the city, the Ambarvalia, superintended by a special guild of priests, the Arval Brethren. The annual ceremony of the Lupercalia (from *lupus*, wolf), in which two young patrician men sacrificed a dog (a wolf might have been difficult) and a goat in a cave on the Palatine, smeared themselves with the blood, laughed, wiped themselves clean with fillets of wool dipped in milk and then, naked except for a loincloth, ran around the sacred boundary of the old city, striking at people with strips of goat's hide, recalls the new bride's apotropaic ritual of anointing the doorposts with wolf's fat. Each individual family's All Souls' Day, the Parentalia, on the anniversary of the relevant ancestor's death, was gradually replaced by the national Parentalia each February.

One final cult was specific to city life, and (despite its origin at the time of the monarchy) essentially to the Republic. When Rome became a city in the late seventh century, the Capitoline Hill was levelled and over the next century an Etruscan-style temple was built on it. This was finally dedicated on the Ides of September, 509, at the inauguration of the Republic. The temple was of the typical Etruscan tricellar type, with an image each of Tinia (Jupiter), Uni (Juno) and Menrva (Minerva). The two goddesses faded into comparative insignificance at that particular shrine, but its presiding god, Jupiter Optimus Maximus (Jupiter Best and Greatest) became the presiding deity of the Roman Republic. It was to him that the victorious generals came and dedicated their spoils in the Etruscan-style triumphs which became the custom after a successful campaign. The cult of Jupiter Optimus Maximus was quite separate from the older cult of Jupiter Feretrius, whose temple was elsewhere on the same hill, and of Jupiter Latiaris, the original god of the Latin League, on the Alban hill. Nor did the ancient priest of Jupiter, the *flamen Dialis*, have anything to do with the Capitoline cult. The latter was national and international, and its epithets were eventually even applied to the name of the supreme god in Christian times, for in 1582 we read Johannes Lasicius, a Polish bishop, praising the cult of 'Deus optimus maximus', i.e. the Christian God.[19] In the Capitoline temple, too, the Sibylline Books were deposited. These were the books of Sibylline prophecies, which were resorted to as oracles in times of confusion, and were interpreted by the two Commissars for the Sacred Rites (*duoviri ad sacris faciendis*), whose number later increased to ten, then to fifteen, following the increase in importance of the Greek rites which they administered.

## FOREIGN DIVINITIES

The Romans allowed incomers to worship their ancestral deities, but the outsiders (*di novensiles*) were kept if possible beyond the *pomoerium*, the inviolate strip of land bordering the old Servian Walls. This reinforced the distinction between the patricians, who claimed to be descendants of the founding families of Rome, and the plebeians, who were not. We have already seen the temple of Diana set up in about 570 to serve the visitors from Latium, and likewise before the inauguration of the Republic the merchants and traders who settled around the Cattle Market had acquired their own temples to Hercules and to Castor and Pollux within Rome itself. Minerva had arrived from Falerii as a patroness of artists and craft workers and been given her temple on the Aventine, dedicated on 19 March. The Aventine became the centre of the plebeian religion, but with no one overriding cult. It seemed obvious to the Romans that different peoples were protected by different divine beings. They did not ask, at this stage in their intellectual history, how the various divine beings interrelated, or rather, they seem to have assumed that they were like human beings, each concerned with their own interests and making alliances mainly for the sake of expediency. When the Romans beseiged a foreign city, they would ritually beseech its protective deity to change sides and come to Rome, where a worthy cult would be set up in the deity's honour. In this way the famous statue of Juno from Veii, the Etruscan city across the Tiber which was captured in 396, arrived in Rome.

## PONTIFFS AND AUGURS

Priests and priestesses were not allowed to hold any secular office of state, although in most cases (with the notable exceptions of the *flamen Dialis* and the Vestal Virgins) they could carry on a normal life as private citizens. They were, so to speak, the executive arm of the divine order. Members of the legislative arm, by contrast, the group of men (no women here) who were empowered to interpret the will of the gods, to write rituals and to determine forms of worship, were also able to hold civil office. They were the colleges of pontiffs and of augurs, and in the later Republic they included such powerful individuals as Julius Caesar, Pontifex Maximus in 63 BCE, and Cicero, who was an augur soon afterwards.

The pontiffs, whose name means literally 'bridge-builders' and is of unknown significance, are said to have been installed by the legendary king Numa Pompilius at some time during the seventh century. They originally numbered five (nine after the democratic reforms of 300 BCE) and were credited with the formulation of the earliest laws and oaths. They arbitrated on matters of divine law and on the relationship between religion and state, including the religious calendar, of which more below. The Romans attached the greatest importance to preserving the 'peace of the gods' (*pax deorum*). This was an arrangement which supposedly assured that the actions of human beings were always in accord with the will of the divine beings, whose intentions, though obscure, were seen as far more influential than the puny impulses of mere humans. These intentions were known as the *lex divina*, the divine law, and they were ascertained in two ways: rationally, by the pontiffs, and non-rationally, by the augurs and the lesser colleges of omen-readers who interpreted the portents of the gods. The defining quality of a human being who acted deliberately in accordance with both the divine will and the civil law was *pietas*, a central Roman virtue which included obedience to all duly appointed authority figures. The English derivative 'piety' became more trivial in meaning, but the Latin *pietas* passed into Roman Catholic Christianity as the virtue of Jesus, the son of God who willingly allowed his father to slay him for the good of the universe, the *civitas Dei* or City of God.

The pontiffs, then, had the important task of guarding the right relationship between humans and deities. The earliest laws lay down the correct times for sacrifice, the forms of ceremony, what to do if a ceremony is carried out wrongly, and how a transgressor against the divine law should expiate his or her crime. One memorable law stipulated that a woman who had sexual relations outside wedlock should not touch the altar of Juno. If she did, she should sacrifice a ewe lamb with her hair unbound. A son who struck his father, however, had offended mortally against the gods and was condemned to death. The father, the *paterfamilias*, was the representative of the divine order to the whole of his family, both blood relations and slaves, and demanded absolute obedience from them. The standard formula for death under the divine law was *sacrum facere*, to be made sacred, or devoted to the deity who had been offended, and thus no longer one of the living. Normally, though, a minor misdemeanour could be rectified by a *piaculum* or expiatory sacrifice, a sort of fine, usually a piglet. For instance, the boundary ceremonies of the Arval Brethren, carried out in their grove at the fifth milestone along the Via Capena between Rome and Ostia, included a taboo against iron. However, the Arvales would sometimes deliberately use this convenient metal, with the wise precaution of two piacular sacrifices, one before and one afterwards.

These, then, were the ceremonies that the pontiffs regulated. They also prescribed the form of words for celebration, for expiation and for 'evoking' (calling out) a tutelary deity from the town it was guarding. They supervised the often archaic rituals of the sacrificing priesthoods and integrated these into the increasingly sophisticated life of the expanding city. They prescribed the forms and occasions of the rituals of the increasing number of foreign deities, and they advised individuals on how to harmonise their daily life with the regulations of the divine law. As guardians of the calendar, which was not published until 304 BCE, the pontiffs alone knew which days were fit (*fas*) for carrying out mundane business, and which were unfit (*nefas*) and had to be devoted to sacred activities. They knew when the feast days of the various deities were, and they announced the beginning of each month. All this information was kept secret until the middle of the fifth century, when the so-called Twelve Tables of the laws published a part of it. Fifty years later, the Lex Ogulnia opened the college to plebeians (non-members of the founding families of Rome), and at around this time the pontiffs' number was increased from five to nine, of whom five had to be plebeians. The pontiffs, like the augurs (see below) nevertheless remained a secretive and self-selecting body until the Lex Domitia in 104 BCE introduced elections.

The college of augurs or diviners had the duty of interpreting omens, which revealed the will of the gods. The chief magistrate or consul would ceremonially observe the omens from a special area, the *templum*, quartered and laid out for the purpose according to the sacred fourfold pattern. As the name 'augury' indicates, the flight of birds (*aves*) was particularly important in this procedure, but other omens could also be asked for by the secular official who was observing them. These omens were consulted before any important state action, such as going to war, to see whether the proposed human change in the *status quo* was acceptable to the deities. Augury was also taken from interpretation of the entrails of a sacrificial victim. Armies would take along whole herds of oxen and sheep for this purpose. During the famines and general civil unrest of the fifth century BCE, Etruscan sooth-sayers, the *haruspices*, were also consulted, and their elaborate techniques of divination from the liver and other entrails were held in high regard. The detailed interpretation of lightning flashes which fell in the quartered field of observation possibly dates from Etruscan times. During the life of the Republic (509–527 BCE), the official practice of augury became more or less a formality, rather like the announcement of *di propitii* by the young son of each family who threw the cake of spelt on the fire at the midday meal. It was the magistrate, rather than the augur, who was held responsible for maintaining the peace of the gods, and accordingly, the augurs had more prestige than power. Cicero, himself an augur, wrote forcefully against what he considered to be superstition in his *De Divinatione*. It was nevertheless thought correct, in a more or less ceremonial way, to consult the will of the gods before undertaking any action, and no doubt individual Romans, like individual citizens when faced with a public ceremony in the modern world, differed in the nature of the importance they granted to such actions.

## THE CALENDAR

The original calendar seems to have been a lunar one. Each month began with the first sight of the sickle moon, which a junior priest would call out (*calare*) to the chief pontiff. When the calendar was eventually based on the solar year (before written records began) the first day of each month was still called the 'Calends', and it was made sacred to Juno and to Janus. The full moon, later the thirteenth or fifteenth day after the Calends, was the Ides, sacred to Jupiter, and between these, the ninth day before the Ides was called the Nones. Since the Romans counted inclusively, the Nones fell at the end of the week before the Ides, thus referring in the original lunar calendar to the first quarter moon. This was supposedly the date on which the king of ancient Rome used to meet with villagers from the surrounding countryside, the *pagus Romanus*, and give out his edicts. In the early Republic it was the day on which the pontiffs announced the holidays for that month. This, then, was the calendar whose inaccuracies Caesar corrected in 45 BCE, giving us the system of months now used throughout the western world.

The major festivals in the calendar were dedicated to the native deities, the *di indigetes*, already mentioned. These festivals described the progress of the natural year. There were springtime festivals of cleansing, riddance and invocation, which cleared the way for a prosperous summer; there were harvest festivals themselves, the October festivals marking the end of the military campaigning season; and there were winter festivals of sowing and purification, the Saturnalia, Sementivae and Lupercalia. Ovid, in the *Fasti* I.163ff., evokes the festival of the Sementivae:

> Stand garlanded, o bullocks, beside the full manger:
>> With the warm spring your labour will return.
> The countryman hangs his deserving plough upon the pole:
>> The cold soil shrinks from every wound.
> Steward, let the earth rest now the seed is sown;
>> Let your men rest, tillers of the soil.
> Let the district [*pagus*] have a feast: purify the district, settlers,
>> And offer the year-cakes on the district hearths.
> May the mothers of corn be pleased, both Tellus and Ceres,
>> With due [offerings of] spelt and the entrails of a pregnant
>> victim
> Ceres and the Earth share a single function:
>> The one gives the grain its origin, the other its location.[20]

The original calendar began with the spring equinox (or with the new or full moon after the spring equinox) in March. It seems to have been a ten-month calendar with what later became the winter months of January and February as a fallow period.[21] From the winter solstice to the spring equinox, time was suspended. (There was a similar feature in Delphi, where, according to Plutarch, Apollo, the god of order, ruled nine months of the year, but the dissolute Dionysos ruled the winter quarter, the season of 'craving'.) The king who introduced the months January and February to Rome must have intended the year to begin with the god of the gateway, the two-faced Janus, and not with the month of Mars as hitherto. Until 153 BCE, the consuls were, however, appointed according to the 'traditional' year beginning in March, rather as the modern British fiscal year begins according to the old 'Annunciation-style' Church New Year, 25 March (corrected by eleven days to 5 April following the calendar reforms of 1752), although the start of the secular calendar year is 1 January. Likewise in Republican Rome, many public festivities still followed the old New Year of 1 March, although the 'hieratic' calendar[22] as regulated by the pontiffs seems to have taken 1 January as its start from an earlier date.[23]

## THE SIBYLLINE BOOKS

Alongside the apparently indigenous priestly system of the pontiffs, augurs and lesser colleges, there was an oracular system derived from the Greek shrine at Cumae, in south Italy. In the basement of the Capitoline temple were housed the Sibylline oracles, a collection of verses supposedly bought from a prophetess by Tarquinius Superbus. These were interpreted by a college of two men (increased to ten in 367, then to fifteen in 81), and resorted to for questions which the officials of the main state religion were not competent to answer. The Sibylline oracles advised the foundation of several Greek temples in the early years of the Republic, all outside the *pomoerium*, or sacred city boundary. As the Republic expanded, the duties of the Sibylline officials became more important. They were responsible for administering all the ceremonies of the Greek rite in the city and presided over public rituals which were not of Roman origin (see next section). What is remarkable about Rome is not that there was from the beginning of the Republic a strong Greek influence in religious affairs, since the international trading links and Hellenised culture of the city's Etruscan developers would have guaranteed that, but that the indigenous, non-Etruscan, non-Greek religion persisted so strongly and centrally alongside these more sophisticated influences.

## ROME EXPANDS

The urban religion of Rome, then, seems to have grown out of the family religion of the individual farmsteads and their *pagi*. Roman religion was essentially a religion of the spirits of the locality, who were seen as the latter's unseen inhabitants. The state was the farmstead writ large. Its routines and ceremonies were similar to those of the family. But as the Roman state expanded, new deities had to be included in the life of the city, and new opportunities had to be found for the vastly expanding 'congregation' to take an active part in religious rituals.

During the last years of the kingship and the first century of the Republic, Rome became a major economic and military power in central Italy, attracting visitors and settlers from the rest of the peninsula and from elsewhere in the Mediterranean. Pressure from the *plebs*, those citizens who could not trace their descent from the original founding clans of Rome, forced the patricians step by step to extend their privileges to the wider population. The laws once guarded by the pontiffs were published in about 450 as the Twelve Tables, and both the pontificate and the augural college were opened to plebeians some fifty years later. The office of praetor was created in 366, so that ordinary citizens could gain advice on the law, and the dates of the Fasti, or festival calendar, were published at the beginning of the third century. Practical power was passing into the hands of the ordinary citizen, and in this way the civil law, or *ius humana*, became more and more clearly distinguished from the divine law, the *ius divina*. Secular life was beginning to detach itself from religious life.[24]

Throughout the fifth century, Rome had been finding its administrative and economic feet without Etruscan guidance, and as a result suffered from continual war, plague and famine. Clearly, so it would seem to the average Roman citizen, the ancient peace of the gods was not being upheld by existing religious practices. Many new temples to foreign and minor indigenous deities were dedicated during that century, including one to Saturn in the Forum in 496, one to Mercury in 495, to Ceres, Liber and Libera (Demeter,

Dionysos and Persephone) on the Aventine in 493, to Castor and Pollux in 484, to the Dius Fidius (Jupiter) in 466, and to Apollo in 431. The Sibylline Books were regularly consulted and were responsible for the introduction both of Greek-style rites and of the worship of Greek divinities into Republican practice. In 399, during a severe plague, the Sibylline Books prescribed a new form of worship, the *supplicatio*. Unlike the old rituals, where the priest or priestess offered a sacrifice or made a vow to the relevant deity, using the prescribed form of words, with the non-participants watching in reverent silence, the *supplicatio* was a colourful procession of ordinary men, women and children, crowned and bearing laurel branches, to the temple of a deity. There they prostrated themselves before the image of the deity, the women with hair unbound, and begged for that deity's favour. For eight days there was also a *lectisternia* (literally, a spreading before the couches), in which food was offered to images of paired deities (Apollo and Latona, Diana and Hercules, Mercurius and Neptunus), which reclined on couches before the tables. The whole citizenry kept open house, and hospitality was the order of the time. It was these Greek-style rites which offered the ordinary people a chance to take part in religious ceremonies, and perhaps for this reason they became increasingly important in the city.

During the following century, the Romans instituted a more open style of government, open to plebeians as well as patricians. They beat back the Celtic threat (the Gauls had sacked the city itself in 390, destroying its Etruscan street planning) and achieved mastery of most of Italy by 330. In 312 the Via Appia was opened, linking Rome with the newly conquered Greek and Etruscan colonies in Campania (southern Italy), and also opening her to increasing Hellenistic influence. During the third century Rome then consolidated her gains, expanded into the western Mediterranean, and of necessity assimilated the knowledge and worship of more foreign deities.[25] Religious life was passing out of the pontiffs' control. The first gladiatorial games (perhaps based on Etruscan funeral games, which included ritual fights to the death) were recorded in 264, and an equally grisly innovation, the human sacrifice of Greek and Celtic victims, was recorded in 216, with the chief of the *decemviri*, the interpreters of the Sibylline Books, conducting the religious part of the ceremony. (To prevent this happening again, in 196 BCE the Senate passed a law forbidding human sacrifice.) In the latter half of the third century Rome battled with Carthage for economic control of the western Mediterranean, and the Carthaginian Hannibal's arrival in Italy during the Second Punic War (218–201) posed a terrifying threat. In 212 an order went out for the registration of all religions. No-one was to sacrifice in public with a strange or foreign rite unless their form of worship had been authorised by the praetor. The praetor, of course, was responsible to the chief pontiff. The tension between the indigenous Roman religion, regulated by the pontiffs, and the multiplicity of cults from outside, under the broad control of the *decemviri*, had come to a head.

In fact, an important point of contact had already been made. In 217 the Sibylline Books prescribed another *lectisternia*, which was organised according to the Greek pantheon in a Roman disguise. Images of Jupiter and Juno, Neptune and Minerva, Mars and Venus, Apollo and Diana, Volcanus and Vesta, and Ceres and Mercury presided at the feast. The deities, with their Roman names, were in fact Greek cult pairs. Mars and Venus, for example, had nothing to do with each other in Roman worship, but in Greek myth Ares and Aphrodite were lovers. The informal assimilation of Roman deities to Greek deities who had a similar function, which had been going on for some time, was thus given official authorisation. From then on the original nature of the Roman deities would fade into obscurity, and their now familiar equivalence to Greek deities become established.

The last foreign deity introduced to Rome by order of the Sibylline Books was the Great Mother of Asia Minor, who has already been mentioned in connection with Greek religion. Although the Romans venerated Vesta, the goddess of the hearth, and Tellus, or Mother Earth, as well as a variety of individual goddesses such as Ceres, it is difficult to find a trace of any worship, however archaic, of a Supreme Mother as recognised in Asia Minor and the Levant. When the Great Mother, in her form as a black meteorite given by permission of the king of Pessinonte, arrived in Rome, scandal ensued. Her priests were castrati, and they practised orgiastic rites of delirium and self-laceration. This was not at all Roman, and although the arrival of the image, in 203, was followed by the successful conclusion of the Punic War, Roman citizens were nevertheless not allowed to become priests of this goddess. In addition, rites of the goddess had to be conducted in private, within the temple precinct. Every effort was made to contain this alien form of worship.

## MYSTICAL SECTS

During the second century Rome expanded eastward, consolidating the gains of the Punic Wars, and more Oriental cults came within her ambit. Given the practical, unimaginative and externally directed nature of the Roman character, these cults were impossible to assimilate. Greek society had developed a greater emphasis on individual experience, both intellectual and mystical, than Rome, and in Greece the eastern cults, though initially resisted and inevitably modified, eventually found their place alongside the native practices of the various city-states. (Compare two Athenian plays from the late fifth century: the *Bacchae* of Euripides, which describes a worst-case scenario of the perceived threat, and the *Clouds* of Aristophanes, which satirises the excesses of contemporary religious and philosophical cults.) Rome simply could not find a place for ecstatic religious experience. Like Greek art and Greek literature, it was seen by the authorities as a decadent and enfeebling influence. The Bacchic rites were banned in 186, and the requirement of 212 for registration of new cults remained. It is a sign of the pluralistic nature of ancient Paganism, however, that even a banned cult like that of Dionysos could be practised in private, within strict limits, if a practitioner succeeded in obtaining special dispensation from the Senate. At the ceremonies of such 'unlicensed' religions (*religiones illicitae*), no more than five people might be present, no permanent priest or priestess could be appointed, and no temple funds were allowed to exist. These restrictions, intended to deprive small sects of any practical power, later determined the much-vaunted form of the early Christian gatherings: small, informal, without permanent officials, and vowed to poverty.

The practically functioning religious cults, then, in an increasingly multicultural Rome, were *religiones lictae*, or registered religions.[26] Interestingly, the Latin word *superstitio* simply meant religious practice which was outside the state rituals: private religion, which could well be duly registered. For the modern meaning of superstition, the excessive fear of spirits, we have to look to the Greek word *deisidaimonia*, which meant just that. The Romans regulated people's actions; the Greeks, with finer sophistication, also judged people's attitudes.

## PHILOSOPHY

In the aftermath of the Punic War, as a result of subduing the eastern Mediterranean countries and the Celts of the Po Valley who had supported Carthage, Rome had effectively achieved mastery of the whole civilised world by the year 160. Roman brutality in maintaining and exploiting her conquests became legendary, but the cultural influence of the newly conquered territories began to provide a counterbalance. Curiously enough, the eastern Mediterranean had become culturally united during the same decade, the 330s, in which Rome had conquered the bulk of Italy. In 336 Alexander the Great began his career, and the following year the philosopher Aristotle, Alexander's teacher, founded his school, the Lyceum in Athens. Aristotle was the last of the scientific philosophers, and by the third century scientists were pursuing their research separately from philosophers, who had become students of the arts of living (ethics) and of understanding (epistemology). Epicureanism and Stoicism developed at the same period, and in the following century the contemplative side of Platonism as well as the teachings of Pythagoras were revived with the addition of a strong ethical component. The much older civilisations with which Rome came into contact began to have their effect. The upper classes began to educate their sons in grammar, rhetoric, gymnastics and eventually philosophy, rather than leaving them to absorb the arts of war and leadership from their elders as hitherto.

In 155 the philosopher Carneades, head of the Academy in Athens, arrived in Rome as part of an embassy. His teaching, carried out as a sideline, put philosophy on the intellectual map. At a time when the cult of the old Roman deities seemed increasingly unsophisticated and irrelevant to personal spiritual needs, but the imported religions of the eastern Mediterranean were chaotic and confusing, the sceptical method of Carneades, intellectually stimulating though it must have been, was thought to be hastening the progress of moral relativism rather than providing any new standard of conduct, and the philosopher was expelled from Italy. But over the next few decades, three ordered systems of thought were seized on by the increasingly well-educated upper classes of Rome. These were the recently founded schools of Epicureanism, Stoicism and, eventually, Neoplatonism.

These systems offered people two main things. First, they offered a description of the nature of the universe, replacing the tacit assumption of the indigenous religion that each locality had its invisible inhabitants, some wiser and all more powerful than human beings, who demanded from their human neighbours a particular way of life, including particular rituals, in order to preserve the peace between them. Second, the philosophical systems offered an ethical account which described a model of human excellence which could be achieved by understanding rather than by obedience, replacing the old Roman *pietas* with a different model, more suitable for people in contact with the differing social norms of an international community.

The first system, Epicureanism, named after its founder Epicurus, was a radical individualism. The universe was thought to be made up of atoms moving in a void, collections of which went to make up physical objects. The prime motive of all beings was to seek pleasure, but the wise human should choose his or her pleasures rationally. Divine beings existed, to be sure, but they took no part in human affairs and were of use to humans primarily as objects of contemplation, inspiring presences which might flash across the mind's eye during meditation and so impel the soul to act more nobly and more wisely. This system never really took root during the second century. In the first century it inspired the wonderful poem of Lucretius (*De Rerum Natura*, published after his death in 55 BCE), and was taken up by people of a contemplative bent, but as a practical philosophy for people of a more active disposition its advocacy of pleasure seemed like a sanction for irresponsibility and hedonism, as recognised by our modern popular use of the name.

Stoicism, named after the porch or stoa at Athens in which it was developed, took hold in Rome immediately. This was probably because of its advocacy at the time by the successful general Scipio Aemilianus Africanus. Scipio was a soldier in the old Roman fashion, whose troops had wiped the resurgent state of Carthage off the face of the earth in 149–146. But he was also an intellectual who was looking for a more abstract guide to life, and he became convinced of Stoicism by his friend and teacher Panaetius of Rhodes. The Stoics saw Nature as an intermingling of mind and matter, with different beings tending more to one than to the other. Thus a rock is predominantly material, a disembodied spirit is predominantly psychic, but no being is devoid of either principle. The Stoics were monists, believing that the divine Being was the hidden intelligence of the universe, the ordering principle of Nature which was nevertheless contained within the latter. This outlook, seeing Nature as an active theophany, was much closer to the traditional religion of the *pagus* than that of the abstract divinities in Epicureanism. The Stoics also understood the different deities of traditional religion to be manifestations of the One divine power, which should be worshipped accordingly. Thus their monism allowed pantheism and polytheism, and so permitted the practice of traditional theistic religion. It generalised the indigenous local cults, even the city-cult of Rome, which was by now itself too parochial for the whole Mediterranean world, into an overarching religion which could in fact serve an international community. Ethically, the Stoics sought conformity with Nature, or rather with what we call 'the nature of things', which is Reason (*ratio*, a translation of the Greek *logos*). If all beings behaved according to their true nature (*logos*), then justice would prevail, according to the orator Cicero (106–43), the second great exponent of Stoicism in Rome. In practice a dichotomy grew up between reason and emotion in the Stoics' minds, as our popular use of the name implies, and the snobbish anti-emotionalism of Stoic doctrine guaranteed that it would not appeal to the followers of the ecstatic cults already in Rome. Nevertheless, it remained influential among the upper classes for a further two centuries, its last great exponent in public life being the Emperor Marcus Aurelius (d. 180 CE), the author of the *Meditations*, who was admired in his lifetime as a wise and just ruler.

In 88 BCE, Plato's Academy in Athens had been taken over by Antiochus of Ascalon, who retreated from the sceptical method of Carneades which had brought a similar questioning outlook to that of modern philosophy. Antiochus favoured a contemplative, some said dogmatic, analysis of the immaterial Forms or Ideas which were thought to exist in the world of thought as invisible patterns underlying material objects. This line of research became the foundation of Neoplatonism, the belief in the progressive emanation of being from the unified spiritual Source through successive layers of increasingly material and dissimilar types of being. Neoplatonism eventually found an expression in Jewish mysticism, via Philo of Megara (25 BCE–45 CE) to the four Worlds of the Cabbala; in Christian mysticism, via pseudo-Dionysius the Areopagite, *c.*500, with his Celestial Hierarchies of Thrones, Powers, Dominions, Angels, Archangels, etc.; and eventually in the cultured humanist thought of the Renaissance with its Great Chain of Being. In the Rome of the late Republic, the birth of Middle Platonism brought an increased interest in the possible divinity and immortality of the soul and of the unified nature of the divine Source. Thus, for example, Cicero[27] argues that death is not to be feared if we accept that the soul is immortal and by its very nature must rise into the ether rather than sink with the body into the earth. This doctrine is far removed, as Cicero points out, from the original Roman assumption that the spirits of the dead lived at ground level or in the family tomb. Under the influence of Greek philosophy, the Romans were beginning to speculate and to reach some un-Roman conclusions.

Another influence was neo-Pythagoreanism, associated with Cicero's friend Nigidius Figulus (praetor in 58) and in the early years of the Common Era with the famous prophet and teacher Apollonius of Tyana. In 181 BCE some documents had been forged to prove that Numa, the legendary king who was supposedly responsible for Roman religion, was in fact a disciple of Pythagoras. One hundred years later the Pythagorean current had reached maturity. A belief in reincarnation and the superiority of the immaterial world (the world of thought, the Pythagoreans being investigators of number-theory) to the material world, led to an ascetic, humanitarian outlook. Because of their belief in reincarnation, neo-Pythagoreans were among the first Romans to be vegetarians, and their reluctance to take part in animal sacrifice caused them some trouble in a world where loyalty to the state implied active loyalty to its deities.

# 4

# THE ROMAN EMPIRE

## THE AUGUSTAN REVOLUTION: 30 BCE–14 CE

Nevertheless, these philosophical movements touched only a handful of people, and the effect of intellectual elitism, though profound, is always delayed. The 173 years from the defeat of Hannibal to the accession of Augustus, in 30 BCE, were years of political and intellectual turmoil. Carthage, Rome's great rival in the western Mediterranean, was finally destroyed in 146 and Africa became a province of Rome. Greek literary, artistic and behavioural influences had already flooded in since the conquest of Hannibal's allies in the eastern Mediterranean, leaving the Romans confused about standards of good conduct. Pressure from the urban poor and from Rome's Italian allies increasingly forced further democratic concessions, but the system of government was not strong enough to withstand the accompanying threats of anarchy and serial tyranny. The Social War with the Italians (91–88) and the Civil War of 83–82 brought the conflict to a head. After the great reformer Julius Caesar was assassinated in the year 44 for having taken too much power to himself too fast (albeit, in his own opinion, on behalf of the Roman people), constitutional reform was essential.

Caesar was succeeded by the Second Triumvirate of Marcus Antonius, Lepidus and Octavian, the dictator's nephew and adopted son. Fifteen years of jockeying for power eventually brought Octavian to the position of supreme authority. In the year 29 he returned from defeating Antony at the Battle of Actium and reigned supreme.[1] He closed the gates of Janus in the Forum, thus beginning what later became known as the *Pax Augusta*, and installed an altar to Victory in the Senate. (In ancient Rome, religious and secular life remained intimately intertwined, even in a cynical age, and public buildings, from assembly halls through baths to circuses, were well provided with statues, altars and small shrines.) Augustus – literally, The Blessed One – as Octavian later became, set about far-reaching constitutional and religious reforms, based on restoring the ancient Republic, the focus of Roman idealism, in an appropriate form for his time. He restored eighty-two temples which had fallen into disrepair during the previous century, and authorised the state to build another thirteen.[2] Over the previous seventy years the state had founded only four new temples (the normal rate since the start of the Republic had been at least two per decade), but the trend was about to be reversed. The forty-four years of Augustus' rule saw the ancient priesthoods renewed and religion incorporated into a focus of national identity and pride.

Augustus seems to have been extremely careful to let his considerable personal power be seen as dedicated to, and exercised only by permission of, the political collective. A state religion, of whatever kind, was a means of strengthening this collective. The genius of Augustus was that he was able to reanimate an ancient and politically significant religion, which gave its followers a sense of ancient justification and of manifest destiny, in a form which also took account of the later religious influences which had almost destroyed it. His revived religion was able to satisfy almost everyone.

The climax of Augustus' restoration took place with the Secular Games in 17 BCE. These were sacrifices and games in honour of Dis (Pluto) and Proserpina, which took place every *saeculum*. The last of the Pagan historians, Zosimus, writing in the early fifth century CE, describes a *saeculum* as the lifespan of the longest-lived human being born at a given time. Although the word later passed into Church Latin as meaning one hundred years, the canonical reckoning in Classical times was 110 years, a reckoning more honoured in the breach than in the observance. Each Secular Games marked an epoch, as an event which no one living had seen before and no one living would see again. Augustus used the Games of 17 BCE to inaugurate his new order. The first three days, 26–28th May, saw a general purification of the Roman people. This was presumably intended as a ritual cleansing from the chaos of the past. On the following three nights, Augustus himself sacrificed black lambs and she-goats to the Greek Fates, then incense to Eileithyia, the goddess of childbirth, and finally a black sow to Tellus Mater, Mother Earth, while praying for the security and prosperity of himself, his household and the Republic. By day, Augustus offered white bulls to Jupiter and white heifers to Juno, who are described in the Sibylline oracle given by Zosimus as the celestial deities. Augustus himself was a devotee of Apollo, a god seen both as the bringer of civilisation to barbarous lands and also as the Sun. On the third and last day, white victims were sacrificed to Apollo at his new temple on the Palatine while two choirs, one of boys, the other of girls, sang a paean in honour of all the divinities, while at Juno's altar Roman matrons prayed to that goddess. The paean of praise had been written for the occasion by the great poet Horace, and after being sung at Apollo's temple it was then sung outside the original temple of the Republic, the scene of the previous two days' sacrifices, on the Capitol.[3] In this way the ceremonies cleansed and unified the Roman people, then placed them under the protection of three sets of divinities: those of the Underworld, whose rites resembled the ancient protective rituals of the farmsteads; the celestial deities of the old Republic; and the new international god who ruled the peace and civilisation of the newly extended Roman world. It was a masterly ceremony, welding what was to become the Empire into a cohesive whole for the next two hundred years, and it was to provide the backbone of the old order during the disintegration of the two centuries after that.

## EMPEROR WORSHIP

Other factors were, however, at work in the religion of the future Empire. Julius Caesar had been posthumously deified after his death in 44 BCE, the first Roman leader to receive this honour, and Augustus openly referred to himself as the 'son of [the] god', presumably to justify his claims to power. Deification is probably best seen as an imported Greek tradition of hero-

*Plate 4.1* Roman tombstone from Spain with swastikas.

worship: Augustus, too, was deified after his death, as were his successors Tiberius and Caligula (who deified himself during his own lifetime). The fourth emperor, Claudius, conqueror of Britain, received a colonial temple during his lifetime, in place of the usual temple to the Capitoline Triad, at Colchester (Camulodunum) in that country, but was deified only post-humously in Rome itself. Thereafter, however, divine pretensions spread according to the taste of the current emperor.

During Augustus' lifetime the emperor was declared 'father of the father-land' (in 2 BCE) and sacrifices were offered to his *genius*, the progenitive spirit by the favour of which he held his office, just as we have seen the ancient households venerated the *genius* of their own *paterfamilias*. Since from the Secular Games of 17 BCE onwards the prince was effectively iden-tified with the state, his *genius* was also seen as a *numen*, a more general divine power. Whatever the fantasies of the later emperors, in practice it was to the Imperial *numen* and to the deities of the Empire that loyal citizens sacrificed in the centuries to come. Following the usual Pagan tradition of free thought, citizens were free to put on this whatever interpretation they wished, and in the eastern parts of the Empire particularly he was often taken quite literally as a god, in accordance with the practice which had arisen when Alexander the Great set up his Hellenistic kingdoms in the 330s and 320s. The Roman emperor, however, held divine status only by virtue of his office. If he were deposed or if he abdicated, his divinity would leave him, just as a modern military officer, however talented, receives formal obedience not as an individual but as the holder of a given rank.

## UNIFYING RELIGIONS – THE CULT OF ISIS

So we see at the start of the Empire three contenders for the new role of unifying divine principle. First, there was the One of the philosophers, iden-tified in practice with Jupiter in Rome and with Zeus in the eastern provinces. Then there was the civilising and, by now, predominantly solar deity Apollo, instituted by Augustus. And finally, there was the Imperial *numen*, the *genius* of the emperor, which was seen as the invisible protector of the state. A proposed religion for the whole civilised world had, of course, already been set up by the Egyptian Pharaoh Ptolemy I, following the conquest of Egypt by Alexander the Great in 331 BCE. It is outside our scope to describe Egyptian religion, its rites and practices, in detail here, but in outline the religion of Isis and Serapis (originally Osiris) had been created, rather like Augustus' revived ancient religion, out of the original pantheon of Egypt. Its central legend gave the new Graeco-Egyptian religion its primary image of the Mother, Son and Consort. Osiris, identified by some Greek commen-tators with the dismembered Dionysos and by others with the dying and resurrected vegetation-god Attis of Asia Minor, was in fact too complex a figure to assimilate completely, and so was replaced in the new religion by a personification of the divine Bull, Apis, into which Osiris was said to have passed after death. The new god, Serapis, could be identified with Zeus, Poseidon, and indeed, Dionysos, all of whom were associated with bulls. Isis, initially identified by Herodotus in the fifth century BCE with Demeter, was later seen as the mistress of magic and the bringer of civilisation to the world. Although in 3,000 years of Egyptian state religion Isis (her name means 'throne') had been only one of the central figures in the pantheon, in the Hellenistic version of the last three centuries BCE her significance far outweighed that of her new consort, Serapis. Identified with many other goddesses of the eastern Mediterranean through the natural process of comparison and assimilation, she had temples throughout the Hellenistic world.

Rome, however, was more suspicious. Isis was a saviour-goddess, and the Romans had no conception of *metanoia* – spiritual transformation or, as Christians call it, repentance. A College of the Servants of Isis was founded in Rome around the year 80 BCE,[4] after the victorious Roman troops under Sulla had returned from subduing Greece and Asia Minor, but Roman citizens looked askance at the wailing penitents beating their heads against the door of the temple and begging for transformation.[5] During the 50s the altar of Isis on the Capitol was destroyed as superstitious by order of Aemilius Paulus, but in 43 the ruling triumvirate authorised the building of further temples to the goddess and her consort. After being banned again following the defeat of Egypt in 31 by Octavian, the cult of Isis and Serapis again became established in Rome, and by the late 30s CE had its own state-funded temple in the Campus Martius. The annual festival of Isis in Rome ran from 28 October to 1 November, followed by that of Osiris, which involved a public ceremony of lamentation for the dying god.[6]

The Isian religion, in most un-Roman fashion, was also one of Mystery initiation. In the mid-second century CE, the African barrister Lucius Apuleius, himself an initiate of the Mysteries of Isis, wrote *The Golden Ass*, an entertaining allegorical tale of one man's conversion from materialistic desire, symbolised by his metamorphosis into an ass and accompanying bawdy adventures, to the state of pure service of the sublime Goddess, who is known by many names in many places, but whose true name is Queen Isis. Isis seems likely to be a prototype of the modern Pagans' Great Goddess, who is known by many names (likewise a goddess for a syncretistic, multinational world). Surprisingly for us and for the hero of the novel, the hero's initiation is followed by one into the Mysteries of Osiris in Rome, 'the great god and supreme father of the gods, the invincible', whose nature is 'linked and even united' with that of Isis, but whose initiation rites, according to Lucius, differ greatly from those of the goddess. Here once more we have a universal religion, one which does not tend towards monotheism, as did those of the philosophers' Jupiter and of Apollo, but one which aims to amalgamate all other pantheons within itself. Syncretism is a natural reaction to the confusions of a multi-ethnic community, and for some time the 'Roman interpretation' of foreign, especially barbarian, deities in terms of the Graeco-Roman Republican pantheon had been carried out in the west. Thus, for example, we have Tacitus identifying the Germanic Woden with Mercury. With the introduction of the religion of Isis into the western Empire the *interpretatio Romana* met what might be called an *interpretatio Aegyptia*, and any tidy-minded soul would have reason to feel uneasy. But somehow neither a clash nor an amalgamation ever occurred. The religion of Isis and Serapis/Osiris was not intimately tied up with the state as its original had been in Egypt and as the Republican religion was in Rome. It flourished as a private cult, with state recognition and support, but Isis, it seems, was never viewed as a contender for recognition as the *numen* which holds the Empire together.

## MITHRAISM

Another cult which arose at the time the Empire was founded, and which became widespread and popular, was Mithraism, an outgrowth of the Zoroastrian religion of Persia. The Emperor Commodus (180–192) was initiated into its mysteries, and the Stoic Emperor Marcus Aurelius founded a Mithraic temple on the Vatican Hill whose eventual desecration by the Christian Prefect of Rome in 376 was later to herald the destruction of Pagan civilisation. Mithraic shrines and inscriptions first appear among Syrian mercenaries in the Danube provinces around 60 CE. At one point there were two dozen shrines in Rome alone, but the inscriptions become far less numerous after the second century CE and the religion is not mentioned by other writers after this time. Brought in by soldiers, Mithraism remained a religion of soldiers, and as far as we know it had no place for women in its rites. Perhaps for this reason it was seen as a private religion, an individual commitment which could find no place in the broader life of the community. The Mithraic shrines were small, capable of accommodating only about one hundred people, and situated underground, either in caves, in the cellars of houses, or in buildings specially constructed for the purpose. Most of what we know about the religion has to be deduced from inscriptions and brief, mostly hostile, allusions in the writings of outsiders.[7]

All social classes were admitted to the rites of Mithras, but a painful and terrifying initiation seems to have been required of them, as suits a soldiers' religion. The god Mithras, originally in Persian the mediator between the god of light and order, Ahura-Mazda, and the god of darkness and chaos, Ahriman, is depicted in Roman iconography as a young man wearing a Phrygian cap, usually in the act of slaying a bull (whether as a sacrifice or as a conquest we have no idea), and surrounded by Zodiacal symbols. One notable image shows the god emerging out of a rock, naked except for his Phrygian cap, carrying a knife in one hand and a burning torch in the other.

This was thought by ancient commentators to represent the sunrise seen over the mountains. Mithras is often described in ancient inscriptions as a solar god, and so seems to have lost his original role as mediator between light and darkness. Altars of the principle of darkness, Ahriman, are, however, also found in Mithraeums, although we do not know their purpose.

The followers of the religion were called *sacrati*, 'Consecrated Ones'. There were seven grades of initiation, the first four of which – the Raven, the Hidden One, the Warrior and the Lion – led to full membership of the cult, and the last three of which – the Persian, the Sun Runner and the Father – were higher grades. The rites seem to have included a communion meal rather than the simple feasting which was normal after ordinary Pagan sacrifices, and other features led the early Christians to see the Mithraic cult as a blasphemous parody of their own. It is more likely, however, that the two cults simply developed along different lines from a similar background. There is no evidence that the Mithraists ever preached a morality of love, rather the opposite; nor is there any that the Christian cult was ever all-male from the outset, as the Mithraic one was, nor that the Mithraic cult ever admitted women, as the Christian cult did. Mithraic dualism sprang directly from its Zoroastrian parent, but Christian dualism was a temporary feature of Jewish thought in the Apocalyptic period, the time of Christianity's origin. Christians called themselves soldiers in virtue of their faith, but many if not most Mithraists actually were soldiers, and their faith was simply suited to their calling. The bull sacrifice of Mithraism can hardly be seen as a parody of the Christian communion, since it stands fully in the tradition of the religions of antiquity.

## DUALISM AND CHRISTIANITY

Mithraism does, however, introduce the Persian dualistic idea of the battle between light and darkness, which are seen as good and evil in a strong sense that is unique to the religions of the Middle East at this time. In most religions, harmful spirits are seen as having their place in the order of things, their influence giving way in time to that of spirits which are helpful to human beings. Many spirits are themselves seen as ambivalent, with the power to blast or to bless. The very strong strain of dualism derived from sixth-century Persia, however, saw a perpetual battle between two eternal principles of good and evil, in which the good had to strive to overcome the evil, which would otherwise win by default. This deeply pessimistic view of the nature of the world contrasts strongly with that of the Pagan religions, which see the rule of nature as either good (e.g. Stoicism) or neutral. It affected some strains of Egyptian and Hellenistic religion, through which the god of the desert, Seth, became magnified into a more threatening adversarial principle, forever pitted against his brother Horus the Elder in a battle of which the outcome was uncertain. Dualism also affected the Jewish religion during the period after the rebellion of Judas Maccabeus (167 BCE). The overwhelmingly hostile social climate of the time led to an accentuated religious emphasis on Satan, the servant of Jahweh and tempter of humanity, in which dualistic tendencies are apparent. Smaller dualistic cults, offshoots of the main Middle Eastern religions, also grew up in the deserts of Syria, Palestine and Persia. The Essenes, many Gnostic sects, and later the followers of the prophet Mani (d. 276 CE) were dualists in varying degrees. Most of them had no lasting effect; Judaism and the religion of Isis eventually returned to a less polarised or more holistic outlook. One small sect, however, did. This was Christianity, whose dualistic tendencies were present from an early stage in its drive to stamp out 'sin'.

The Christians, followers of the early reform rabbi Jesus of Nazareth, had grown invisibly during the first century CE by appealing to a wide range of people. Many of their followers were insignificant in political terms and so we hear nothing of their early growth, but by the year 64 they must have had the necessary combination of a high public profile and a low level of influence in order to be selected as scapegoats by the Emperor Nero for the fire which ravaged Rome for nine days. In the year 90, twenty years after the destruction of the Temple at Jerusalem during the Jewish Revolt of 66–73, the Jewish community reorganised itself, abolishing the Temple priesthood and its sacrifices, replacing it by the rabbinical structure and, along the way, excommunicating the Christians. Christianity then became a separate religion in its own right.

It introduced several attitudes which were not shared by the many cults of the Pagan world.[8] The first of these was charity, the idea of the spiritual worth of the poor. Pagan society was deeply stratified and snobbish, and both rich and poor knew their place. Families could advance over several generations, and individuals could be respected beyond their economic class for good manners and learning, but there was no idea that people were intrinsically equal simply as they were. Christianity was from the start a socially revolutionary movement. Second, its notion of sin was foreign to Paganism. Pagans could do unworthy deeds, or make mistakes, or be unenlightened (in terms of the Mysteries), but sin and guilt were meaningless concepts, as was the Christians' third concept, heresy. 'Heresy', in the original Greek, simply means a choice, and in the Pagan world the choice of cults multiplied almost daily. People could serve many cults at once, and they took it for granted that these were not incompatible with the deities of the Empire or with the supreme source of divine Being (if they thought there was one). Pagan religions have guidelines and precedents but no dogma, and the idea of a Devil, a subverter of the One Truth, is not found in Paganism. The Christians also based their salvific story on history rather than myth; they sought revelation rather than Mystery; and where the Pagans honoured and prayed to the dead, the Christians prayed for them.

Conceptual innovations apart, the Christians also had one rule of conduct which even the broadest Pagan tolerance could not stomach. Like their parent body, the Jews, they refused the obligatory sacrifice to the deities of the Empire, who, as we have seen, were regarded as guarantors of the material and spiritual stability of all of Rome's dominions. Sacrificing to the emperor's *numen* was understood in much the same way as the American custom of saluting the flag or the British custom of standing when the national anthem is played. The Jews were strict monotheists and iconoclasts, but they did not impose their religious tastes on those around them, they sought no converts, and so (especially after losing their home base in Palestine) they were generally tolerated as visiting aliens. Christianity, however, rapidly developed into an otherworldly religion, not only democratically ignoring, but ascetically eschewing, the benefits of material existence, and Christians sought both converts and martyrdom on the slightest of pretexts. The records are full of accounts of Pagan magistrates desperately offering Christian non-sacrificers the chance to make the most nominal of offerings to the Imperial *numen* so as to save their skin. To the Pagans' utter incomprehension, the Christians generally refused. Despite their political disruptiveness, in the early years the Christians seem to have had little impact on Pagan thought, and their theories were not discussed in Pagan circles until the end of the second century.

## POLITICAL INSTABILITY: THE THIRD CENTURY

By this time, the scope of the Empire had widened far beyond Rome and its traditions. Trajan, 'the best of princes' (98–117), was the first emperor not born in Rome, and his successor Hadrian (117–138), also successful and also a Spaniard, travelled far and wide throughout the Empire inspecting the state of the provinces. Hadrian, a keen amateur architect, was responsible for the building of the Pantheon, the temple to all the deities. The second century continued the comparative stability and civilised way of life inaugurated by Augustus. Cults and philosophies came and went, political turmoil arose and was dissolved, and what later citizens looked back on as the Golden Age of the Empire lasted until the death of the Stoic Emperor Marcus Aurelius in the year 180. By then, signs of instability were showing. A trade recession was beginning and the birth-rate was falling. To the north-east of the Empire, the Goths were pressing forward and seeking entry into the Danube provinces. In 165–167 the legions had brought back a plague from the eastern provinces, and for all these reasons the Empire was finding difficulty in mustering the internal resources to meet its external challenges. Rome had survived similar periods of disintegration before, but it had never previously had so much territory to administer.

At times of economic stress, religious innovations often occur. The *Meditations* of Marcus Aurelius had demonstrated the persistence of Stoicism, the cults of the various deities and the increasingly philosophical pronouncements of oracles continued to flourish,[9] and a biography of the Pythagorean teacher Apollonius of Tyana was compiled by the philosopher Philostratus for the Empress Julia Domna, the wife of Septimius Severus (193–211). In 178 the Platonist Celsus wrote *True Reason*, a refutation of Christianity, and around the year 200 the Christian Tertullian wrote extensive criticisms of the Pagans as well as of Gnostics and other Christian schismatics. Christianity had reached intellectual maturity and was now considered worth disputing with by the intellectual establishment.

Meanwhile, on the political scene migrating tribespeople were beginning to infiltrate the Empire. Population movements had forced the nomads of the Asian steppes to press on Rome's northern frontiers, and from the beginning of the third century they were invited not only to serve in the legions as mercenaries, but actually to settle within the Imperial boundary in exchange for military service. Control of the military soon passed to able barbarians, and the troops developed the habit of electing emperors. Nobody could quarrel with the soldiers' choice except another body of soldiers, and of the twenty emperors between 235 and 284, all but three died by the assassin's hand.

In Rome itself, however, a new growth of philosophy and literature was taking place. Ammonius of Alexandria (*fl.* 235), Plotinus (204–275) and Porphyry (*fl.* 270) brought Neoplatonism from Alexandria to Rome. Plotinus was a contemplative mystic, asserting the ultimate unity of all religions, teaching the doctrine of emanation from the spiritual Unity to the material multiplicity, but denying any evil or 'fallen' quality of the material world, because, as he said, he had seen no evidence of it. His disciple Porphyry was to become one of the most bitter enemies of Christianity, and his works were banned by the later Christian administration in 333. By contrast with Plotinus, the Persian teacher Mani (d. 276), also a visionary, taught the evil of the material world and the necessity for human beings to 'purify' themselves in order to approach the eternal Light. Mani's doctrines led to many Christian sectarian movements, even as late as the thirteenth century, when Waldenses, Cathars and other Christian schismatics came to the notice of the Papal authority. In Mani and Plotinus we see the contrast between Middle Eastern dualism and the broader Pagan holism against which it stood out.

From 222 to 226 the Empire was ruled by Elagabalus, scion of a family of Syrian sun-worshippers. The Syrian religion was not dualistic, was of great antiquity and had doubtless influenced the attribution of solar qualities to the Greek Apollo in the fifth century BCE. Now it met its distant heir in the Roman Imperial cult of Apollo, but when Elagabalus, Hellenistically renaming himself Heliogabalus, instituted the religion of his solar deity El Gabel, the culture shock was too much to bear. After his death the cult was erased and the Imperial cult went back to its old pragmatic ways. But in 274 the troops of the Emperor Aurelian (270–275) were inspired in battle by 'a divine form',[10] which turned out to be the Syrian El Gabel. Honouring the god who had given him victory, Aurelian modified the cult to suit the established outlook of the Empire and instituted the worship of *sol invictus deus* – The Sun, the Unconquered God – whose temple on the Campus Agrippa was dedicated on the winter solstice, the feast day of Mithras, 25 December, 274. Aurelian was a successful emperor, attacking corruption in the civil service, reclaiming the ravaged eastern frontier and describing himself on his coins as 'Recreator of the World'. The Unconquered Sun was clearly intended to be a unifying factor in the Empire, coexisting with other divinities but taking into himself elements of the solar deities who already existed in Rome and her provinces. Aurelian's successors, Tacitus, Probus and Carus, continued to revere the sun-god.

Between these two solar cults, however, came the first systematic persecution of the Christians. In 249–251, Decius used his short reign to institute an absolute requirement for all citizens to swear allegiance to the state and its deities in order to receive the coveted certificate of loyalty. The aim was to restore unified central government, and the means chosen was the old Roman appeal to conservatism and continuity. Clearly, by this time those foreign cults which devalued practical duties in favour of spiritual duties were seen as a real threat to the Empire. The Christians themselves later admitted that this campaign nearly wiped them out.[11] But the Emperor Gallienus (260–268), who himself invoked the protection of Mithras, suspended the persecution and so the dualists and semi-dualists could regroup while the unifying religion of the Empire reverted to solar worship.

## DIOCLETIAN: STATE PAGANISM RESTORED

Around the year 275, Porphyry wrote *Against the Christians*, an attack against which, like that of Celsus one hundred years earlier, the newcomers felt obliged to defend themselves. The political chaos of fifty years was then reversed by the accession of Diocletian (284–305), a Dalmatian provincial, in no way a noble, a professional soldier and an organising genius. Like Augustus three hundred years before him he radically reorganised the administrative hierarchy and reasserted the old religion of Republican Rome in a form adapted to contemporary circumstances. He disestablished the cult of the Unconquered Sun and reinstituted the traditional cult of the Empire, with Jupiter, Hercules and Victory at its head. His edict of 287, 'On Malefactors and Manichees', was an ideological attack on dualist believers, who were to be burned 'along with their abominable writings' for 'futile, evil and superstitious teaching' which was 'contrary to human nature'.[12] This is the first instance of censorship of thought rather than simply of practice (as when the Bacchic rites were banned as a 'depraved foreign superstition' in 186 BCE) that we have from the Roman world. It shows that the fashion for dogmatic religion was beginning to infect Paganism itself. Diocletian was not as successful against the Manichees as Pope Innocent II was to be against the (more geographically localised) Cathars more than nine hundred years later. Manichaeanism went underground and persisted, and Christianity grew by leaps and bounds.

In 298 the emperor instituted a disciplinary purge of the army by making the statutory oath of allegiance to the Imperial cult an individual rather than a collective obligation. This made it impossible for Christians and Manichaeans to continue their military service, and their presumably subversive influence was thereby eradicated. In September 303, following continued inflation and natural disasters, the emperor instituted the 'Great Persecution' of the Christians, ordering the destruction of their churches and sacred writings. Perhaps this was the normal cynical Imperial scapegoating of the handiest minority group, but to judge from Diocletian's edicts he believed, as his more easy-going Pagan subjects did not, that the dogmatism of the dualists and semi-dualists could not be accommodated within the open-minded polytheism of the Pagan consensus. It would be natural for Pagans to assume that the monotheistic and dualistic cults would take their place among the multiplicity of other cults in the Empire. Diocletian clearly perceived that the dualists 'set their own beliefs against the old cults',[13] actively trying to undermine them, and he obviously did not trust that time and revelation and rational debate would bring about eventual integration.

Diocletian also moved the capital of the western Empire from Rome to Milan and eventually to Ravenna. As a provincial, he felt uncomfortable with, and was loftily ignored by, the old aristocracy of Rome, and when the time for the twentieth anniversary of his rule came in 303–304 he ill-advisedly cut short the celebrations, including the all-important Secular Games, which he was attending in the old capital, and fled to Ravenna, where he contracted a fever and became so ill that he eventually abdicated. This insult to the city and its ancestral divinities was bound to strike a blow at the morale of the whole Empire. The Pagan historian Zosimus attributes the whole decline of Rome to this act of sacrilege. Even if we do not take such divine intervention literally, it could be said that Diocletian's action, incongruous in such a master strategist, knocked the heart out of the Empire and the self-confidence out of its people. At any rate, over the next century Rome itself became increasingly marginal and ineffective. Pagan arts and letters flourished there as if in a backwater, but had no practical effect on day-to-day government.

Diocletian was followed in 305 by his Caesar in the east, Galerius, such a rough man he was nicknamed 'the Drover' even by his own soldiers, who intensified the persecution of Christians and other un-Roman sects. But, strangely enough, on his deathbed in 311 he issued an edict of toleration, and this was a turning-point in religious history. From this time on the Christians grew stronger and intensified their own campaign against the old polytheism. The years 313–314 saw the building of the first Christian basilica in Rome. Meanwhile, the rulership of the Empire went through several coups and changes during which the temple of Fortune burned down in 309. However, the new eastern emperor, Maximin Daia, responded to petitions from cities such as Nicomedia and Aricanda in Lycia to reinstitute anti-Christian legislation throughout his area of jurisdiction. He founded the shrine of Zeus Friend of Humanity in Antioch, and set up an organised Pagan priesthood in every town in the area. This was imposed from above rather than growing up organically from local shrines as in the past, just as the Christian Church organisation was delegated from above on the model of the secular Imperial administration. Daia also introduced anti-Christian schoolbooks which described Jesus of Nazareth as a slave and a criminal rather than as one inspired prophet among many, which is how the liberal Pagans of the time saw him.

Daia's edicts caused tremendous hardship among the Christians who were driven out of their homes and countries, but aroused great enthusiasm among local Pagans, not so much for the persecutions but for the restored opportunity of serving their communities and representing their divine protectors in the age-old tradition, which by conventional reckoning was by now over 1,000 years old. It was at this time too that Hierocles, governor of Bithynia, added some imaginative reconstructions of miracles to Philostratus' *Life of Apollonius* and presented it as a Pagan alternative to the Christian Gospels. Once more this shows that in terms of organisation the Pagans were on the defensive, trying to match the miracles as well as the teachings of Jesus with similar prodigies by Apollonius. It is interesting that at a time when politically so much power depended on the whim of the chief emperor of the time, in the religious sphere what seems to have been sought were miracles showing the inspirational power of a single great leader, and a priestly hierarchy with autocratic power delegated from above rather than one developing organically from tradition in the manner of the old Republican religion. The cult of the individual had arrived.

## CONSTANTINE: PAGANISM DISESTABLISHED

The reforms of Daia were to last only three years. The power struggle among the would-be emperors continued and in 312 Constantine, the son of Galerian's western Emperor Constantius Chlorus, seized power in Rome. By 313 Daia was dead, having succumbed to cholera after his army had been routed by Constantine's future co-emperor, Licinius. The victorious army had marched under the battle-cry *Summe sancte deus* – 'O Supreme and Holy God' – although its general was notoriously irreligious.[14] Daia's partisans were massacred and his new administration dismantled.

Constantine's father, a devotee of the Unconquered Sun, had been lax in implementing Diocletian's acts of persecution in his territory. Constantine himself had no obvious religious allegiance, but (as John Holland Smith explains in detail[15]) he seemed keen to appear inspired in a general way. The triumphal arch erected after his victory over the western Emperor Maxentius at Mulvian Bridge reads:

> To the Emperor Caesar Flavius Constantine who being instinct with divinity and by the greatness of his spirit with his forces avenged the commonwealth in a just cause on both the tyrant and all his party.

The panegyric read before the new emperor at a celebration several months after his victory includes the question:

> What god was it that made you feel that the time had come for the liberation of the city against the advice of men and even against the warning of the auspices? Assuredly, O Constantine, there is in you some secret communication from the divine mind which delegating the care of us to lesser gods, deigns to reveal itself to you alone.
>
> (*Paneg. Lat.* XI.3.4–5)

In a series of later accounts, the first one published about a year after the event, an answer is constructed. Constantine was variously directed in a dream on the eve of battle to mark the Christian chi-rho sign on his soldiers' shields (Lactantius), or thus directed in a vision on the march before the campaign, or directed to add to the monogram the words 'Conquer in this sign', according to subsequent versions. At any rate, with each new telling the original intimation of a divine mission became more specifically Christian, and like Aurelian before him Constantine was able to present himself before the people as a man divinely guided. But unlike Aurelian, he did not immediately offer his saving god to the people as a unifying symbol for the commonwealth.

What Constantine actually did was to grant freedom of religion to all within the Empire, under the Edict of Milan of 313. He did not especially favour the Christians, but as we have seen he was personally inclined to the worship of a supreme and nameless deity, as the philosophers had been before him. His mother, however, was a Christian. At his tenth anniversary in 315 (he had declared himself emperor during the power struggle with Galerius in 305), he insulted the ancient divinities by refusing to take part in sacrifices and allowing only prayers of thanks without flames and smoke. From then on there was an increasingly tight partnership between the emperor and the extremely well-organised Christians, who had begun their career as 'soldiers of Christ', dying for their cause in the arena, and who had modelled their organisation on the lines of the Imperial administration itself, with terms such as 'vicar' and 'diocese' taken directly from Diocletian's administrative remodelling. The otherworldly Manichees had no such organisation, and neither, apparently, did the various priests of the Unconquered Sun, which may have been Constantine's original deity. The 'Sunday Observance' laws of 321 forbade all but essential work on that day, not described as the Sabbath, as in Jewish usage, nor as the day of the resurrection of Jesus, as Christian understanding now has it, but simply as the 'Venerable Day of the Sun'. In 326 Constantine gave the shrine of Helios Apollo in Nero's circus to the Christians for the foundation of their new church of St Peter.

To direct the emotional sympathies of his many subjects, Constantine used the superb administrative network of the Christian Church. By 318 the bishops had been given all the civil rights and privileges of the Pagan high priests, and the Christian ministry had become a career rather than a vocation. In 323, under the chi-rho sign and the battle-cry of *Deus summus salvator!* – 'God the Highest, Saviour!' – Constantine had attacked and defeated his co-emperor, Licinius, who according to Eusebius was now fighting under the Republican deities and was accompanied by a corps of augurs working from a shrine in a sacred grove. Three explanations are possible for this. The first is that Licinius had simply transferred his allegiance to a different set of deities under the free-market regime of polytheism. The second is that he had experienced a conversion (or an apostasy) in the Christian sense, turning bitterly against the Supreme and Holy God who had once given him victory over his eastern rival. And the third is that Eusebius was simply inventing the story in order for Constantine's victory to

*Plate 4.2* Roman altar with swastikas, lunar horns and Daeg rune. Inscription reads: 'I, T. Licinius Valerianus, tribune, make this for the genius and colours of 1st Cohort of Varduli.

be presented as a religious one, just as that of Licinius had been described to be when he was fighting against an emperor who happened to be Pagan.

In order to organise the Christian Church still further, Constantine convened the Council of Nicaea in May 325, instituting the famous Nicene Creed which laid down a clear set of beliefs for Christians to subscribe to, and effectively making the bishops a branch of the Imperial civil service. In 328 the emperor transformed the town of Byzantium, once protected by the goddess Hecate, into the city of Constantinople, which was to be the capital of the new unified Empire. Constantine looted Pagan shrines in the Aegean to enrich his newly founded city. The temple of Asclepius in Agis in Cicilia and Venus Ourania near Mount Lebanon were ransacked.[16] On 4 November, Constantine himself cut the furrow defining the walls of the new city. The whole ceremony was conducted according to the 'ancestral rites', with the help of the high priest and the Neoplatonist Sopater, who presumably drew up the horoscope for the occasion – Sun in Sagittarius and Cancer rising, indicating a religious city which would be a home to the Empire. The temple on the acropolis (actually and symbolically the strong-point) of the new city was a Christian church, but elsewhere there were four other religious shrines. Three of these were Pagan: shrines to Castor and Pollux (gods of the cavalry), Holy Peace, and the Fortune of the city. The last was a shrine to Constantine himself, constructed with the utmost symbolic care.

It consisted of a huge statue containing in its base the sacred Palladium which Constantine had reputedly removed from the house of the Vestals in Rome two years before. The Palladium, the 'attribute of Pallas', was a relic whose appearance is now unknown, which had supposedly been brought from Troy by Aeneas and which therefore, placed in the sacred hearth of the city, guaranteed the lineage of Rome from the most ancient Mediterranean civilisation known to its mythographers. By removing the Palladium, Constantine had symbolically destroyed the power of Rome. By placing it in the foundation of his own statue, he had placed himself at the head of the spiritual and political lineage which it represented. The whole foundation of the new Empire was a careful piece of symbolic and spiritual engineering, conducted according to the age-old techniques of Pagan magical technology.

On the practical level, the capital of the Empire had to move east, since it was the eastern frontier that needed securing. Practically also, this put the western Roman religion into close contact with eastern practices and philosophies which had hitherto been contained within private devotions rather than public ceremonial. The rituals of public life were going to have to change to take account of this. Syrian sun-worship had already been Romanised and presented as a framework for such a change, and would have fitted seamlessly into the pantheon of the Roman ancestral deities, but it lacked the bureaucratic structure which Christianity offered. Likewise, the religion of Isis had no political organisation worth mentioning, and although massively popular among the citizens of the Empire, it seems not to have appealed to the more action-minded, military emperors, who offered their personal devotions to Sol, Mithras or Jupiter. Constantine, then, was looking for a religion which would unify the eastern and western provinces of the Empire. In the orb which his statue carried, symbol of world dominion (Pagan scientists had already demonstrated that the Earth was round) was embedded a fragment of what was claimed to be the True Cross of the Christians, discovered by the emperor's mother. Symbolically, according to the 'ancestral rites', this would be seen as representing not simply Christianity, but also the cross of the four quarters of the Earth and heavens, the ancient *templum* of the augurs and land-surveyors. Alexandria, Rome, Constantinople and Jerusalem were the cities which quartered the Mediterranean, at least according to ancient symbolism, and according to that same tradition, their axes crossed at the site of Troy, the mythical source of Roman civilisation and the home of the Palladium, which Constantine had adopted as the foundation of his rule. Through both Christian and Pagan spirituality, the new emperor was mastering the world. He seems in fact to have been a normal polytheist and he both permitted and founded shrines to other divinities. In 320 he passed a law authorising augury to interpret lightning strikes on public buildings. Pagans did not understand the exclusive nature of Christianity and would naturally see it as one cult among the many to which they could subscribe, under the philosophical aegis of the Supreme Divine Principle – whatever It is.

In the 320s, a new form of Christianity was developing. Arius, a teacher in Egypt, had begun teaching a form of Neoplatonism which denied the absolute identity of the Supreme God and the prophet Jesus (the 'consubstantiality' doctrine). This allowed all kinds of philosophical and mystical Pagan teachings to coexist with the thoughtful sort of Christianity, but ironically, the Arian missionaries were also successful at converting northern 'barbarian' tribes. It was not a Catholic Christian but an Arian, Alaric the Goth, who was eventually to bring about the fall of Rome.

## THE PAGANS FIGHT BACK

Constantine was baptised into Christianity by an Arian bishop on his deathbed, on Whitsunday 337. Constantine never followed the Christian sectarians in persecuting non-Christians, but his three sons did. In 340 a ban was put on Pagan sacrifices, 'superstition' and 'unsoundness of thinking' in the east, and in 342 this edict was extended to the whole Empire. In 346 public sacrifices were banned and Pagan observance was made a capital offence. The Pagans kept their heads down and waited for the tide of history to sweep the new sect away. Never before had a new cult tried to stamp out the established religion of the state. The dualism of Christian thought was completely unprecedented and presumably incomprehensible to Pagans.

In 349, Pagan sectarians backed the political rebellion of one Count Magnentius, commanding officer of the elite Jovian and Herculean legions set up by Diocletian. He was bought off by the youngest emperor, Constans, but renewed his efforts the following year, taking the whole of the western Empire. His Pagan regime was received with great rejoicing by the majority of the population, who obviously only needed a champion in order to reassert their own beliefs. Yet at the same time Christian conversions were multiplying rapidly, especially in the cities. It is at this time that the word 'pagan' ceased to be used by the Christians simply to refer to a cowardly non-combatant in the army of Christ, and regained its literal meaning: a country person, a rustic, a yokel who was too slow-witted to take up the religion of the modern age. Magnentius was defeated after some diplomatic realignment of forces by the eastern emperor, Constantius, in September 351 and committed suicide two years later in Gaul or Britain, to which he had retreated. In the campaign against Magnentius, however, Constantius had had to give power to the only male relatives (apart from his brothers) whom he had not butchered on his accession, his cousins Gallus and Julian. It was Julian who was to lead the next Pagan restoration.

Julian was a thoughtful young man, prickly and defensive, who eventually developed the eccentric habit of dressing like a Hellenistic philosopher, with an unkempt beard and wearing a rough robe. He and his brother had been brought up in seclusion as Arian Christians. Julian completely lacked the courtly manners of a gentleman of whatever faith, but when called to military command distinguished himself as a brave leader, a fair disciplinarian and a just victor.[17] When his duties took him to Greece the young prince reconverted to Paganism at the shrine of Athena of Ilium – once more the purported site of ancient Troy, the symbolic home of the mysterious Palladium. The following year he experienced an ecstatic vision during his initiation into the Mithraic Mysteries at Ephesus (the site of Maximin Daia's shrine of Zeus Friend of Humanity), and became a committed Pagan missionary for the rest of his life. Clearly, private Pagan worship including the Mysteries was still going on, but Julian noted with bitterness the decay of the public temples.

Julian's military appointment under Constantius took him as Caesar to Gaul, where the Germanic tribes, pressed by Gothic invasions from the east, had been ravaging the province. The new Caesar restored order and, it would seem, prosperity there, then duly rose against the emperor in what had become the time-honoured way of taking power. After more diplomatic intrigue, Constantius died on 3 November, 361, naming Julian as his successor, and the new emperor marched into Constantinople on 11 December, 361. He did not institute a massacre of the Christians, which led them to complain that they had been cheated of martyrdom.[18] He reduced corruption in the administration, repealed the laws of religious persecution, but prevented Christians from serving in the army (because their law forbade killing), from receiving grants and gifts (because their religion preached poverty) and from using Pagan texts in schoolbooks (because Pagan myths demonstrated Pagan ethics, which could only mislead Christian children). It is unclear whether these rulings were superbly cynical or naively sincere.

Under Julian the temples were reopened and the marauding bands of Christians who had become used to pillaging and destroying Pagan shrines became subject to the usual penalties of the law. Julian himself seems to have been a philosopher at heart, and this may have been the climate of the times, with people fighting over ideas, whether rational or revelatory, and seeking to put into practice an ethical rule of life. There is some evidence that Julian intended to set up a Pagan 'church' preaching Pagan 'doctrines', with authority imposed from above by himself as supreme pontiff. This is the religion of a Follower of the Word, whereas for the bulk of Julian's subjects the many divinities of what we can now see as the Pagan religion were simply unseen presences whose existence was proved by their effects, *numina* whose presence people would be mad to deny. The climate of thought was changing, whether because of the dogmatic preaching of the Christians and Manichees or as the precondition of this. Julian's version of 'Hellenism' reflected the change in the times.

In 363 the emperor went to secure the eastern frontier against the Persians and died in battle. Christianity became the official religion once more, but Paganism was tolerated until the accession of Theodosius in 379. Meanwhile, Pagan art and literature had taken heart again in Rome and the so-called 'Aristocracy of Letters' flourished in that backwater until the Pagan rebellion against Theodosius in 394. After Theodosius declared Catholic Christianity the only permissible faith in 381, the western emperor, Gratian, snubbed the Pagans of Rome by declining the title of Pontifex Maximus and then enacting a series of deadly laws against the cults of the old Republic. State funding was to be withdrawn from Pagan shrines and ceremonies, the Altar of Victory was to be removed from the Senate, and, perhaps worst of all, the Vestals were to lose their privileges and immunities and their sacred fire was to be put out. The Roman establishment was stunned. By the end of the year, however, Gratian was murdered by his barbarian Master of Cavalry at Lyons.

After Gratian's assassination, a patrician called Symmachus became Prefect of Rome in 384. He fronted the Pagan party in the argument over the Altar of Victory, arguing that ancestral usage ought to be maintained, for different nations have different faiths. Rome should be allowed to live in her own way.

We ask peace for the gods of our fathers, peace for our nature divinities. It is only just to assume that the object of all people's worship is the same. We look up to the same stars, one sky covers us all and the same universe surrounds us. Do the means by which a man seeks the truth really matter? There is no single road by which we may arrive at so great a mystery.

(Symmachus, *Relatio* 3, in Smith (1976), p. 152)

The Christian emperor, under the guidance of Bishop Ambrose, refused to restore the Altar, Symmachus was assailed by a whispering campaign and resigned as chief magistrate in 385, just before Emperor Valentinian held his ten-year jubilee in Rome. That year, 386, saw Libanius publish his *Defence of the Temples*, but it also saw the fanatical ex-monk John Chrysostom appointed as archbishop of Constantinople. In 392, thoroughgoing laws against Pagans and non-Catholic Christians made Pagan wills invalid when contested by Christian heirs, banned all celebratory games and Pagan holy days, and forbade even the worship of the household deities in private. In the west, however, Valentinian was assassinated in 392 and Eugenius (392–394) restored the image of Victory in the Senate and payments to Pagan priests began again. Pagan shrines were restored ceremonially by senior officials, including that of Hercules at Ostia.

Theodosius had been principal emperor since 379 and in his eastern area of jurisdiction anti-Pagan legislation had been continuous. Given the un-stable nature of the times, he had a horror of secret societies and of magic, so private Pagan rituals were forbidden from the start of his reign. Monasteries and nunneries had been founded in the east, and gangs of black-robed monks would roam the cities and countryside desecrating temples and inciting mobs to destroy them, while the civil authorities turned a blind eye. In 390 a mob burned down the library of Alexandria, an irreplaceable collection of documents dating back to remotest antiquity, and in the following year the Serapeium (temple of Isis and Serapis) was destroyed by order of Archbishop Theophilus of Alexandria. After decades of expecting the Christians to go away, the Pagans finally fought back. The old Roman habit of obedience to authority was perhaps weaker in the east, and there were battles in the streets. One Bishop Marcellus, having sent a party of soldiers and gladiators to destroy a temple, was seized by the local populace and burned alive.[19] At Alexandria, some of the wreckers were crucified. But the Pagan cults were disunified, there was no concept of a general Pagan religion (Julian's 'Hellenism' had not been tested for long enough), and Libanius' 'men in black, who show their piety by dressing in the clothes of mourning' ultimately had their way, destroying most of the artwork and the learning of the ancient world in their zeal to discover and eradicate 'sin'.

In 394, Theodosius took over the whole Empire and announced that the state could not afford to pay for Pagan rites, as the money was needed for the army. Official Paganism was forced underground, and Pagans were perse-cuted. The civil rights of Pagans continued to be suppressed, culminating in 416, when Pagans were barred from the Imperial Service. But by then, the Empire was divided, ravaged by Goths, Vandals and Huns, moving west under pressure from the Huns who had recently been expelled from China. Many of these were Arian Christians. The Roman troops who defeated Eugenius, the Pagan emperor in the west, in 394 were under the control of an Arian, a Vandal named Stilicho, and included Gothic Arian mercenaries under one Alaric. Alaric next appears the following year pillaging and largely destroying the Pagan shrines of Greece. Some Pagan commentators of the time[20] were convinced that this was a religious crusade. The Mystery shrine, still functioning at Eleusis, was destroyed then, and the Erechtheum, the shrine of Poseidon on the Acropolis, became the first Pagan site on the peninsula to be converted into a Christian church.

Stilicho the Vandal, a naturalised Roman, was now chief of staff under the western Emperor Honorius (395–423), who instituted the long-feared decree to destroy the temples in 398. The law attacking the temples was, however, repealed, and the Empire relapsed into its previous state of confusion. At some time after 402 Stilicho burned the Sibylline Books, perhaps to demonstrate his contempt for the Pagans' explanation of the chaos as a consequence of abandoning the ancestral deities. In 405 more than 200,000 Goths, under a Scythian Pagan called Radegais, flooded into Italy from the north-east. They were defeated, but only just, by Alaric. More pretenders to the throne arose and were defeated, Stilicho was executed on a pretext by Honorius, and then in 409 Alaric found himself on the receiving end of a new persecution. The administration was to be purged of 'barbarians'. Briefly, Alaric, although Christian, set up a new Pagan Imperial administration in Rome, but the experiment failed to impress Honorius, and in a fit of frustration on 24 August, 410 Alaric sacked the city.

As a Christian, Alaric allowed one sanctuary to be spared, the church of St Peter on Vatican Hill. In it were kept the valuables of as many Christians as could get them there, and their girl children. The new city was set up as a Christian foundation. Further edicts referred to Pagan practices as an error on the part of Christian believers, rather than as part of a separate and independent religion. One thousand years of Pagan tradition had come to an end.

## THE LEGACY

However, the common people remained Pagan in fact if not in theory, as decrees and the writings of observers show. The writings of Church fathers from Augustine (354–430) through to the antiquarians of the nineteenth century (e.g. J.B. Andrews' observations of the Italian *streghe* reported in the journal *Folk-Lore*, vol. VIII, no. I, March, 1897) variously condemn, bewail or simply observe the remnants of ancient belief and practice among unlettered folk. The temple of the Mother of Heaven (i.e. Isis) at Carthage, disused and overgrown by the early fifth century, was made into a church. But in the year 440, bishops noticed that worshippers there were continuing to worship the old goddess, and had the temple demolished.[21]

A few Pagan intellectuals managed to salvage and transmit the learning and values of the past during that first bleak century. We have already mentioned Zosimus the historian, writing at the end of the fourth century, whose account of Roman civilisation fills out with its own bias the biased record of his Christian contemporaries. In addition, the lawyer Martianus Capella, a contemporary of Augustine at Hippo, compiled *The Marriage of Philology and Mercury*, a great compendium of what became known as the seven liberal arts, including long quotations from Classical authors. Platonic teaching continued in Alexandria, a hotbed of Christian missionary zeal, but in 415 the head of the school, Hypatia, was torn apart by a Christian mob on her way to the lecture theatre. In 432–433 a young visionary called Proclus studied in Athens under the Pagan philosophers Syrianus and Plutarch. After further wandering under the guidance of his goddess Hecate, the divine patroness of his birthplace, Byzantium, Proclus himself became head of the Academy in around 450. He wrote and taught voluminously, and when in 529 the eastern Emperor Justinian closed down the Pagan schools in Athens, the remaining philosophers, rather than recanting, fled to Persia and taught at the university of Jundishapur.[22] Greek learning was thus preserved and built upon by the Persians and also by the Arabs, who had received it through centuries of interaction with the Graeco-Roman Empire. It was eventually returned to the western world when the Christian Frankish Empire clashed with the Islamic Moorish Empire in Spain in the ninth century.

Cultured Christians such as Boethius (480–524) and Cassiodorus (*c.*477–*c.*565) were rare but invaluable in the transmission of learning. Boethius translated Aristotle into Latin, wrote several treatises on logic, music and arithmetic, and used quotations from Classical authors freely in his work *The Consolation of Philosophy*. By applying philosophical categories to questions of Christian theology, he prepared the way for the later re-admission of intellectual speculation into the theological fold. Cassiodorus was a pupil of Boethius, who extended Capella's work on the seven liberal arts and eventually founded a house of contemplatives which included a well-stocked library of many ancient texts. Boethius and Cassiodorus gave medieval philosophy the intellectual nicety for which we respect it today, much of which is derived from Pagan thought.

After the death of Emperor Theodosius in 395, the old Roman Empire with its two Christian capitals split once more into east and west. This time there was to be no co-ordinating authority. In 381 Theodosius had declared the eastern patriarchate in Constantinople equal in authority to the western pat-riarchate in Rome, and after that the two Christian dominions went their increasingly separate ways, as the political strength of the western Empire diminished following the sack of Rome. Despite localised fanaticism, such as that of the Christian mobs in Egypt, the Byzantine Empire retained the Greek respect for intellectual and visionary information, and preserved many ancient documents as well as incorporating some mystical teachings into its form of Christianity. By contrast, as Neoplatonism grew during the second century, the Christians in Rome had abandoned Greek, their original liturgical language, and began to distrust it as sophistical and dangerous to honest minds. Western Christianity based on Rome was politically active, considering itself a moral counterbalance to the ignorance of its new political rulers, the one-time warrior nomads who knew little of urban civilisation, but in its initial years it also set itself against speculative thought, both intellectual and mystical.

Divided by conflicts between Catholics and Arians, the western Empire grew increasingly weak, its last emperor being deposed in 476 in favour of a barbarian king of Italy. The Goths and Vandals who held Italy and Spain, however, saw themselves as custodians of an ancient civilisation which they, as newcomers, did not share. This civilisation was, of course, Pagan. The Catholic Church in these countries adopted many of the outward forms of Pagan ceremonial. For example, the Goths wore their hair long and their tunics short, but Christian priests retained the short hair and long robe of a Roman gentleman. A shaven head had been characteristic of a priest of Egyptian religion, so much so that St Jerome (b. 348) stated that Christian priests should not appear with shorn head lest they be confounded with priests of Isis and Serapis.[23] Yet by 663, the Synod of Whitby included an argument not over whether priests should be tonsured, but over what style of tonsure to adopt. Christianity was vehemently opposed to the worship of goddesses. Yet one of the earliest churches dedicated to Mary Mother of God was on the site of the temple of Diana at Ephesus. A synod held at Ephesus in 431 first designated Mary as Mother of God.[24] The procession celebrating the beatification of Mary used smoking censers and flaring torches, as were once used in the processions of Diana. The use of holy water and incense, solemn processions (the old lustrations), religious rites of passage marking the turning-points of human life, the veneration of local saints, and the great feast of the dead, the annual Christian Parentalia on All Souls' Day, can all be seen as direct imitations of Pagan tradition.

St Augustine proposed the 'christening' of Pagan objects as well as of Pagan people, to convert them to Christian use. Notoriously, in 601 Pope Gregory I advised his missionaries in northern Europe to do the same thing with holy places. We have already seen the unexpected result of an early attempt to do this (the temple of the Mother of Heaven at Carthage, above). In Rome, the Litania Major of the Catholic Church was held on St Mark's Day (25 April), the day of the Roman Robigalia. In that city, it included a procession that took the same route as the Pagan procession.[25] During the following centuries, Church directives become full of orders to Christian priests not to allow, for example, 'carols' of dancing and singing, especially by young women, in their churches.[26] Priests even took part in the rites of the Calends of May.[27] The orders were mixed and *ad hoc*, because they were fighting against the inevitable. The Roman midwinter feast of Saturnalia (17 December), the winter solstice or Brumalia on 25 December and the New Year feast on the Calends of January persisted in their Pagan form through an accident of Church doctrine. In theory they were Pagan holidays, not Christian ones. New Year celebrations had been inveighed against by Bishop Martin of Braga in 575:

> You shall not perform the wicked celebration of the Calends and observe the holiday of the Gentiles, nor shall you decorate your houses with laurel and green branches. This whole celebration is Pagan.
> (*Acta Conciliarum* V.iii.399, quoted in Tille (1899), p. 103 n. 2)

In 742 the Northumbrian missionary Bishop Boniface warned his German converts against celebrating the solstice. However, they said they had seen the same done in Rome outside St Peter's Church and not forbidden. In fact, the winter solstice or Brumalia, by now the feast of Mithras and the Unconquered Sun, had been associated with the birth of Jesus in 354 by Bishop Liberius of Rome.[28] This move had been made in order to accommodate the new doctrine, one move in the continuing battle against Arianism, that Jesus had been divine from his birth rather than receiving divinity when he was baptised by John, which latter occasion was celebrated as the Epiphany on 6 January. ('Epiphany', of course, is the old word for a Pagan god or goddess showing themselves to their worshippers in a vision.) The new feast of Christ's mass at the winter solstice was exported to Constantinople in 379, and in 506 the Law Book of Alarich designated it as a public holiday. As we have seen, in the time of Constantine, the new faith of Christianity was taken to be similar to that of the Unconquered Sun, whose feast day, together with that of Mithras, was also at the winter solstice. Why Bishop Liberius chose the winter solstice as the birth of Christ we do not know, but we can assume that his choice took account of the historical conflation of Christ, Mithras and Sol.

What is certain is that once the choice was made the old Pagan celebrations were almost bound to attach themselves to the new date. The name of Saturnalia died out, but its celebrations, such as decking houses with evergreens, giving presents and feasting, were attached to Christmas. Some features of the New Year, such as the keeping of a perpetual fire in the hearth and the laying of a table for the goddess Fortuna (later for local spirits or for Father Christmas), were transferred to the new feast. But New Year, which corresponded to a genuine turning-point in civic life each year, also remained as a (heretical) feast in its own right and was never assimilated by the Church. It is not generally true to say that the Church adopted Pagan feast days as its own feast days, but it did adopt the celebrations of adjacent ones, such as the Saturnalia, into its own liturgical year, and it did lend its blessing to local events which would have been celebrated anyway, such as Plough Monday, St George's Day, beating the village bounds, and May Eve, as we shall see.

The western Empire was broken up eventually by the continuing rivalry between Catholics and Arians. In 534, the eastern Emperor Justinian reclaimed Africa from the (mostly Arian) Vandals and was hailed as a liberator by the Catholic Church there, and between 535 and 555 he took Italy back from the (Arian) Goths, all in the name of religion. The wealth and infrastructure of the country were almost destroyed in the process,[29] and it did not have time to recover before the next wave of barbarian invasions, led by the Lombards in 568. Any pretence at a western Empire was now over, and yet the ideal remained, to be revived as the Holy Roman Empire by Charlemagne the Frank (741–814). The eastern Empire remained politically and liturgically intact (though held by the Franks on behalf of Rome for fifty years until 1261), until it fell to the Islamic Turks in 1453. After that the self-appointed championship of the Holy Roman Empire of the east, with its Orthodox rite, differing from that of the Catholics, was taken on by Russia.

## ISLAM

Between 580 and 632, the prophet Mohammed lived, worked as a merchant and taught his new monotheistic faith, a reworking of Jewish, New Testament, Parsee and Gnostic influences current in the Levantine countries at the far end of his caravan journeys. The new religion, Islam ('obedience'), swept away the old Paganism of southern Arabia, with its aniconic shrines including that of the Caba at Mecca, which Mohammed later declared to be the temple of Abraham, and its moon-god Sin, who had already subsumed the worship of the three goddesses Al'lat, Al-Uzzah and Manat, later mentioned by Mohammed in the famous 'Satanic verses' of the Koran. The crescent and star motif of Islam recalls the emblems of the moon-god Sin and the evening-star god Attar, and, indeed, Mohammed changed the original luni-solar calendar of the Arabs to the purely lunar one which is still used today. Mohammed's inspired reworking of a moon-god monotheism which was already in progress led to a conquering religion which was as successful as that of ancient Rome or those of Catholic and Orthodox Christianity. It was following the Arab conquest in 637 that the Parsees, followers of Persian solar dualism, fled to India and Persia became Islamic. Arab rulers, fanatically anti-Pagan, were on the whole tolerant of the other monotheisms, Judaism and Christianity, and many parts of Europe came under their control in the following centuries.

The Christian kingdom of Spain was taken over by the Arabs under Islam, with Berber troops, in 711, so linking this western peninsula with eastern art and scholarship in a generally tolerant, multicultural society under Islamic control. In 870, the library of Al Hakem at Cordoba boasted books from all over the world. Classified and catalogued in order were 600,000 volumes.[30] The few tiny Christian kingdoms, huddled up against the Pyrenees, began their reconquest of the south in 1085 and finished it in 1266, with Portugal founded in 1147. Strangely enough, it was not only the Christians who fought against the Arabs. Sardinia, itself Islamic from 720–740, sent Pagan missions to Spain in about the year 1000. In the late sixth century, Pope Gregory the Great had found Sardinia to be a stronghold of Paganism, with the people bribing the governor to turn a blind eye.[31] In the eleventh century, Paganism was strong in Sardinia, and 'many professors of it'[32] went into Spain, where they attempted to spread their belief, but were driven out by the Catholics and also, presumably, the Arabs. Crete was Islamic from 823 to 961, Sicily from 832 to 878, Corsica from 852 to 1077 and Malta from 870 to 1090. Southern France was invaded by Arab forces in 720, but after a decisive defeat by the northern French at Poitiers in 732, the raiders made no more serious attempts at settlement and were eventually beaten back over the Pyrenees.

Islam spread north from its home to Egypt, Persia and Syria, where it inherited the intellectual legacy of the Classical world, which it retransmitted to the Roman kingdoms in the west. Spain and southern France became centres of learning under their Islamic overlords, and this learning was disseminated further north after the Berber invasion of Castile in 1195, which forced many Christian and Jewish intellectuals to flee north into the Christian kingdoms, taking with them logic, astronomy and other aspects of Greek learning which had been nurtured by the Arabs. (In 1492 Ferdinand and Isabella expelled these same intellectual classes as actual or potential heretics, and Spain became a doctrinaire outpost of militant Catholicism.) By the eleventh century Islam had spread far north in the old Hellenistic world and was the antagonistic neighbour of the eastern Roman Empire, where we shall meet it again in the penultimate chapter. Meanwhile, the Celto-Roman west was becoming Germanic.

# 5

# THE CELTIC WORLD

The Greeks gave the name *Keltoi* to the barbarian peoples of central Europe, who came down in their raiding parties from the fifth century BCE and terrorised the settled city-states of the Mediterranean. During the late fifth century these tribes expanded westwards into Gaul, Britain and Ireland, southwest into Iberia, southwards into northern Italy and eastwards through the Balkans and into Asia Minor. Tribes now considered 'Celtic' include the Helvetii in the area of what is now Switzerland, the Boii in what is now Italy, the Averni in what is now France, and the Scordisci in what is now Serbia. Nineteenth-century historians set great store by the supposed difference between 'Celtic' and 'Germanic' root-stocks, but modern research indicates that these were originally part of a common north European tradition, already differentiating into separate linguistic groups when they were geographically split apart by the Romans. We use the word 'Celtic' as short-hand for the indigenous peoples of north-west Europe who, apart from the Irish, were colonised by Rome and in all cases were cut off by the boundary of the Roman Empire from the 'German' tribes east of the Rhine and north of the Danube.[1]

Celtic civilisation emerged around 700 BCE in Austria: the so-called Hallstatt culture. The wealth of Hallstatt was based on salt, which was traded for goods from Greece and Etruria. A development took place around 500 BCE in north-east France and the middle Rhine, the early La Tène period, after which the Celts became noticeably mobile. When they swept down into the Italian peninsula, they won the Po Valley from the Etruscans, founded Milan in the fifth century and sacked Rome in 390. They reached their widest area of influence in about 260, and were seen, together with the Persians and the Scythians, as one of the three great nations of barbarian Europe. During the seventh century the Celts arrived in Gaul, where from the third century onwards, under Roman influence, they took up a semi-sedentary life in towns, and began to act as merchants, travelling across Europe to buy, sell and often plunder goods. They had settled Britain in the sixth century BCE and at intervals thereafter, parts of Spain during the third century, and during the same century they colonised the Dalmatian coast (part of what was until recently Yugoslavia), Thrace (modern Bulgaria) and parts of Asia Minor, where they became known as the Galatians. Strabo reported that the Celts were quarrelsome, brave, quick to fight, but otherwise not uncouth.[2] Under the name of Gaesatae, they often worked as mercenaries, e.g. for Dionysius of Syracuse (Sicily) in the early fifth century, for the Macedonians, including Alexander the Great (336–323), and later for Hannibal (247–182).

During the third century, the Mediterranean nations developed an effective resistance against them. In 225 a Celtic invasion of Italy was defeated by the inhabitants under Roman leadership, and in 201, after defeating Hannibal's Carthaginian invasion, Rome reclaimed the Po Valley from its Celtic settlers and began to enslave or exterminate Celtic tribes including the Cenomani, the Insubres and the Boii. Spain and Gaul were conquered by the Romans over some two hundred years, beginning with the second Punic War, when the strongholds of Carthage in Spain and southern France were captured, and ending with the final conquest of north-west Spain in the reign of Augustus. During the early third century the Celts had attacked Macedonia and Greece but were routed at Delphi in 279, with the result that the deity of that shrine, Apollo, was taken for ever afterwards as the champion of civilisation against barbarism.

Nevertheless, the nomadic Celts and the settled cultures of the south did interact. Cultural interchange with the Mediterranean civilisations seems initially to have been one-way. Around 650, through contact with the Greek and Etruscan civilisations, the Celts began to absorb elements of Mediterranean culture. Through these contacts, the characteristically Celtic style of art came into being as the development of the central European Hallstatt style with modified Greek (Etruscan) elements. The figurative art of Greece and Etruria seems to have had less impact than the more abstract elements, which were transmuted by the Celts into their unique style. Despite contact with the alphabet-using Greeks and Etruscans, there was no written Celtic language. Thus, names of deities and religious meanings of artefacts come down to us only from a later period, after the Roman conquests. The Celts were renowned for their reverence of the spoken word: Bards were respected members of society, and Druids maintained their knowledge through highly developed memory. In the first century BCE, when the Roman conquest of the Po Valley had settled down, the old Celtic lands produced many outstanding men of letters, among them Catullus, Cato, Varro, Virgil and others. Much later, after the fall of the Empire in the fifth century CE, the provinces of Spain and what is now southern France likewise became tenacious strongholds of Roman social, artistic and literary culture under the rulership of their new Visigothic overlords.

To the Greeks and Romans, the Celts were barbarians (people whose language sounded like 'ba ba ba'). They were nomads who lacked the arts of civilisation and they were thoroughly despised by their settled neighbours.

But in religious matters, to the modern eye they were part of the same broad Pagan grouping: Nature-venerating, polytheistic and recognisant of female divinities. Their deities were easily, if not accurately, Romanised (just as those of the Romans had been easily Graecised), in a way which the Jewish and then Christian divinities never were. They venerated both local and general deities, usually in natural sanctuaries, especially shrines at springs, rivers, lakes and in woodland. The water-spring goddess Sirona was revered at Pforzheim, Germany, and continuity of water-cults is known at hundreds of holy wells in Britain and Ireland, for example the hot springs at Buxton in Derbyshire, known in Roman times as Aquae Arnemetiae (the waters of the goddess of the sacred grove). Certain rivers have their own deities, many recalled by their still-Celtic names, e.g. Axona (Aisne), Nechtan (Neckar, Neckinger), Sequana (Seine), Sinend (Shannon), Deva (Dee) and Belisama (Mersey). Important shrines of water-deities existed at the sources of rivers, such as that at the source of the Seine. Here, healing shrines developed. Major British examples are Sul, divinity of the hot springs at Bath, identified by the Romans with Minerva, and Nodens, who was perhaps equivalent to the Irish god Nuada Argetlám, revered in the forest sanctuary at Lydney, Gloucestershire. In the late fourth century CE this site expanded and became a pilgrimage sanctuary of healing, equipped with rich temples, baths and accommodation for visitors.

## RELIGIOUS PRACTICES

Like the Mediterranean civilisations, the Celts worshipped in sacred groves or *Nemetona*, but unlike them they did not have elaborate temples to house the images of their deities. In his *Pharsalia*, Lucan refers to the Gaulish Druids who live in deep groves and sequestered uninhabited woods. The Scholiast's comment on this passage is 'They worship the gods in the woods without using temples'.[3] Dio Cassius wrote that the Britons had sanctuaries in which they offered sacrifice to Andraste, goddess of victory.[4] These groves were dread places, held in great awe and approached only by the priesthood. The place-name *nemet-* indicates the site of a sacred grove. They may also have been administrative meeting places: Strabo reports that the main meeting place of the Galatae, the Celts who had settled in Asia Minor, was called Drunemeton, or Oak Grove.[5] As centres of native loyalty, they were sometimes destroyed by conquerors. Julius Caesar cut down a sacred grove near Marseilles, which had tree trunks carved into the likeness of gods, and Suetonius Paulinus destroyed the Druidic groves on Anglesey during his sack of the island in 61.[6] The Celtic practice of tree veneration continued into Christian times, when priests like St Martin and St Patrick also found groves to desecrate.

The *Temenos* (ditched enclosure, literally 'place set apart') was the major place of worship, the temple inside it being a secondary consideration, as it

*Plate 5.1* Image of the goddess Sequana, deity of the river Seine, France, from the Romano-Gallic shrine at the river's source. Nigel Pennick.

had been in the early days of Greece and Rome. The enclosure was usually square or rectangular; if irregular, it still had straight sides. Sometimes, the enclosure contained a sacred tree or pillar, perhaps carved or adorned like modern Maypoles. A circular ditched enclosure at Goloring (near Koblenz, Germany; sixth century BCE) had a post hole at the centre. There is archaeological evidence for the perambulation of shrines, perhaps in circle dancing, as in Maypole traditions. Inside a wide ditch at the late La Tène II barrow at Normée (Marne, France) is a 20-metre-square floor, compressed hard as if people had walked or danced in large numbers around a central point.[7] In Roman Imperial times, there was continuity of shrine-sites in England. At Frilford, near Abingdon, Oxfordshire, two Roman shrines were erected on the site of an earlier wooden structure, whilst at Gosbecks Farm near Colchester, Essex, a Roman temple of Celtic style was erected in an earlier ditched sanctuary. A bronze image of Mercury was found there.

Wells were also sacred, often associated with healing, as we shall see below. Each well was associated with a particular deity, as, for example, Coventina at Carrawburgh. In the north of England, the ancient territory of the Brigantes, and in Ireland, well-worship continues in a modern form, sometimes as a local folk-observance but more often by adoption into Christianity

*Plate 5.2* Well-offering in the form of a 'dolly' from Kilmacrenan, Donegal, Ireland, 1894. Those visiting the well for its healing properties would leave a 'dolly' in acknowledgement and thanksgiving, continuing ancient Celtic Pagan practice.
© 1992 Nigel Pennick.

in the form of 'well-dressing'. Pictures made of flower petals are carefully constructed the night before and then carried to the well in a procession, sometimes with floats and dancing children, sometimes more soberly, where the vicar blesses the well as a source of water for the community. Originally, a local saint was associated with the well, the successor of the original Celtic deity, but this feature has sometimes been lost in Protestant times.

Although the Celts had been in contact with the Mediterranean world since at least the seventh century BCE (through trading) and had become settled agrarians since occupying the Po Valley in the fifth, Caesar, writing in 53 BCE, can still report that the Celts in the main part of Gaul beyond the Alps practised human sacrifice. The Celts were 'slaves to superstition', he says, and believed that in order to preserve their own lives in battle they must sacrifice an equal number of others.[8] The Druids presided over these regular public sacrifices, which among some tribes were accomplished by burning the victims in huge wickerwork effigies. By the Imperial age, some fifty years later, travellers no longer report human sacrifice, and so it may be that Caesar was recording the last evidence of an earlier phase of Celtic culture. Strabo, writing at the beginning of the Common Era, says as much:

> The heads of enemies held in high repute they used to embalm in cedar oil and exhibit to strangers, and they would not deign to give them back even for a ransom of an equal weight of gold. But the Romans put a stop to these customs, as well as to all those connected with the sacrifices and divinations that are opposed to our usages. They used to strike a human being, whom they had devoted to death, in the back with a sabre, and then divine from his death-struggle. But they would not sacrifice without the Druids. We are told of still other kinds of human sacrifices; for example, they would shoot victims to death with arrows, or impale them in the temples, or having devised a colossus of straw and wood, throw into the colossus cattle and wild animals of all sorts and human beings, and make a burnt-offering of the whole thing.[9]

Similarly, Homer described the Greek leader Agamemnon's sacrifice of his daughter in the Trojan War of 1180 BCE, likewise the sacrifice of Trojan prisoners of war before the pyre of Patroclus, but there is no evidence that Homer's Greek contemporaries three hundred years later practised or even countenanced human sacrifice. On the contrary, nations who called themselves civilised rejected it as an abomination, and as we have seen, the Romans passed a law explicitly forbidding it.

We do not hear of women as priestesses or as seeresses among the earliest reports of the Celts. The Druids and their associated male colleges, the Vates and the Bards, seem to have monopolised the field. According to Pliny (IV.4), the Bards were singers and poets, the Vates were seers and scientists, and the Druids were both scientists and moral philosophers, the judges and arbitrators of both private and public disputes. Pliny mentions that the Druids and 'others', presumably the Vates, taught the immortality of the soul; Caesar had mentioned that they taught that the soul would pass into another body after death. In the Mediterranean world, such beliefs were only held among the Pythagoreans, and so the Druids were sometimes described as such. Pliny echoes Caesar's earlier report (which he may simply be repeating) that the Druids also used to decide matters of public policy such as the decision to go to war. We have already seen that the main political meeting place of the Celts in Asia Minor was a sacred oak grove. In Caesar's time, the main centre of Druidism was in the area of the Carnutes, after whom Chartres is named. There, Druids met annually at a shrine believed to be the site of Chartres Cathedral. This was the omphalos of Gaul, the sacred though not the geographical centre of the country.

It seems, then, that the Celtic priesthood had much more direct political power than that of Greece or Rome, where magistracies were a secular appointment, augurs had only the power to advise, not to direct, and secular officials, however many priestly obligations they might have in virtue of their office, were chosen for their rationality, good judgement and perhaps good luck, rather than for any direct line they had to the gods. After the Roman conquest of Spain, Gaul and Britain, reports of the Druid priesthood are few, presumably since the political structure of decision-making had changed. Both Claudius and Tiberius attempted to stamp out the 'religion of the Druids',[10] and the altars for the 'savage superstition' of human sacrifice were destroyed,[11] but we do not hear details of a general persecution. Occasional reports of single Druids and Druidesses surface in the later Empire, and in Ireland, which was never Romanised, the traditional tales mention Druids and *fili*, poets or seers whose pronouncements were highly valued and often feared by their communities. In historical times too the Irish *fili* and Druids travelled around and were known as 'hedge-preachers', like the wandering *sadhus* of India, passing on their teaching to anyone who would have it.

Tacitus, towards the end of the first century CE, also reported that the Celts made no distinction between male and female rulers. In Britain, the famous revolt led by Boudicca (60 CE) seems to have inspired unhesitating loyalty throughout the province. Queen Cartimandua, leader of the neighbouring Brigantes in the north-east, clearly enjoyed absolute authority over her tribe. She handed over Caratacus, the leader of an earlier rebellion, to the Romans in the year 47, and in the year 53 we hear of her again, having divorced her husband in favour of his presumably younger and more virile charioteer. But the ancient authors tell us little of priestesses. Strabo[12] repeats a report by Poseidonius of an island off the coast of Gaul, on which the women of the Samnitae lived without men, devoted to the ecstatic worship of Dionysos, to whom they devoted mystic initiations as well as other rites. This would be a female college similar to the Vates, the Celtic seers. There is also a report by Artemidorus, as saying that on an island near Britain women perform sacrifices like those in Samothrace, devoted to the (all-female) worship of Demeter and Kore. Unfortunately, these reports were never confirmed by later travellers and are sometimes dismissed as apocryphal. Tacitus, however, mentions black-robed women rushing between the ranks of British warriors, waving firebrands, before the battle of Anglesey, but it is not clear whether these are Druidesses or laity. These are tantalising hints, but there is little more. In medieval and modern times, the Celtic countries have boasted of many female well-guardians, often seeresses who presumably follow in direct line from the ancient healing and prophetic sanctuaries evidenced by archaeology and the ancient authors. But in between the line is obscure.

## THE CELTIC DIVINITIES

The Celts seem to have been devoted to individual achievement and prowess, rather than to collective pursuits such as nationalism. Tribal warfare, which was frequent, seems to have been as much an occasion for individual heroism as for national prestige (as among the Germans and Romans) or even for booty. Celtic gods later identified with Mars appear in inscriptions to hybrids such as Mars Rigisamus (West Coker, Somerset), Mars Corotiacus (Martlesham, Suffolk) and Mars Loucetius (Bath). In the north of Britain the gods Belatucadrus and Cocidius were invoked and occasionally depicted, with helmet, a spear and a shield. In particular there were many battle-goddesses, for example Nemetona. The Irish myths, written down by monks in the ninth century, name a triple goddess called the Macha, one called the Morrigan and one called Badb, but both from these later tales and from ancient artefacts it seems that almost any goddess has at least a subsidiary role as a deity of battle.[13] The ancient writers report that the Celtic women were tall, fierce and strong, and as terrible in battle as their men, and Celtic coins often depict a naked woman on horseback triumphantly brandishing a spear or a sword. Being naked, perhaps she is a deity of battle or a personification of victory rather than an actual warrior. The Gaulish goddess Epona, whose name means 'Divine Horse', was adopted by many soldiers in the Roman cavalry and her cult spread across the Empire.

Romano-Celtic shrines, like later Celtic myths, tell of triple goddesses such as the Proximae (kinswomen), Dervonnae (oak-sprites) and Niskai (water-goddesses). These are often known as the three Mothers and are particularly numerous in the Rhineland. Some of these have nurturing attributes, such as baskets of fruit or flowers; others are more enigmatic, as in the triads of goddesses carrying two discs and a chain, provisionally identified by one writer[14] with goddesses of Earth, Sun and Moon. These triple goddesses are usually named as guardians of place: the Mothers of Britain and the Mothers of Nîmes, the Mothers of the Homeland and the Mothers of the Celts.[15] In

Wales, the fairies, who were considered to be the source of esoteric knowledge, especially foretelling the future, are known still as 'The Mothers' (Y Mamau). They are not necessarily called 'Mothers' on account of their childbearing capacity, however. 'Mother' and 'Father' in the ancient world were often honorific titles, referring to a mature and authoritative person of the relevant sex, as in ecclesiastical titles today. Irish myths, however, tell of a father god, the Daghda, who has a cauldron of plenty and of the renewal of life, and (in the tenth-century *Cormac's Glossary*) of a mother of the gods, Dana, whose name also appears in the Irish tales as the mother of her human tribe the People of Dana, or Tuatha de Danaan. An inscription of the mid-third century CE from Lanchester invokes the *numen* of the emperor and the goddess Garmangabis, together with a carving of a knife, a jug, a patera or ritual plate, and a disc. This goddess was presumably a deity of prosperity and plenty.

There were many local gods and goddesses, the 'spirits of place' which we have already seen in local cults around the Mediterranean. Herodian, writing in the early third century CE, tells that Belenus, the god of Noricum, was venerated greatly at Aquileia, where he was considered the same as Apollo.[16] Penninus or Poeninus, god of mountain ranges, was revered at the Alpine pass now called the Little St Bernhard. A shrine containing numerous offerings of Celtic and Roman coins was excavated when the modern road was driven through its site. In Roman times, Poeninus was assimilated to Jupiter Dolichenus. Also in the Alps, Brigantia, later Christianised as St Brigida, was guardian of mountain passes. Both names appear in northern England, where

*Plate 5.3* First-century BCE hill-figure at Uffington, Berkshire, England, marking a sacred hill, and perhaps serving as a tribal totem, visible from afar. Ministry of Defence, Crown Copyright reserved.

a similar cult appears to have existed among the Brigantes, who lived on and to the east of the Pennines. Possibly this tribe once controlled the passes which cross those inhospitable hills. Esus, the totemic god of the Essuvii, was worshipped in that region of Gaul, and several cities including Lyons in Gaul, Leiden in Frisia and Carlisle in Britain were named after the god Lugh, as was Mainz (Maguntiacum) after Mogounus. Lugh is one of the few truly international Celtic deities, but he is thought to be a late import into some countries. Caesar speaks of Dis, the lord of the Underworld, as the ancestral god of the Gauls. For this reason, Caesar says, the Gauls count each day as beginning with the preceding night.[17]

Sul was goddess of the hot springs at Bath. Her name means 'Sun': the underground Sun which heats the waters. In Celtic lands the Sun was thought to sink under water each evening, according to the brothers Grimm, and 'Sun springs' are commonplace names, e.g. Sunnebrunno near Düsseldorf. Sometimes these springs were thought to cure eye diseases, bringing the light of the Sun to the eye of the sufferer. A similar complex of associations can be seen in the case of the solar god Apollo: healing, prophecy (clear-sightedness), a spring (at Delphi) and the Sun. Apollo presided over many healing springs in Iberia and Gaul, but the Celtic sun-deities, however, were often (perhaps originally) feminine. The Matres Suleviae are found in Hungary, Rome, Gaul, Germany and Britain, linked with healing and the Sun,[18] and large numbers of female figurines decorated with solar discs are found at Celtic healing springs throughout France and Germany, with a single example in Britain.[19] The Gaelic for 'Sun' is *grian*, a feminine noun, and the modern Irish *grian na maighdean*, meaning the fairest of maidens, is literally 'the Sun among maidens'. J.F. Campbell, the nineteenth-century folklorist, reported that 'Dia Greine' was the old Scottish name of the sun-goddess.[20] The Megalithic sites now known as Newgrange (in Ireland), Granja de Toniñuelo (in Spain) and Bois-de-la-neuve-Grange (in France) may also carry this element in their names. Where the Sun strikes into the heart of the tomb at the winter solstice at Newgrange, we are reminded of the Baltic (and Japanese) stories of the sun-goddess hiding in a cave at midwinter, a theme which is echoed in the later legend of Grainne (the name means 'hateful' but could be derived from *grian*) and her lover Diarmat. This tells of the lovers fleeing from Grainne's husband and travelling around Ireland in a year and a day (one 'circuit' of sunrises and sunsets moving along the horizon), sleeping in a different cave every night. In the same way the Persian solar god Mithras was associated with a cave. The god Apollo bears the Celtic solar title at the shrine of Apollo Grannus near modern Grand in France and that of Grannus Phoebus in Trier. According to Dio Cassius the Emperor Caracalla paid an unsuccessful visit to the healing shrine of Grannus in 215 CE.

In Romano-Celtic iconography, under the *interpretatio Romana*, the sky-god Jupiter also appears with the spoked solar or sky disc of north European palaeolithic art. Gods identified with Jupiter under the *interpretatio Romana* included Ambisagrus (the persistent) as well as Taranucus (the thunderer), Taranis and Uxellimus (the highest one). Many inscriptions and place-names are dedicated to the worship of Minerva and Mercury, deities of civilisation and commerce. Minerva was most famously commemorated as Sulis Minerva at Bath. The gods identified with Mercury include the people's god, Teutates, Atesmiius, Caletos and Moccos. Those identified with Mars include Albiorix (king of the world), Caturix (battle-king), Dunatis (god of fortresses), Leucetius (lightning-god), Vintius (wind-god) and Vitucadrus (brilliant in energy). Surviving sacred objects bear images of the more important deities of the pantheon. The Gundestrup Cauldron, which has Thracian and Celtic elements, the result, it is thought, of cooperation between Triballian (Thracian) and Scordiscan (Celtic) silversmiths, bears images of the Lord of Animals (Dionysos), the war-god (Perun-Ares), the Great Mother (Kybele), and the antlered god (Cernunnos).[21] An altar found at Notre Dame in Paris bears an image of the axe-god Esus, a bull and three cranes, with the inscription 'Tarvos Trigaranus'.

Animal deities and animal totems continued throughout the Romano-Celtic period: the horses of Epona and 'Jupiter'; the dog of Nehalennia; Arduina, the mistress of the wild boars of the Ardennes; Artio, the bear-goddess of Berne and Berlin; the ram-headed serpents which are never named; and, of course, the Gaulish antlered god named on one inscription as [C]ernunnos, the Horned One, who is paralleled by bull-horned deities in Britain. There appears to have been a belief that members of certain clans were magically descended from totemic beasts.[22] They are reflected in the names of animal-linked deities such as Tarvos (the bull), Mullo (ass), Moccos (the god of swine), and Epona, Artio and Damona, goddesses of horses, bears and cattle respectively. Gallic Celtic names such as Brannogenos (son of the raven) and Artogenos (son of the bear) parallel the comparable totemic warrior-cults of Scandinavia (the Berserkers etc.). According to Caesar, the Britons kept hares, chickens and geese, but did not kill them. They were held in supreme respect. Before her final battle against the Roman troops, Boudicca is said to have released a hare which she had carried under her cloak, presumably to propitiate the deities or perhaps to consult the omens. Later, the cat, too, joined these respected beasts. The Helvetii, who migrated from the area of modern Bavaria south into Switzerland, seem to have placed themselves under the protection of the bear-goddess Artio. An image of this goddess was found at Muri near Berne in Switzerland. In the thirteenth century, a revelation of a bear to a knight led to the foundation of the city, where bears are kept to this day as totems of the city.

## THE SACRED YEAR OF THE CELTS

In Gaul and Ireland, the year was divided basically into two halves: winter and summer. The winter half was the beginning of the year, starting at

Samhain (1 November). This was the most important festival of the year, showing the pastoralist, rather than agricultural, origin of the calendar. Samhain was the end of the grazing season, when flocks and herds were collected together, and only the breeding stock set aside from slaughter. It was a time of gathering-together of the tribe at their ritual centre for rituals of death and renewal, dedicated to the union of the tribal god (in Ireland, the Daghda) with a goddess of sovereignty, the Morrigan, or, more localised, Boann, deity of the River Boyne.

The second great festival of the year was Beltane or Cétshamhain (1 May, May Day). This was the beginning of the summer half of the year, also a pastoralist festival. As at Samhain, the lighting of bonfires was an important rite. Cattle were driven through the smoke to protect them in the coming season. Beltane may be connected with the Austrian deity Belenos, who was particularly associated with pastoralism,[23] or it may simply take its name from the bright (*bel*) fires which were part of its celebration. Beltane is the only festival recorded in the ninth-century Welsh tales, a time when the Otherworld communicates with the world of humans, either through portents such as the dragon fight in the tale of Lludd and Llevelys, or through apparitions such as the hero Pwyll's sighting of the goddess Rhiannon. The Romanesque church at Belsen, on an old Celtic holy hill

*Plate 5.4* Samhain Cake, Cambridgeshire, England, 1987. Private ceremonies continue to use traditional designs knowingly. © 1987 Nigel Pennick.

near Tübingen, Germany, has contemporary images of Béél, with ox- and sheeps' heads.

In Ireland, the year was further subdivided by two more festivals. (The solstices and equinoxes do not have corresponding Celtic festivals.) In the story of the wooing of Emer by the Irish hero Cú Chulainn, the maiden asks her suitor to go sleepless from 'Samhain, when the summer goes to its rest, until Imbolc, when the ewes are milked at spring's beginning; from Imbolc until Beltine at the summer's beginning and from Beltine to Bron Trogain, earth's sorrowing autumn'.[24] Like Samhain and Beltine, Imbolc (1 February) was a pastoralist festival, celebrating the lambing, the first lactation of the ewes. It was sacred to the goddess of healing, poetry and smithcraft, Brigit, who was assimilated by the church into St Brigit, still fêted on the same day. It is possible that Imbolc was a festival specific originally to a single cultural or occupational group, later being absorbed into general recognition.

Lughnasadh (1 August, also called Bron Trograin) appears to have been imported into Ireland at a later date, perhaps by continental devotees of Lugh, who in the Irish pantheon is a latecomer, the *ildánach*, master of all skills, more modern in character than the other goddesses and gods. Correspondingly, Lughnasadh differs from the other three festivals in being agrarian in character, marking the harvest, and baking of the first loaf from the new grain. The deity honoured at Lughnasadh was Lugh, who was said to have instituted the games in honour of his foster-mother, Táiltiu. 'Táiltiu' (Teltown) is in fact the name of the site of the festival in Tara. It is an ancient burial ground, and its name is thought to mean 'fair' or 'lovely',[25] so if it ever was associated with a presiding goddess of that name, like Demeter in Greece she would have ruled both the Underworld and the fruits which sprang from it.

The most complex known Celtic calendar is from Roman Gaul, recorded on a bronze tablet, from Coligny, Ain, France. Dating from the first century BCE, it is fragmentary, but enough survives to indicate that it was divided into sixteen columns showing sixty-two consecutive lunar months, each divided into a bright and a dark half, the changeover-point being marked ATENOVX. There are also two intercalary months, used to realign the lunar year with the solar one. All months are named; good months are marked MAT and inauspicious ones ANM. The days are numbered from I to XV in the light half of each month, and from I to XIV (or XV) in the dark half. Certain significant days are marked by abbreviations, but festivals are not marked.[26]

## THE CELTS BECOME ROMANISED

The Phoenicians had set up a trading post at Gades (modern Cadiz in Spain) and one at Massilia (modern Marseilles, France) before the eighth century BCE, but otherwise the hinterland of the western Mediterranean was untouched by the old eastern civilisations and the Celts swept down towards the coast in the seventh century. Iberia (modern Spain and Portugal) seems to have had a mixture of inhabitants; writing in the fifth century BCE, Himilco the Carthaginian reports seeing Ethiopians living there.[27] Strabo, at the beginning of the Common Era, says that there were no indigenous altars in the south of the country, but only stones 'lying in groups of three or four, which in accordance with a native custom are turned round by those who visit the place, and then, after the pouring of a libation, are moved back again'.[28] It looks as if the inhabitants were using megalithic sites for contemporary worship, a practice which continued into historical times and was forbidden by the seventh-century Edict of Nantes. Strabo adds that the inhabitants forbid people to offer sacrifice there or even to go there at night, because the gods occupy the place at that time. Modern Westerners in such a situation would say that the place was haunted, or that the Little People were there. For the ancients, however, full Olympian sacrifice (*thuein*) was debarred, yet the spirits there were seen as *theoi*, divine and deserving of libation. This gives us an interesting insight into the nature of ancient Pagan thought and also into our own assumptions, whether we accept modern folkloric practices as 'survivals' or, alternatively, dismiss them as 'superstitions'.

In northern central Iberia lived the Celtiberians, who apparently were once the most savage of all the inhabitants, but who by the time of Strabo spoke Latin, wore the toga and were thoroughly Romanised.[29] However, they retained at least one non-Roman custom, that of sacrificing before the doors of their houses to an unnamed deity on the night of the full moon every month, then dancing the whole night through. Strabo unfortunately had never been to Iberia and was only reporting other travellers' tales, but at least his is an early record and his story, if true, forms an engaging parallel with modern Pagan full moon celebrations. He also gives details of sacrifice and of divination similar to the unpleasant rites described by Caesar fifty years before and repeated by Tacitus more than fifty years afterwards.

The Carthaginians had occupied Iberia from about 240 BCE, followed by the Romans beginning some twenty years later. Roman expansion into the north-west of the province took another two hundred years, but by then Celtic culture was almost invisible; the Iberians were becoming Romans. (Iberia later produced not only the writers Seneca and Lucan, but also the Emperors Trajan and Hadrian.) Indeed, it seems that Roman Paganism survived there into the sixth century CE, for the Bishop of Braga, St Martin, who was appointed in 560 to convert the Arian inhabitants of the north-west, the Galicians, to Catholicism, describes the old practices as still extant:

> Observing the Vulcanalia and the kalends, decorating tables, wearing laurels, taking omens from footsteps, putting fruit and wine on the log in the hearth, and bread in the well, what are these but worship of the

devil? For women to call upon Minerva when they spin, and to observe the day of Venus at weddings and to call upon her whenever they go out upon the public highway, what is that but worship of the devil?[30]

Southern Gaul was invaded by Rome at the beginning of the second century BCE, after the defeat of Hannibal, and effectively annexed one hundred years later. It was the first 'province' outside Italy and the eastern part of it still bears that name: Provence. During the century of Roman occupation, the Celts settled and developed commercial towns throughout the whole of what is now France. The conquest of 'long-haired Gaul' (*Gallia comata*), the area north of *Gallia togata*, the modern Provence and Languedoc, was carried out by Caesar in 57–55 BCE. His description of it in the *Gallic Wars* has given us our only first-hand account of tribal Celtic life. After Caesar, there were regular revolts in northern Gaul until Augustus annexed the province and saved it from a German invasion. After this, the Druids fade from view, and during the first fifty years CE Tiberius and Claudius tried to suppress their remnants; but otherwise there was no interference with the worship of the Celtic divinities. The Gauls, as several ancient writers mention, soon became accustomed to Roman ease and were rather despised for it by their conquerors. Nevertheless, five centuries later they were to become the guardians of Roman organisation and culture, which they, like their kins-people and neighbours the Iberians, managed to impose on their conquerors when overrun by the Goths, the Alemanni and the Franks in the fifth century CE. The system of Roman law as codified by Theodosius and Justinian has survived to form the basis of European Union law today.

Britain, conquered by Claudius in 43 BCE and initially milked for taxes, slaves and auxiliary troops, attempted to expel the Romans in Boudicca's rebellion of 60 CE. The rebellion nearly succeeded, but after it was put down and the punitive victor, Suetonius Paulinus, discreetly removed to another command, a series of new governors and their financial directors set about a systematic process of Romanisation. As Tacitus observed with some acerbity, 'Among the conquered it is called culture, when in fact it is part of their slavery'.[31] Britain, in contrast to Gaul and Iberia, is known for two great queens: Boudicca and Cartimandua. Once more in Tacitus' words, 'They do not distinguish among their rulers by sex'.[32] Boudicca, the widow of King Praesutagus of the Iceni, devoted the spoils of her battles to the goddess Andraste,[33] and as already mentioned, ceremonially released a hare onto the battlefield before her final standoff with the Romans under Paulinus. Cartimandua's decisive role has already been described.

The Romano-Celtic phase in both Gaul and Britain was characterised by three main features. First, there is the comparative absence of the Druids, and the total absence of their bloodthirsty sacrifices and divinations. They may possibly have become the temple-priests of the newly expanded religion, but if so it is strange that we have no records of this, nor hear of them as official augurs, perhaps in a college in their own right, like the Etruscan *haruspices*. In Gaul there was a rebellion in 69–70 in which Druids are mentioned,[34] but thereafter both Druids and Druidesses appear only occasionally, as freelance seers. One Druidess is said to have been an innkeeper, who prophesied to the soldier Diocles that he would one day become emperor – which indeed he did, as Diocletian.[35] Next there is the appearance of native monuments and images, which had been more or less absent in the pre-Roman phase. There is some evidence that the pre-Roman Celts had images made of wood, but only after the Romans came did they start carving in stone. Celtic square temples have already been described, and so

*Plate 5.5* 2,000-year-old Celtic images kept at Newhouse Farm, Stretton Grandison, Herefordshire, England. ©1991 Nigel Pennick.

94

have some of the native divinities. Images of triple goddesses are specifically Celtic, as are gods carrying or adorned with wheels. Other wheel-gods are identified with Jupiter (see below). The Roman Jupiter ruled the sky, thunder and lightning, but the Celts, especially the Gauls, had a specific god of thunder, Taranis. He is often shown carrying a hammer, like Thor in later Germanic art. Sucellus, 'the Good Striker', is specifically a hammer-god, and he is sometimes shown with an elaborate headdress of thin-handled hammers radiating out from his head in what could equally well be a solar motif. The Celtic deities often remain obscure to us, since the Romans did not comment on them in any detail but preferred to assimilate them to Roman ones.

The third feature of Romano-Celtic religion is that of assimilation. Many dual deities are depicted and also mentioned in dedications. These range from ill-assorted hybrids like Sulis Minerva and Mars Loucetius to genuinely new departures in syncretic religion such as the famous Jupiter columns which are found all over the northern provinces of the Empire, especially in the east. Maximus of Tyre stated that the representation of Zeus to the Celts was a high oak,[36] and Celtic columns are often decorated with tree imagery, for example with oak leaves and acorns at Hausen-an-der-Zaber. Often, the figure at the top of the column is a mounted god trampling a snake-limbed monster. The Celtic sky-god here is given the name of his Roman equivalent, but his horse, spoked wheel, celestial column, sacred tree imagery and fight with the underworld snake look forward to the Germanic sky-god Odin, fully described only as late as the thirteenth century by Icelandic writers, using identical celestial symbolism. Here an enduring north European tradition has found expression within a Classical framework. Some 150 Jupiter columns have been documented, and it would be interesting to know whether they served, in true sky-pillar fashion, as the omphaloi of their settlements, the symbolic and practical centre of the built environment.

# 6

# THE LATER CELTS

The north-west provinces, the 'Celtic' lands, developed an identity of their own and declared independence several times in the late Empire. During the third century, seaborne pirates from Saxony and from Ireland started to harass Britain and northern Gaul. Since the eastern Imperial frontier was already being attacked by the Goths, troops could seldom be spared to defend the northern provinces. Around the year 260, the Rhine commander Marcus Postumus declared Spain, Gaul, Britain and the Rhineland to be the Empire of the Gallic Provinces. This Empire lasted until 274, during which time the Alemanni, a confederation from east of the Rhine, invaded and devastated northern Gaul. The towns were unwalled and fifty to sixty of them were captured. British towns, meanwhile, expanded, perhaps taking refugees from the continent. Country villas in Britain also show signs of building, since the rich landowners would be the first to be able to retreat to the comparative safety of the island, and some superb mosaics, including the Orphic pavement at Littlecote House in Oxfordshire, date from this time. In Gaul, the years 284–286 saw another secession by the unemployed and homeless whom the Alemanni had dispossessed, and in 287 Britain seceded from the Empire under Carausius and then Allectus.[1]

This outer threat coincided with the inner turmoil caused by (or addressed by?) Christianity, as the Roman body politic struggled to formulate a unifying religious system. The turn of the century, the time of Diocletian's persecution of the Christians followed by Constantine's toleration of them, saw many new temples built in Britain. The Gallic provinces must also have been a comparative haven for Christians during Diocletian's reign, because their Caesar, Constantius, husband of the Christian Helena and father of the future Christian Constantine, was lax in implementing the anti-Christian edicts. The new administration following the reconquest of Britain by the Empire in 306 in fact expedited Christian rule. Britain, Frisia, the Rhineland, Gaul and Spain were formed into a new prefecture with its capital in Trier (the site of a healing shrine of Apollo on the modern French–German border). This had its own civilian administration independent of the central power based in the western capital, and under the rule of Constantine, this bureaucracy became dominated by Christians. As Constantine's favour for Christianity grew, the Pagan temples were starved of funds. In Britain, which had not suffered as Gaul and Spain had from the Gothic invasions, this had the curious result of a general increase in civic prosperity as the funds of the temples were recycled into the Christian-controlled community.

The western Empire as a whole, including Italy and Illyricum (Dalmatia) as well as the Gallic provinces, was also involved in the battles of the Imperial succession: when the Pagan Count Maxentius opposed Constantine from 306 to 312, and when Magnentius, who tolerated Paganism as well as endorsing official Christianity, battled with the last of Constantine's sons from 350 to 353. The short-lived revolt of Magnentius (see above, p. 70) was a time of great hope for Pagans, who by now were losing their property through fines and their income through exclusion from office in the newly confident Christian Empire of Constantine's sons. In Britain the revolt was put down with great savagery by a tidy-minded bureaucrat, an Imperial notary who earned the nickname of 'Paul the Chain' from the paranoid link-age of associations he constructed so as to acquire new victims for his reprisal tribunals. Luckily for Pagans, two years later Emperor Julian came to the throne, and although his influence was as short as his reign on the continent, on the island of Britain there are signs of a new-found Pagan confidence. The healing sanctuary of Mars Nodens in Gloucestershire was expanded and became an enormous centre, and at around this time the Pagan temple at Verulamium was rebuilt. The Mithraeum in London was dismantled and then rebuilt, indicating that an expected attack either did not happen or had been survived (although the dating here is uncertain), and it was perhaps at this time that the governor of southern Britain restored the Jupiter column at Cirencester. This had either crumbled through neglect or had been destroyed by Christians. His inscription reads:

> To Jupiter, Best and Greatest, His Perfection Lucius Septimius . . .
> governor of Britannia Prima, restored [this monument], being a citizen of Rheims.
> This statue and column erected under the ancient religion Septimius restores, ruler of Britannia Prima.[2]

Whether this temporary revival extended for long, had any deep-reaching effect, or even existed at all, is a matter of dispute among scholars. Inscriptions by Roman soldiers are mostly Pagan, but probably the civilian administration was Christian. Certainly, when a continental bishop, Germanicus, was called to Britain in 429 to dispute on matters of Christian heresy, he described a ruling class which was entirely Christian.

On the continent, militant Christianity began again. This was not a time of multifaith tolerance, at least among adherents of the new religion. From 380 to 385, St Martin of Tours inspected northern Gaul, destroying Pagan shrines and particularly trees. One story has it that the Pagans in one town challenged him to perform a miracle. He could cut their sacred tree down if he would stand under it as it fell. St Martin declined their challenge and went elsewhere.[3]

The Emperor Theodosius (379–395) extended the draconian laws against Paganism which had lapsed since Julian, but fortunately for Pagans in the north-west prefecture, they were largely ignored by the praetorian prefect in charge of the area, a Pagan Frankish barbarian named Arbogast. The Franks, who had crossed into Gaul from the eastern bank of the Rhine at the time of Carausius' Empire, had already been Romanised by their conqueror Constantius, and we can assume that Arbogast was defending Roman rather than Germanic Paganism. When Theodosius passed his famous law forbidding even household Pagan worship in private, Arbogast installed a puppet western emperor, Eugenius, who immediately rescinded the anti-Pagan legislation and ordered the restoration of the Altar of Victory to the Senate (see chapter 4) as well as the revival of some very odd and recondite Pagan cults. But Theodosius fought back, and Eugenius and Arbogast died in the battle of Flavia Frigida on 6 September, 394. Iberia and Gaul were swept into the chaos of Christian infighting that was to lead to Alaric's sack of Rome in 410, the Rhineland did battle with invading Germans (see chapter 7), who followed the basic tribal form of north European Paganism, and of Britain we know little apart from monumental inscriptions.

In 409–410, Britain and Armorica (modern Brittany) seceded for the last time from the Empire, taking responsibility for their own defence against the marauding Saxons and Irish who had been harassing the coast for the last century. The Irish had never been part of the Roman Empire, and so what we know about them has had to be deduced from archaeology and the careful interpretation of ballads and stories written down by monks centuries after the world they described had disappeared. The Irish tales describe the same proud, superstitious warrior-aristocracy as Roman observers saw in Britain and on the mainland. They also add a tradition of powerful, autonomous women and battle-goddesses which is absent from Romanised areas after the initial decades during which such rulers as Cartimandua and Boudicca played a decisive role. Like the Galatians in Asia Minor, the Irish regularly met in cult centres which were huge earthworks, the most famous being that of Tara in County Meath. Like the Gaulish Druids, whose meeting place at Chartres was thought to be the centre of their country, the Irish saw Meath as the centre of their island, with the four provinces of Ulster, Leinster, Connaught and Munster encircling it. Ulster in the north was seen as the odd one out, being at one time opposed by a coalition of the other provinces led by Queen Maedb. Whether the north was symbolically the unlucky quarter (it is the quarter of the gods in Germanic tradition), or whether the story is less overtly symbolic, we cannot tell. An echo of this tradition was preserved in the Celtic outpost of Cornwall. Medieval Cornish miracle plays, performed at permanent circular earthworks (the Plen an

Gwary), retained the tradition of the north as the direction of the Pagan gods. 'Bad or Pagan characters in the Cornish Plans are grouped near the North, and in Meryasek we find this confirmed as the only proper arrangement, for a demon and Jupiter are each called there "our patron saint on the North Side."'[4]

Nodens, the healing god of the Gloucestershire spring sanctuary, has a name cognate with 'Nuada', the name of a legendary Irish king who lost his arm, had it replaced by a silver one, and later was miraculously healed. It is interesting that the shrine of Nodens only came into prominence at the time of the Irish sea-raids, although it seems unlikely that the people of the area would adopt one of the heroes of their enemies as a god. In the late fourth century, a king known as Niall of the Nine Hostages was raiding Britain. There is a symbolic tale told about him, too, to the effect that he went into the forest on a survival test with his brothers, and was the only one of them to recognise the disguised maiden who was the Sovereignty of Ireland, only by union with whom a man could be pronounced High King. It was quite possibly Niall who kidnapped the future Saint Patrick, Christian converter of Ireland, and kept him in slavery for seven years in Ireland. Patrick had returned to Britain and was living with his family around the year 418, so he is broadly contemporary with Niall.

Irish Paganism was very tolerant to Christianity. In 438, the High King, Laighaire, held a folk-moot at Tara on the question of faith. To accommodate Christianity, he called together a committee to draft new laws for Ireland. The committee comprised three kings, three *Brehona* (Pagan law-speakers) and three Christian missionaries. The laws they drew up became the *Seanchus Mór*, which contained elements from Pagan and Christian law. This remained valid until superseded by English law in the seventeenth century. In 448, St Patrick arrived and established Christianity as the official religion of Ireland, and we hear no more of the country for the next century.

*Plate 6.1* Sheela-na-gig and beastie on mid-twelfth-century church at Kilpeck, Herefordshire, England. © 1990 Nigel Pennick.

Meanwhile, in Gaul and Spain the ruling classes were becoming absorbed into the new Christian administration. Church officials, like the old temple-priests and priestesses, were exempt from many taxes as well as from the swingeing burden of public finance, much of which came out of the pockets of the city notables. For this reason as well as because the effective power was now in the hands of avowed Christians, the Romano-Celtic aristocracy became Catholic and, on the continent, relied on Gothic Arian mercenaries to run their armies. In Britain the troops are likely to have been Saxon mercenaries, Pagans rather than Christians, and when after 430 King Vortigern's foreign troops turned against him the island degenerated into chaos. The traditional date for the Saxon invasion of Britain is 449, under Hengist and Horsa, whose names are totemic: they mean 'stallion' and 'mare' respectively.

In 460 many Britons migrated to Gaul, where they moved into Armorica, a part of the country which had never been properly reabsorbed after the secession of 409, and, being pugnacious and dominant according to Gildas, took it over and founded Brittany. It is at this time that the semi-legendary Ambrosius Aurelianus appears in British history, fighting against the Saxons and routing them at Mount Badon at the turn of the sixth century. This is the historical basis for the King Arthur legends. After Ambrosius' victory there was said to be peace for two generations. Gildas, writing in the mid-sixth century, speaks of 'our present serenity' and mentions a generation which had no experience of 'the great storm'.[5] However, this peace is likely to have been kept by small-scale warrior-chieftains on the old tribal Celtic model, not by a national government based in cities. Gaul, by contrast, was settled under the old Roman civic bureaucracy by the Frankish monarchs, the fabled Merovingians or descendants of Meroveus, the 'sea-fighter' who had captured Tournai in 446. Their Germanic Pagan tradition forbade them to cut their hair, and they retained this tradition even after converting to Christianity in 503 or thereabouts.[6] They eventually became ceremonial monarchs in the style of the late Empire, rather than Germanic fighting kings, until they were deposed by their chief minister Pepin in 751 when he founded the Carolingian dynasty. So, by the sixth century, the north of modern France then was ruled by the western Germans, the (Catholic) Franks, and the south, the old Roman Provincia, together with Spain, by the eastern Germans, the (Arian) Goths. However, Paganism remained in vernacular practice. In 589 the third Council of Toledo thundered that 'the sacrilege of idolatry is rooted in almost the whole of Gaul and Spain'. Ireland, too, swayed back and forwards between official Christianity and official Paganism. In 554, the geomantic centre of Ireland, Tara, was cursed by the Christian monk Ruadhan of Lothra, presumably because people still venerated its sacred nature. Five years later, the king Diarmat McCerbaill celebrated the *feis* or ceremonial marriage with the goddess of the land, part of the traditional inauguration of Irish kings, at the last Assembly of Tara.

*Plate 6.2* Chalk graffito of labyrinth and 'Celtic Rose' pattern (*c.*1600) in the abandoned medieval stone mines at Chaldon, Surrey, England. Believed to be the relic of Pagan miners' rites. © Jeff Saward, Caerdroia Archives.

But Diarmat died in 565, probably the last Pagan king of Ireland, and we hear no more of official Paganism. Diarmat must have been part of a Pagan restoration, for the next High King, Ainmire (565–571), was so concerned at the decline of the Christian religion that he invited Gildas and other monks from Britain to revive it.

There were no more sacred marriages in Ireland, but the cult of St Bridget retained its vitality. Bridget is generally agreed to be a Christianisation of the goddess known as Brighde in Ireland, Bride in Scotland and possibly Brigantia in the north of Britain. She had to do with warmth, fire, summer and possibly the Sun, since an Irish legend tells that in winter she was imprisoned in an icy mountain by a one-eyed hag.[7] In some places she presided over thermal springs, presumably as the underground Sun, and in Scotland until the mid-twentieth century she was welcomed in at Imbolc (1 February) by the symbolic rekindling of the hearth fire after the house had been spring-cleaned from top to bottom. In County Kildare Brighde had a shrine with a sacred flame, which was tended by a college of women rather like the Vestal Virgins in Rome. This is not simply a Roman story, since the flame was kept burning into historical times after the purported temple became a Christian nunnery. In 1220 Archbishop Henry of Dublin ordered the flame to be extinguished. In 722 St Bridget, as she now was, appeared to the Irish army of Leinster, hovering in the sky before they routed the forces of Tara, rather as the sun-god El Gabel had appeared to Aurelian in 273 and as the Christian chi-rho sign had appeared to Constantine in 312.

In Britain the Saxons invaded again after the peace of Ambrosius, probably in about 570. History then is silent until the mission of Augustine in 597, when the Roman monk found a country which was entirely Germanic, ruled by Saxon kings who traced their ancestry to Woden, who lived in townships or villages rather than cities, who spoke Anglo-Saxon rather than Celtic or Latin, and who followed German laws which were almost identical with those noted five hundred years before by Tacitus. The Saxons had obviously been impervious to the blandishments of Romanisation, unlike their continental neighbours the Franks and the Goths. Pockets of resistance held out in the north of Britain. In Strathclyde a struggle for supremacy broke out. There were four British kings in Strathclyde; the Angles had invaded and conquered the Lothians. Under Anglian influence, the Picts and the Welsh returned to Paganism, and around the year 550 the missionary Kentigern undertook a crusade to extirpate it.[8] This was a spectacular failure, however, as a great part of the British population in the south of Strathclyde restored their ancestral faith 'fostered by their bards, who recalled the old traditions of the race before they had been Christianized under the Roman dominion',[9] or at any rate adopting a different form of Paganism under the influence of the invaders. (It should, however, be noted that the Cumbrian language was used in the area until the fourteenth century, and so the traditional Pagan tales carried in its ballads would be accessible until that time.) In 573, the four kings fought for supremacy over the area. Three of them (one Christian, Uriens, one anti-Christian, Morcant, and one unknown, Gwenddoleu) claimed descent through Coil Hên, the 'Ancient One' of Wales, from Beli and Anna, the divine ancestors of Celtic myth.[10] The other king, Rhydderch Hael, was a keen Christian, descended, according to the Four Books of Wales,[11] from the Emperor Magnus Maximus (383–388), the Christian Roman commander who had been raised to western emperor by the troops while serving in Britain. At the Battle of Arderyd, on the River Esk eight miles north of Carlisle, the Christian Rhydderch won the victory, the Welsh Gwenddoleu was slain, and Kentigern and his priests were invited back into Cumbria to extirpate native tradition.[12] The tradition of kings who claimed descent from divine ancestors, which we shall see more clearly among the Germanic tribes, in this part of Britain had come to an end.

We are now moving away from official Paganism into the time of folklore and Christianised practices. Finding that it could not stamp out the small rituals of life, once presided over by the ancient divinities, the Church took many of these on board. May Day processions were blessed, helpful deities like Brighde were adopted as saints, together with the trappings of their old cult, and troublesome deities like Woden were anathematised as devils. The *Capitularia Regum Francorum*, published at Paris in 1677, lists rural practices then in use, but forbidden in France by the Church. Among them were

*Plate 6.3* May Garland, Northampton, England, 1826. Nideck Picture Collection.

ceremonies for the deceased, known as *Dadsissas*, and ceremonies at their tombs. The ceremonies of Mercury and Jupiter were forbidden, along with sacrifices made to any other divinity. This included the observance of the festivals of Mercury or Jupiter and *Vince Luna* (eclipses of the moon). The Church condemned 'those believing that because women worship the moon, they can draw the hearts of men towards the Pagans'. In true dual faith manner, the Mother Goddess was petitioned in the form 'of that which good people call St Mary'. Doubtless, she still is. French Pagans worshipped at 'the irregular places which they cherish for their ceremonies', which included 'water-springs as the sites of sacrifice', also moats around houses and stones. As in England, they also processed through churches and along 'the Pagan trackway, which they name *Yries*', which was 'marked with rags or with shoes'. Certain ceremonies involved the construction of small huts known as sanctuaries, connected with 'the ceremonies of the woodland, known as *Nimidas*'. Seventeenth-century French Pagans made images of flour sprinkled on the ground (step patterns and the like); images made from rags; 'the image which they carry through the fields', and 'the wooden feet or hands used in Heathen ritual'. Pagan amulets included horns and snail-shells, phylacteries and 'things bound'.

Pagan deities were also venerated into historical times as folk-spirits, not simply as Christian saints, as will be described below. This is entirely of a piece with a properly Pagan outlook which recognises many sorts of spirits, each having their place and function, and which in the early days of the Church, of Islam and of Judaism (if the Book of Kings is to be believed) would simply take the monotheistic deity as one among many, perhaps the supreme among many, pre-existing deities. This is a Pagan outlook and it has continued in Europe up to the present day.

## VERNACULAR PAGANISM

In Wales, Scotland, Ireland and Brittany, the old gods, worshipped sometimes under the guise of Celtic saints (i.e. those not canonised by the Pope), were revered in truly Pagan fashion. For example, at Llanderfel, Merionethshire, Wales, Darvel Gadarn was revered in an image 'in which the people have so great confidence, hope and trust, that they come dayly a pilgrimage unto hym, some with kyne, other with oxen and horses'.[13] Taken to London, the image was burnt at Smithfield in the same year. In 1589, John Ansters reported that bullocks were sacrificed 'the half to God and to Beino' in the churchyard at Clynog, Lleyn, Wales.[14] Cattle born with 'the mark of Beyno' were literally earmarked for later sacrifice. Such cattle were later sold for slaughter by the churchwarden on Trinity Sunday. The custom fell into disuse in the nineteenth century.

Worship of goddesses continued under several names. Until the seventeenth century in Brittany, there were shrines kept by old women known as Fatuae or Fatidicae, who taught 'the rites of Venus' to young women, instructing them in shamanistic practices.[15] In Wales, the Goddess of Heaven or Mother of all human beings was known as Brenhines-y-nef.[16] In Brittany, the cult of St Anne 'stepped into the place of one of the Bonæ Deæ, tutelary earth goddesses . . . themselves representing the Celtic or pre-Celtic Ane, mother of the gods'.[17] Sometimes actual Pagan images were revered:

> In 1625, whilst ploughing a field at Keranna, in the parish of Plunevet, in Morbihan, a farmer named Yves Nicolayic turned up out of the ground a statue, probably a Bona Dea of the pagan Armoricans, numbers of which have been found of late years . . . the Carmelites, who had been zealous advocates of the cult of the Mother of Our Lady . . . constructed a chapel for the image, and . . . organized pilgrimages to it, which met with great success. The image was destroyed at the Revolution, but the pilgrimages continue.[18]

Gwen Teirbron, three-breasted patroness of nursing mothers, was also revered in Brittany. Nursing mothers offered Gwen Teirbron a distaff and flax to secure a proper quantity of milk for their babies. A major shrine was at the chapel of St Venec between Quimper and Châteaulin. In the 1870s, most images of Gwen Teirbron were got rid of by the priests, 'who have buried them, regarding them as somewhat outrageous and not conducive to devotion'. In Britain, churches of St Candida, St White and St Wita are sites of the devotion of Gwen Teirbron.[19]

Paganism flourished in Scotland after the break-up of the Catholic Church. In the region of Gaerloch, Wester Ross, the 'old rites' of the divinity Mhor-Ri, the Great King, transformed into St Maree, Mourie or Maelrubha, were observed until the nineteenth century. In 1656, the Dingwall Presbytery, 'findeing, amongst uther abhominable and heathenishe practices, that the people in that place were accustomed to sacrifice bulls at a certaine tyme upon the 25 of August, which day is dedicate, as they conceive, to St Mourie, as they call him . . . and withall their adoring of wells and uther superstitious monuments and stones', attempted to suppress the observances of Mhor-Ri, which, according to the Presbytery Records, Dingwall, included 'sacrificing at certain times at the Loch of Mourie . . . quherein ar monuments of Idolatrie', also 'pouring of milk upon hills as oblationes'. Strangers and 'thease that comes from forren countreyes' participated in the 'old rites' of Mhor-Ri.

The attempted suppression failed. Twenty years later, in 1678, members of the Mackenzie clan were summoned by the Church at Dingwall for 'sacrificing a bull in ane heathenish manner in the island of St Ruffus . . . for the recovering of the health of Cirstaine Mackenzie'.[20] In 1699, a man was arraigned before the Kirk Sessions at Elgin, Morayshire, charged with idolatry. He had set up a standing stone and raised his cap to it.[21] In 1774, Thomas Pennant wrote of the sacred places of Mhor-Ri: 'if a traveller passes any of his resting-places, they never neglect to leave an offering . . . a stone, a stick, a bit of rag'.

During the nineteenth century, sacred places, such as standing stones, hills and holy wells, were spoken of generally as shrines of goddesses and gods, for example: 'In the north end of the island of Calligray there are faint traces of a very ancient building called Teampull-na-H'Annait, the temple of Annat, a goddess . . . having for her particular province the care of young maidens. Near the temple is a well of water called Tobar-na-H'Annait'.[22] On the Isle of Man, Odin's Cross at Kirk Andreas, Thor Cross at Kirkbride and the Heimdall stone at Jurby maintained their Pagan identity.[23]

Hills continued to be used as the *loci* of Pagan observances. The Fairy Goddesses, Aine and Fennel, were honoured at two hills near Lough Gur, County Limerick, Ireland, 'upon whose summits sacrifices and sacred rites used to be celebrated according to living tradition'.[24] Sir A. Mitchell, writing in 1860 of the sacred places in the landscape around Loch Maree, stated: 'The people of the place often speak of the god Mourie.'[25] A hill called Claodh Maree was sacred to the cult. Dr Reeves, writing in 1861, observed: 'it is believed . . . that no-one can commit suicide or otherwise injure himself within view of this spot.'[26]

On the island of Maelrubha in Loch Maree, the sacred oak tree of Mhor-

*Plate 6.4* Thirteenth-century graffito of a dancer wearing the Pagan 'Celtic Rose' pattern, in the church at Sutton, Bedfordshire, England. This design, known as far back as a Bronze-age stone carving at Tossene, Sweden, always had a Pagan connotation, and was rarely if ever used officially in ecclesiastical buildings. Nigel Pennick.

Ri was studded with nails to which ribbons were tied. Buttons and buckles were also nailed to the tree.[27] This tree was associated with a healing well, reputed to cure insanity. The Dingwall Presbytery Records tell of the *derilans* who appear to have been officiating priests on the island. Dixon suggests that this title comes from the Gaelic *deireoil*, 'afflicted', inferring that the priesthood was composed of people enthused by 'divine madness', in the manner of shamans the world over.[28] In 1774 Thomas Pennant[29] visited Loch Maree and witnessed the rites. A person suffering from insanity was brought to the 'sacred island' and 'made to kneel before the altar, where his attendants leave an offering of money. He is then brought to the well, and sips some of the holy water. A second offering is made; that done, he is thrice dipped in the lake'. The shrine was profaned in 1830 by a man who attempted to cure a mad dog there.[30] Then its healing virtue was lost for a time, until around 1840, when visits resumed.

Holy wells are revered all over Europe. There are myriad examples, whose customs show continuity both from antiquity and across the continent. In the nineteenth century, a famous dripping well at Kotzanes in Macedonia had curative water 'said to issue from the Nereids' breasts, and to cure all human ills'.[31] In Vinnitsa, Ukraine, there was a holy well where sick people, after bathing, hung handkerchiefs and shirts on the branches as votive offerings.[32] The holy well Ffynnon Cae Moch, near Bridgend, Glamorgan, Wales, was visited by supplicants who then tied a rag to a tree or bush growing next to it. The rags were tied to the bush by strands of wool in the natural state.[33] At Ffynnon Elian, at Llanylian yn Rhos, near Abergele, Denbigh, Wales, corks studded with pins floated in the water of the well.[34]

Many holy wells had guardians who looked after them and oversaw observances there. In the early part of the nineteenth century, the hereditary well-guardian of Ffynnon Elian, Jac Ffynnon Elian (John Evans), was imprisoned twice for reopening Ffynnon Elian after it had been sealed by the local Christian priest.[35] The holy well 'stood in the corner of a field, embosomed in a grove . . . Sometimes, and that during its most flourishing period latterly, it had a "priestess", one named Mrs Hughes'.[36] Speaking in 1893 at a joint meeting of the Cymmrodorion and Folk-Lore societies in London, Professor John Rhys made the following telling statement about the famous Ffynnon Elian:

> Here there is, I think, very little doubt that the owner or guardian of this well was, so to say, the representative of an ancient priesthood of the well. His function as a pagan . . . was analogous to that of a parson or preacher who lets for rent the sittings in his church. We have, however, no sufficient data in this case to show how the right to the priesthood of a sacred well was acquired; but we know that a woman might have charge of St Elian's Well.

The well was finally destroyed in January, 1829.[37]

*Plate 6.5* Scouring the White Horse hill-figure at Uffington, Berkshire, England, 1889. This was a regular event, the 'pastime', which included traditional country sports, feasting and drinking. Nideck Picture Collection.

Sacred fish were kept in some holy wells. St Bean's Well at Kilmore, Argyll, Scotland, held two black 'mystical or sanctified fishes' known as *Easg Siant* (The Holy Fishes).[38] Ffynnon Wenog in Cardigan, Wales, held a trout with a golden chain, as did the Golden Well at Peterchurch, Herefordshire, England.[39] The fish at Ffynnon Bryn Fendigaid, at Aberffraw on Anglesey, were used in rites of divination. The *Liverpool Mercury* (18 November, 1896) reported the placing of two new fish in Ffynnon y Sant at Tyn y Ffynnon, Nant Peris, Llanberis, Wales. They replaced two others which had died. In the early part of the nineteenth century, Garland Sunday observances at the sacred lake called Loughharrow, in County Mayo, Ireland, continued ancient practice:

> The people . . . swim their horses in the lake on that day to defend them against incidental ills during the year and throw spancels and halters into it which they leave there . . . they are also accustomed to throw butter into it that their cows may be sufficiently productive.[40]

Throwing offerings into lakes or rivers was known in ancient Ireland, Britain and Denmark. It continues today.

Pagan observances continue in the twentieth century in Celtic countries.

A Pagan prayer, collected around 1910 by W.Y. Evans-Wentz from an old Manx woman, invokes the Celtic god of the sea:

> Manannan beg mac y Leirr, fer vannee yn Ellan
> Bannee shin as nyn maatey, mie goll magh
> As cheet stiagh ny share lesh bio as marroo 'sy vaatey'.
> [Little Manannan, son of Leirr, who blessed our land,
> Bless us and our boat, well going out
> And better coming in with living and dead in the boat.]

This prayer had been used by the woman's father and grandfather. Her grandfather had addressed the Celtic sea-god Manannan, but her father had substituted St Patrick's name for Manannan.[41]

In the Scottish Highlands, libations of milk are poured on a special hollowed stone, the Leac na Gruagach (Dobby Stane), in honour of the Gruagach, a goddess who watches over the cows.[42] At Samhain, it is a Breton custom to pour libations over the tombs of the dead. On the island of Lewis, ale was sacrificed at Hallowtide to the sea-god Shony.

> After coming to the church of St Mulvay at night a man was sent to wade into the sea, saying: 'Shony, I give you this cup of ale hoping that you will be so kind as to give us plenty of sea-ware for enriching our ground the ensuing year.'[43]

Evans-Wentz records (1911) that in his day, Lewis people poured libations to Shony for seaweed.[44] Also, 'Until modern times in Iona similar libations were poured to a god corresponding to Neptune'.[45] In Brittany, the equivalent deity Yann-An-Ôd appears sometimes on the seashore, lurking among the sand dunes. He has the habit of shape-shifting, changing from a giant to a dwarf at will. Sometimes he is seen wearing an oil-cloth seaman's hat, and at other times a broad-brimmed black felt hat. Similar apparitions of Odin are known in Northumbria.

James Anderson, writing in the *Journal* of the Society of Antiquaries of Scotland in 1792 about customs in the Lothians thirty years earlier, stated:

> The celebration of the Lammas Festival was most remarkable. Each community agreed to build a tower in some conspicuous place, near the centre of their district . . . This tower was usually built of sods . . . In building it, a hole was left in the centre for a flag staff, on which was displayed the colours on the great day of the festival.

On Lammas Day, the participants danced and sang, took part in sports and banqueting, 'drinking pure water from a well, which they always took care should be near the scene of their banquet'. In Ireland, the Pagan celebration of Lammas continued into the twentieth century. Sometimes, the festivities were held on the nearest Sunday to Lammas Day, known as Garland Sunday. The ceremonies centred on a girl, seated in a chair on the hilltop, who was

*Plate 6.6* Eighteenth-century milkmaids' dance with silver plate, London. May Morning dances continued until the end of the century.

garlanded with flowers. In some places, a female effigy was set up, decorated with ribbons and likewise garlanded with flowers. Round this, dancers circled, the girls picking flowers or ribbons off the figure as they danced.[46] Research conducted in Ireland in 1942 by the Irish Folklore Commission identified 195 assembly sites.[47] Most were hilltop sites; of the 195, only seventeen had any connection with the Christian Church.[48]

Thus Pagan ceremonies have continued until the present time. A few of them have continued directly, others have been amalgamated with Christianity, and yet more have turned into folklore and undeciphered tradition.

# 7

# THE GERMANIC PEOPLES

Between the Rhine and what is now Lithuania, northern Europe was inhabited by peoples whom the Romans called Germani. In Latin, the name means simply 'related', and might refer to the Germans' kinship with the Celts, but Tacitus tells us that it was originally the name of one tribe and was later generalised to the whole people (*Germania* 2). Whatever the origin of the name, the tribes living east of the Rhine did not seem to think of themselves as a collective, and modern scholarship is equally disinclined to speak of any deep distinction between the peoples living east and west of the Rhine at the beginning of the Common Era.[1] Their differences, linguistic and cultural, seem to have been intensified by Julius Caesar's creation of an artificial boundary between them. In what follows we trace the religious history of the people who lived, or at least originated, east of the Rhine in Roman times.

The culture which grew up in the region of modern Copenhagen was rather simpler than the 'Celtic' cultures of Hallstatt and La Tène to the south. There were no large metal deposits on the German plains,[2] and perhaps for this reason the western Germanic tribes did not develop sophisticated weaponry until their meagre resources were exploited in the third and fourth centuries CE.[3] At that time the peoples of the Baltic peninsula stayed in their homeland and became the Scandinavians, but some had earlier migrated and set up home on the eastern mainland. One of these eastern tribes, the Bastarnae from the Carpathian Mountains, menaced the Greek cities of the Black Sea around 200 BCE, and in the following century the western Germans were pressing on the Rhine frontier and southward into the Alps. Here they forced the Celtic Helvetii into Switzerland and the Celtic Boii, whose original home, Bohemia, is still called after them, down to the Po Valley. The western Germans of the Rhineland skirmished with the Celts of Roman Gaul and eventually confederated to become the Franks and the Saxons. In 9 CE these westerners had beaten back a Roman invasion force with the massacre of three legions, but they did not attempt to advance beyond the Rhine frontier. They stayed, with their primitive weapons technology, east of the river until weapons-grade iron became available four centuries later and the smith-god gained a heroic place in their mythology.

The eastern Germans, who in Tacitus' time were called Suebi and later Goths, seem to have had access to better technology. Tacitus describes them as carrying round shields and short swords (*Germania* 43.6), and the ritual hoard found in Pietroasse, Romania, dated to the third century CE, consists of elaborately worked and inlaid gold vases, cups, necklaces etc. in Germanic, Greek and Iranian styles.[4] Their origin myth, reported by their historian Jordanes in the seventh century, claims that they originated in south Scandinavia (the Suebi share their name with the Swedes) and crossed in three ships to the Baltic shore of what is now Prussia, where they defeated the Vandals and others. It was their fifth king who took them south to the Black Sea, where, however, Graeco-Roman armies contained them until the time of Aurelian (270–275 CE). Then they invaded Dacia, pushing out the Celtic inhabitants who had settled there in the fifth century, and became known as the Visigoths. The tribes who stayed in the Ukraine became the Ostrogoths, who built an enormous empire from the Don to the Dniester, from the Black Sea to Belarus. However, in 370 they themselves were conquered by the invading Huns (although the Gothic language continued to be spoken in the Crimea until at least 1554), and the great Gothic migration began. We have already seen how Italy was conquered by the Ostrogoths, southern Gaul and Iberia by the Visigoths and Africa by the Vandals, another east Germanic people. In 568 Italy, only recently reconquered from the Goths by the Emperor Justinian, was again captured by the Lombards, a Gothic people who had originally lived near modern Hamburg at the mouth of the Elbe.[5] Even when they were Christian, the Goths still enacted laws based on Germanic customs, which were eventually codified when they settled in Spain. As for the western Germans, by 487, when Clovis defeated the last of the independent Gallo-Roman leaders, the Franks had effectively founded France. In Italy, France and Spain, the Goths became somewhat Romanised, and so 'Latin' culture prevailed, whilst Latin-derived languages took over from Gothic. In Germany and Britain, this did not occur and the languages and initial culture remained Germanic, with Celtic enclaves persisting on the western fringes. By 550, the Angles and then the Saxons were taking control of what was to become England, and the ruling classes of Europe, whether Latinised or not, had become German.

## EARLY GERMANIC RELIGION

Tacitus, writing in the last decade of the first century CE, says that the Germanic peoples committed their history only to songs. Theirs was an oral culture like that of the Celts, but they did have a kind of sacred script, which was carved on strips of wood in the drawing of lots.[6] Their origin myth was one of patrilineal descent: the story of the god Tuisto, a son of Earth, who sired three sons who gave their names to the three groups of German tribes. Tuisto is the tribal god (Gothic *thiudisko*, like the Celtic *Teutates*), and his epithet 'Son of Earth' is echoed in a Norse legend written down much later. *The Deluding of Gylfi*, recorded in the mid-thirteenth century, describes how the Earth was made from the body of a giant and the human race sprang from two ancestors made out of tree trunks: Ash and Elm. Here, too, human beings are described as springing from the life force of Earth. In the earlier myth, Tuisto's three sons gave their names to three peoples: the Ingaevones, those nearest the sea; the Herminones, those of the interior; and the Istaevones, 'the rest' according to Tacitus, but according to Pliny the dwellers near the Rhine. Two of these race-names emerge later in the names of tribal gods. The Swedish kings of the *Ynglingasaga*, rulers of some of the 'peoples nearest the sea', traced their ancestry to the god Ingvi, and the inhabitants of central Germany were conquered in the ninth century by the Frankish King Charlemagne at the sacred grove whose image was the Irminsul, or 'Pillar of Heaven', a tall wooden post reminiscent of the Jupiter columns of the Romano-Celtic Rhineland. The name of the Istaevones does not recall any Germanic god, but Pliny might have been wrong about the river. From the time of Herodotus (II.33) and

*Plate 7.1* Maypole at Winterbach, near Esslingen, Baden-Württemberg, Germany, May 1992, showing symbols of the village trades, spiral bindings, garland, ribbons and uncut branches at the top.
© 1992 Nigel Pennick.

for centuries afterwards it was not the Rhine but the Danube which was known as the Hister or Istar. The Istaevones could have been the eastern Germans and Ista the deity of their river.

All the Germans, according to Tacitus, were extremely strong and hardy, but unlike the Celts they dressed plainly and in some cases hardly at all, the men going naked except for a cloak. Their tribal loyalty was strong, and it was seen as a disgrace for a man to outlive his leader in battle. Unlike the Celts, they did not live in fortified towns but in villages with widely spaced huts, and they hunted, fished and cultivated grain. Their national drink was beer, and as the Celts did with Mediterranean wine, they drank a great deal of it. The western Germans were democratic (or practical), electing their leaders by merit, but civil order and punishment were in the hands of their priests – 'not as a punishment or by their leader's command, but as if by order of the god whom they believe to be with them in battle'.[7] This would seem to indicate a cult of symbolic atonement rather than of individual responsibility, rather as the Druids were said to offer innocent victims to the gods if enough criminals were not available. Images and signs or perhaps banners (*signa*), normally kept in the Germans' sacred groves, were carried with them into battle, and their special gods were, in the *interpretatio Romana*, Mercury (Woden?), Hercules (Thunor?) and Mars (Tiw?). Tacitus mentions that one of the eastern confederations, the Suebi, also sacrificed to Isis, whose sign was a ship, a Liburnian galley, showing that the religion was imported (*Germania* 9.2). However, the image of Sequana, goddess of the Seine, was also a ship, and with modern hindsight we can allow that the cult of 'Isis' was possibly indigenous. The form of the ship nevertheless suggests that the Suebi had once had contact with the goods of the eastern Mediterranean. In Tacitus' time, the river Oder was known as the Suebus, so a water-deity might well have ruled that confederation, and as we shall see, the eastern Germans were better known for their goddesses than those of the west.

All the Germans believed in women's prophetic power, as both Tacitus and Caesar agree, and the prophetesses were sometimes seen as divine. Veleda, who sang the Germans into battle during the reign of Vespasian (69–79 CE) and was taken to Rome in 78 CE,[8] was one such, and an earlier prophetess Aurinia and other women were similarly revered. Deification of an inspired sibyl paralleled Roman Pagan practice and the modern Shinto tradition where a departed worthy becomes *kami*. Another famed sibyl was the Alemannic-Frankish wise woman, Thiota. The seeress of the Semnones who went to Rome with King Masyas in 91 CE was called Ganna (the old German magic was called *gandno*). Waluburg (after *walus*, a magic staff) was in Egypt with Germanic troops during the second century.[9] The wise women called Haliarunnos, who consulted the shades of the dead, were expelled from the lands of the Goths by King Filimer in the fifth century. Later, the famous Icelandic sibyl Thordis Spákona is known from the *Biskupa*, *Heiðarviga* and *Vatnsdoela* sagas. There is some evidence of rapport with animals. In Sweden there lived the Vargamors, wise women who inhabited the forests, communing with wolves. The sagas also describe ordinary women routinely foretelling the future and working protective and healing spells for their men. This seems to have been part of the normal business of the household for Germanic wives.

Divination, according to Tacitus, was also carried out by the father of the family or, in cases of tribal augury, by the priest of the people, by means of strips of wood cut from a nut-bearing tree and carved with sigils,[10] which were then spread out at random on a white cloth and selected by the diviner whilst looking up at the heavens. A similar procedure is reported in medieval times as divination by runestaves: strips of wood with runes carved on them. The phonetic runic alphabet was, however, not introduced until the fourth century; these earlier sigils were probably ideograms. Divination by means of the flight of birds and the movements of horses was also practised. The sacred white horses were taken from the groves where they were kept and then yoked to a ceremonial chariot, after which their neighing and snorting were observed.

*Plate 7.2* Early runestone with horseman, dog and wend-runes (runes written from right to left with magical intention), Moybro Stenen, Uppland, Sweden. Nigel Pennick.

115

Public meetings were held at the new and full moon, which were said to be auspicious times for conducting business. Crime and responsibility obviously were recognised in some areas of life, because punishments varied for different kinds of offence. Traitors and deserters were hanged from a tree, but cowards and practitioners of 'bodily abominations' were plunged into marshes and held down by a hurdle. Several such bog burials have been excavated in recent years, although they do not all seem to have been punitive. Once more there is a similarity between Celtic and Germanic practice. According to Tacitus morality was strict, by contrast with the dissolute Romans and the soft-living Celts of Gaul. The Germans were fit, law-abiding and monogamous. But days spent lying around the fire in idleness were not counted as degenerate, and all the Germans drank heavily. Burial customs were simple: men were burned on a pyre with their arms and perhaps their horse, then a turf mound was raised above them. We do not hear how women were buried.

These were the warlike western German peoples. The eastern Germans, whom Tacitus calls the Suebi, were rather different. They, too, were warlike and unsophisticated, but one characteristic of theirs was their elaborate hair-styling. The men drew their hair back and knotted it, either at the nape of the neck or at the crown, in order to make themselves look taller and more terrifying. Their religion seems to have been shamanistic – involving trance and possession – and devoted to goddesses as much as to gods. The Semnones, who in Tacitus' time lived in Brandenburg, near modern Berlin, but who later migrated south and became the confederation of the Alemanni, would meet at regular intervals in an ancient forest, long hallowed by time, and would sacrifice a human life before beginning their rituals. The meeting place included a grove which no one could enter unless they were bound and thus 'had diminished themselves so they could openly carry the power of the deity'.[11] This reads like an account of trance possession, as in the Santeria concept of being 'ridden' by a deity. At the very least they would be personating the deity, as in modern Wiccan practice. If the person in the grove fell down by accident (again, another likelihood in a trance situation), they were not allowed to get to their feet but had to squirm out of the place along the ground. Tacitus dismisses this as a 'superstition' in the modern sense, and mentions that it arose from the Semnones' belief that the grove was the home of the god who was the origin of their race and who ruled over all things, everything else being subject to him and part of his household. As holders of the grove, the Semnones considered themselves to be the chief clan of the Suebi.

This Suebic outlook sounds rather similar to that of the Romans, whose sense of manifest dominion over all other peoples and whose ever-expanding household religion it echoes. But unlike any of the other peoples we have encountered so far, the German tribes all traced their human ancestry back to a god. Jordanes, the historian of the Visigoths, reports that these peoples worshipped their ancestors under the name of the Anses, as well as a god who was equivalent to Mars. To this god they gave the first-fruits of their battle-spoils, hanging the booty on tree trunks. The northern Pagan tradition of sacrificing booty to the gods is also reported by Orosius in his account[12] of the defeat of a Roman military force by the Cimbri in the lower Rhône valley in 105 BCE. The Cimbri captured two Roman military camps, and proceeded to sacrifice everything in fulfilment of a vow to the gods.

> Garments were torn apart and thrown away, gold and silver hurled into the river, the soldiers' armour was chopped in pieces, the horses' harness destroyed, the horses themselves thrown in the river, and the men hanged from trees, so that there was neither booty for the victor nor mercy for the vanquished.

Similarly, Caesar reports that the Celts dedicated the spoils of war likewise,[13] though the loot was piled up in heaps on consecrated ground rather than hung on trees or in temples. Jordanes mentions that the Visigoths too used to practise human sacrifice, but that this custom had ended by the time they reached the Black Sea.

It is not clear whether the goddesses worshipped by the eastern tribes were also seen as divine ancestresses or simply as divine protectresses. The tribes

*Plate 7.3* Romano-Frisian altar-shrine of the goddess Nehalennia from her shrine on the sacred island of Walcharen, the Netherlands. Nideck Picture Collection.

117

around the mouth of the Elbe and in the south of modern Denmark are the ones who, as is now well known, worshipped Nerthus, Mother Earth. They saw her as intervening in human affairs and riding among her people in a wagon drawn by cows. The priest of Nerthus would sense when she was ready to leave her island shrine, and then with deep reverence would follow the wagon on its tour through the lands of her people, which would be the occasion for a general holiday, the only time when these warlike people put down their arms. At the end of the perambulation, the wagon and its contents would be washed in a lake by slaves who were then drowned. No-one was allowed to see the goddess on pain of death. We have seen images being paraded and then ritually washed by the Greeks and Romans, but the gruesome sequel is an archaic touch which they did not share.

The Naharvali, who lived nearer the source of the Oder, on the Riesengebirge, practised an ancient religion which involved a priest in women's clothes presiding over the rituals of twin gods, the Alci (which probably means simply 'gods'), who were equated by the *interpretatio Romana* with Castor and Pollux. The priest in female clothes is typical of trance religion. We have already seen the *Galli*, the castrati priests of the ecstatic cult of the Great Mother of Asia Minor, who according to Apuleius dressed as women, and in eastern shamanism the male shaman also cross-dresses as a sign of his separateness from normal life. However, Tacitus does not let us know the details of the worship of the Alci. Even further east, in what is now Lithuania, Tacitus tells us the tribe of the Aestii (whose name survives in that of the Estonians), spoke a language like that of the Britons, worshipped the mother of the gods and took her emblem, the figure of a wild boar, as a protection even where arms would normally be needed. It would seem that those devoted to the service of this goddess were considered taboo, protected from the rough-and-tumble of normal life. The boar was a sacred animal to the Celts also, and in later Germanic religion it was sacred to Freya and Frey, the bringers of success and of plenty. The Aestii were also harvesters of amber, another emblem of Freya in later mythology, and Tacitus tells us that they were unaware of its value to the Roman traders. This seems unlikely, because the amber routes had operated between the Baltic and the Mediterranean since the time of the Etruscans.

Finally, Tacitus mentions the Sitones, who were like the other tribes in all respects except that they were matriarchal. It seems that among the eastern Germanic tribes a female figure, a goddess or even an actual woman, carried greater authority than among the western Germans, whose deities are all described as gods and among whom we never hear that, like the Britons, they 'do not discriminate among their rulers by gender'. The ancient Germanic tribes of the east overlap with the Slavic peoples of that area, who are described in chapter 8. When the Ostrogoths and Visigoths emerge from ethnography into history, however, we hear little of their religion. The story of the martyrdom of St Saba in the late fourth century by the Visigoths describes death by drowning, which might have been a ritual method of death, as in the case of the slaves of Nerthus. In addition, the tribes around the Black Sea, including the Goths, are described by several writers as honouring a god of the sword. According to Ammianus Marcellinus, the Alans (a Mongolian people, but typical of this area) 'thrust a drawn sword into the ground which they honour as the god of war and protector of their homes'.[14] An identical emblem of a war-god who is also a god of justice is found in accounts of the Norse god Tyr, whose attribute is the sword and whose rune, which shares his name, is in the shape of an upwards-pointing arrow or stylised sword. Records from the time of the Gothic incursions, however, tell us nothing of their goddesses.

## SHRINES AND SANCTUARIES

Germanic and Nordic sacred places show the same evolution recorded in the other areas considered so far. The most basic were natural features. In tenth-century Iceland, the *Landvættir* (land-wights, earth-spirits) had fields or fells hallowed for them. *Landnámabók* (5.6), the record of the settlement of Iceland, describes worship at waterfalls, caves and sacred hills into which souls passed at death. Helgafell was so sacred that no person was allowed to look at it unwashed.[15] On these sacred lands, no person should urinate, no fetid smell should be made and no living thing might be destroyed there.[16]

Sacred places in the landscape were marked by hill-figures, Maypoles, cairns and labyrinths. Cairns were built where important offering ceremonies, known as *blóts*, had been celebrated. (The word *blót* means a blood sacrifice. It is cognate not only with modern English 'blood', but also with 'blessing'.) Each cairn had a commemorative name (e.g. Flokavarda, *Landnámabók* 1.2). Often, they were at important boundaries. Weland's Stock, a boundary-marker near Whiteleaf, Buckinghamshire, mentioned in a charter of 903,[17] was a 'Maypole' or phallic image sacred to the smith-god Wayland. The most celebrated of these poles was that called Irminsul, which existed at the Eresburg (now Ober-Marsberg, Westphalia, Germany). The *Translatio S. Alexandri* (ch. 3) states that the Saxons worshipped 'a large wooden column set up in the open. In their language it is called *Irminsul*, which in Latin is "a universal column"'. Labyrinths were used in spring rites, weather-magic and ceremonies of the dead (as at Rösaring, Laåsa, Uppland, Sweden, where a straight 'road of the dead' and a stone labyrinth adjoined a grave-field).[18]

The Anglo-Saxon *Wih* was an unsheltered image standing in the open. An important example of this class of site, where worship was out of doors, is the Norse *Vé*: a sacred enclosure, rectangular, lenticular or triangular, surrounded by standing stones or a consecrated fence of hazel poles (and ropes) known as the *Vébond*. These could be set up temporarily, as when the community gathered to witness the paying of a debt or the swearing of an

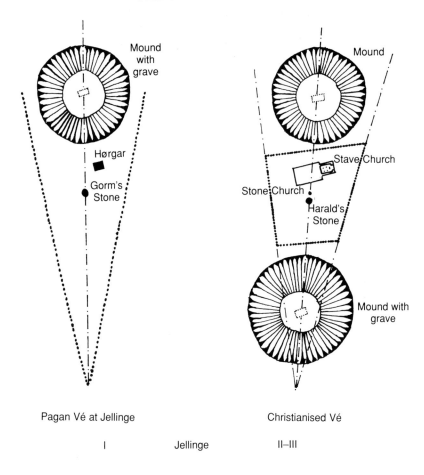

Mound with grave

Mound

Hørgar

Gorm's Stone

Stave Church

Stone Church

Harald's Stone

Mound with grave

Pagan Vé at Jellinge

Christianised Vé

| I | Jellinge | II–III |

*Plate 7.4* Plan of the royal Vé (sacred enclosure) at Jellinge, Denmark, in Pagan (left) and Christian (right) forms. The boundaries of the sacred enclosure remained almost unchanged, whilst the holy centre-line was used to define the positioning of the later church. Thus the advent of the church altered little the Pagan traditions of geomancy and the use of sacred places. Nigel Pennick.

oath. Ritual combat also took place in the *Vébond*, and the modern boxing 'ring' (in fact a square) is a survival of this practice. More developed is the *Træf* (Anglo-Saxon), the Scandinavian *Hørgr* or *Hörgr* (literally, 'rocky outcrop'), which was a tented shrine, tabernacle or pavilion sheltering an altar or a sacred image. An enclosed sacred building was the *Hof*, an ordinary farm hall, where regular festivals such as those to mark the seasons were observed. The *Hof* was divided into two areas: the *skáli*, or hall proper, and the *afhús*, a sanctuary, where the sacred objects and images were kept.

Although most religious observances took place in a *Hof*, there were also fully enclosed wooden temples (the Anglo-Saxon *Ealh*). Important temples to deities of the Nordic pantheon stood at Jellinge in Denmark, Sigtuna and Uppsala in Sweden, Trondenes, Lade, Skiringssal and Mæri in Norway, and Dublin in Ireland. The temple at Uppsala had a square plan, like that of the Prussian god Svantovit at Arcona on the Baltic holy island of Rügen. In Iceland, every farmer in the locality paid dues to a temple, though it was the temple-priest's duty to maintain the temple at his own expense. *Erbyggja Saga* records a temple built by Thórólf Mostrarskegg at Thórsness on Snæfellsness. Thórólf brought with him the high-seat pillars of his original temple in Norway, and cast them overboard from his ship, so that, where they came ashore, the new temple would be built. This seems to have been a common practice, for when Thorhadd the Old, temple-priest at Thrandheim in Mæri, emigrated to Iceland, he took the earth beneath the temple and the pillars with him (*Landnámabók* 4.6). After the earth upon which they stand, trees, poles and posts are the most hallowed features of sacred enclosures, including the holy grove, *Vé* and temple. Pilgrimage to ancestral sites was not unknown in the north: the Icelander Lopt made a pilgrimage to his grandfather's temple in Norway every third year to worship (*Landnámabók* 5.8).

The entrance to Thórólf's temple was in a side wall, near the gable. Immediately inside the door were the high-seat pillars, studded with the 'divine nails'. They marked the boundary of the sanctuary. Inside the temple was a chancel containing an altar, around which were images of the gods. On this altar was a sacred ring, worn by the temple-priest at all public gatherings and upon which oaths were sworn. The altar also held a sacrificial bowl, with a blood-sprinkler. The temple at Uppsala was described around 1200, perhaps one hundred years after its destruction, by Adam of Bremen: 'In this temple, ornamented entirely with gold, the people worship images of three gods . . . Priests are assigned to all their gods, to offer sacrifices for the people.' The temple of the Black Thor at Dublin, called 'the golden castle', was sacked by the Irish King Mæl Seachlainn in 994, who looted it of its sacred treasures, including the golden ring.[19]

When Christianity was imposed, the most important Pagan sacred sites were occupied and churches built upon them. The *Vé* at Jellinge, Denmark, is a prime example. Similarly, at Gamla Uppsala in Sweden, a great wooden temple existed until around 1100. It is thought that this site originated as a sacred grove, then evolved into a *Hørgr* and then a temple. A cathedral was built upon the temple site. On the other hand, during Anglo-Saxon, and later, Viking times, Pagan burials were made in sacred enclosures that had been re-Paganised. Peel Cathedral in the Isle of Man had Norse Pagan interments after earlier Christian burials. The Viking-age runic-inscribed Pagan tombstone found in 1852 in the churchyard of St Paul's Cathedral in London, which may have been carved by a Swedish rune-master, is a notable example.[20]

## THE GERMANIC FESTIVAL CALENDAR

Tacitus, in *Germania* 26, tells us that the Germans had only three seasons: spring, summer and winter. Some 1,000 years later, the Law Book of Iceland described the year as divided into two: winter and summer. In fact, it seems that the ancient Germans had a sixfold year made up of sixty-day tides, or double months as we should call them. In the Viking Age (post-eighth century) there were two Roman-style months called Litha in summer, and the sixth-century Gothic Church calendar calls the Roman month of November 'the first Yule', indicating that there was once a second Yule, i.e. December. The Venerable Bede, an Anglo-Saxon monk writing in about 730, likewise records a double Litha in June and July, plus a 'Giuli' tide in the months of December and January. Thus we have the names of two of the presumed old sixty-day tides, but unfortunately none of the others. The sixfold Germanic year, apparently divided by three major festivals, has given us the year of the legal and university terms.[21]

Like the Celtic year, the Germanic year started at the beginning of winter with a feast equivalent to the Celtic Samhain. In Germany and France this feast was eventually absorbed into the Christian Martinmas (11 November), and in England into All Hallows (1 November). It was the beginning of the financial year: church-scot (tax) had to be paid then, as had other dues such as the first of three annual instalments of the wages of female servants and the first instalment on a lease. Appointments were made from Martinmas to Martinmas, and accounts ran over the same period. In Scandinavia, where the winter sets in earlier, the festival was known as 'Winter Nights' and began on the Thursday between 9 and 15 October.

The second term began in mid-March, later equated to Easter, mid-Lent or St Gertrude's Day (17 March). Pagan festivities at this time have been included in Easter, such as Easter eggs, taken from Baltic Paganism (see chapter 8) and the Easter rabbit or hare, which recalls the sacred hares of the British tribes. March or Easter was the second of three instalments in the paying of dues, in the inspection and culling of livestock, and in the three terms of the ploughing year. In Holland, the four months from 15 March to 15 July were called May.[22] In Scandinavia, where neither Roman nor Christian influence was strong until about the year 1000, the year began one month earlier, in October, and its second festival, four months later, is recorded in the *Saga of Olaf the Holy* (ch. 77) as 'the principal blood-offering of Sweden . . . at Uppsala, in the month of Gói [February]'. A market and a fair were held then for a week, but with the coming of Christianity there the market was moved to Candlemas (2 February) and held for only three days.

The final term began in mid-July, later equated to Lammas (1 August). In Germany, France and England it survives as a legal and farming date. Sheep were not to be shorn before Lammas, and in the weeks leading up to Lammas

# HOROLOGII ICONISMUS.

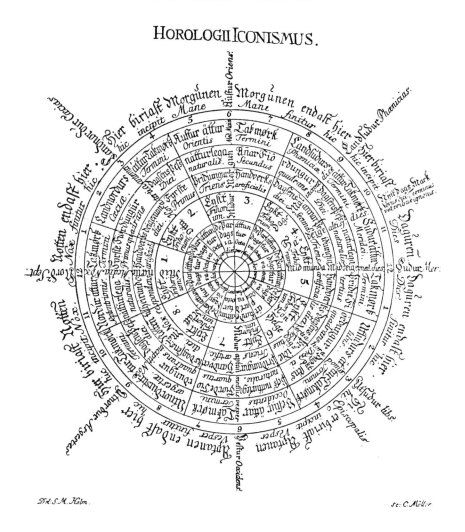

*Plate 7.5* Northern tradition eightfold time-space wheel from *Rímbegla* by Stephán Björnssen, Copenhagen, 1780. Nideck Picture Collection.

the weaklings were to be put out to fatten for an early sale.[23] Summer grazing for sheep and cattle often finished at Lammas, and 'Lammas Land' denotes a pasture leased until this date each year. In Scandinavia, the third division took place a month earlier and was known as 'in summer', a sacrifice 'for peace and the plenty of the year' (*Saga of Olaf Tryggvason*, ch. 74). It began on the Thursday between 9 and 15 June. In Iceland this feast became the date of the annual General Assembly, or Althing.

The Germanic half-year division is better known, as its Scandinavian version has been preserved in the twelfth-century Icelandic Law Book. Summer's Day, the beginning of the summer half-year, was on the Thursday between 9 and 15 April, opposite to Winter's Day, which fell between 9 and 15 October. In England, Germany, the Low Countries and northern France, half a year after the beginning of winter brought the beginning of summer to mid-May. This was later assimilated to Whitsunday or the Rogation Days, and in France and England it took on some of the characteristics of the Celtic Beltane. Throughout medieval Europe, the two divisions of Martinmas (November) and Whitsun (May) dated the half-yearly accounts of boroughs until the sixteenth century, when Easter and Michaelmas superseded them. Whitsun was celebrated in the normal Pagan fashion with games, processions, horseraces and feasting.[24] The Whitsun games continued into the High Medieval period as the tourneys familiar to all readers of the Arthurian romances, and in modern times in the north of England they survived as local carnivals including bands, floats and dancing flower-maidens.[25]

In the Viking Age, the year seems to have been quartered, and references to the dates of the three and four festivals are ambiguous. Scandinavian sources describe a midwinter feast between 9 and 15 January, halfway through the winter half-year. In Norway, the Christian King Håkon the Good (940–963) 'made a law that Yule should be held at the same time that Christian men hold it. But previously Yule had been held on *höku* night, that is midwinter night, and it was held for three nights'. Now in the original Germanic year, Yule was not the name of a feast, but of a two-month tide. According to Tille,[26] the *Ynglingasaga* makes no mention of a Yule feast before 840: the main feast is that of the 'Winter Nights' in mid-October. From 840 to 1000 Winter Nights and Yule are mentioned with equal frequency, and after the year 1000 Yule becomes the main feast. Since Scandinavia adopted official Christianity around this time, the change is not surprising. Was there, however, a Pagan festival at the winter solstice?

The English monk Bede, writing around 730, states that the ancient Angles began their year on 24–25 December. He calls this not Yule (for him, that is the name of the months December and January), but 'Mothers' Night'.[27] In the eighth century the Church started its year at Christmas, but the Roman calendar, from which that of the Church was derived, began its year at the Calends of January. All other evidence shows the north European year starting with Winter Nights or Samhain. Was Bede reporting an otherwise unknown Anglian custom, perhaps sacred to the three goddesses known as the Mothers? Possibly, but as Tille argues, he could equally likely be describing a Pagan adaptation of the imported feast of Christmas. During the eighth century at least one Church decree (from the Council of Trullus, 706) had forbidden some rather crude ceremonies carried out by the faithful honouring the confinement of the Mother of God. The round, flat cakes or *placentae*, once used at the Roman domestic festivals, were baked in honour of the afterbirth of the Divine Mother. Christmas Eve was her night. Even in the nineteenth century a symbolic lying-in was enacted by households in country districts in Scotland. One member of the family would get up early on Christmas morning and bake 'care cakes', which would be eaten in bed by the other family members.[28] Bede's assertion that the Germanic year began at the winter solstice remains an isolated claim, contradicted by other sources.

The midwinter customs which became attached to the birth of Christ were, as we have seen, northern adaptations of the Roman Saturnalia. But the summer solstice, under its statutory date of 25 June, became a popular festivity early in Germanic history. The German word *Sonnenwende* always refers, in medieval texts, to the summer solstice, not to the winter solstice. At the end of the first century CE some German troops in the Roman army at Chesterholme listed their supplies for the celebration in a record which has come down to us. In the early seventh century, Bishop Eligius of Noyon in Flanders criticised the chants, carols and leaping practised by his flock on 24 June.[29] In medieval Germany this same date, adopted into Christianity

*Plate 7.6* Eighteenth-century Yule pastry mould from Frisia, showing the spinning, horned goddess. Like the traditional cake designs, pastries and biscuits are remarkably conservative in design, retaining Pagan motifs. Nigel Pennick.

125

as St John's Eve, was a night of revelry, when apprentice boys in particular ran wild. In some Scandinavian settlements the solstice replaced the summer offering-tide of 9–15 June. The Isle of Man in Britain retains its Viking-founded parliament, held at an artificial hill called Tynwald (assembly plain) on 25 June every year. Christianisation has ensured that each delegate wears a sprig of St John's Wort on the day. In modern Scandinavia, midsummer bonfires are lit to this day, and the custom of rolling flaming wheels down hills at midsummer still persists in northern Europe.

## THE FRANKS AND SAXONS

By the mid-third century, the tribes nearest to the Rhine had grouped together and called themselves the Franks, meaning the bold or spirited ones. In the south, some of the Suebians had reformed themselves into the 'All-men' or Alemanni, and began to harass Italy and southern Gaul. Towards the end of the century, the central tribes had confederated as the Saxons and were beginning to expand. They forced the Franks westwards and also began sea-raids on southern Britain and northern Gaul, causing devastation, as we have seen in chapter 6. The Saxons remained Pagan for another half-millennium. In Britain, their arrival was seen as a clash of faiths as well as a battle between civilisation and barbarism, and it was the barbarians who won. The bloodiness of the confrontation is attested by its only historian, Gildas, writing about a century after the invasion. Britain became a Germanic Pagan confederation ruled by kings who traced their divine ances-try not to Beli and to Anna, but to Woden.

In Britain the conversion to official Christianity took place in the seventh century more by argument and petty legal constraints than by massacre and the demolition of temples. The Christian mission sent from Rome to Britain under Augustine in 597 visited the king of Kent, who agreed that it would be politically valuable to have continental support, and so became Christian. The Church authorities in Rome decided that Britain should be converted (ignoring the existing sect of Celtic Christianity which existed in non-Saxon parts, but which itself had ignored the opportunity to convert the incomers). Following Roman practice, the missionaries divided Britain into a southern province ruled by London, and a northern one ruled by York. Mellitus, one of Augustine's assistants, visited London in 603 and convinced Sebert, king of Essex, that he should become Christian, as his powerful neighbour and potential enemy in Kent had done. The Pagan temple in London was taken over and became Paul's Cathedral. But this did not last long, as on the death of Sebert in 614, his three sons, Saxred, Sigebert I and Seward, who were Pagan, expelled the Christians, who fled back to Canterbury and even considered quitting England altogether. Paul's Cathedral was reconverted to a Pagan temple, and the Elder Faith flourished in London for another forty-one years. During this time, the ecclesiastical system became established in its temporary headquarters, and so Canterbury instead of London remained as the centre of the new religion.

The politico-religious wars of Europe have been elevated into heroic struggles between good and evil, following Christian authors, when in reality, religion and politics were intertwined. For example, the Celtic Christian king of Wales, Caedwal II, fought on the side of Penda, the Pagan king of Mercia, against the Roman Christian King Edwin of Northumbria, killing him at the Battle of Hatfield on 12 October, 633. When Caedwal II died, he was buried in Pagan London at the place which is now Martin's Church in Ludgate. Following the downfall of Romano-Celtic society, there was no good-and-evil Christian versus Pagan battle which apologists often portray. Kings converted to the god who brought them victory and prosperity, and for many kings the Christian god was successful. In England the perceived good-versus-evil conflict dates from the Anglo-Saxon wars against the Danes in the eighth and ninth centuries.

In Saxony itself, by contrast, the Pagan inhabitants were persecuted from outside by their old tribal enemies the Franks, who had meanwhile become fanatical Christians. Once more religion was used to rationalise old political hatreds. At the end of the eighth century, the Frankish monarch Charlemagne led a religious as well as a territorial crusade against the Saxons. In 782 he slaughtered 4,500 Pagan prisoners who refused to convert at a grove which has given its name to the modern town nearby, Sachsenhain-bei-Verden. Frankish troops cut down the sacred icon of the Saxons, Irminsul, the Pillar of Heaven, and in 785 the Pagan leader Widukind was baptised. Charlemagne instituted the death penalty for refusing baptism and for other aspects of continued adherence to the Pagan faith.[30] 'With respect to trees, stones, and fountains, where certain foolish people light torches or practise other superstitions, we earnestly ordain that that most evil custom detestable to God, wherever it be found, should be removed and destroyed.'[31] Despite this repression, the Saxons rebelled in 793. Mass deportations followed, when one in three of the inhabitants of Saxony was expelled on the orders of Charlemagne.[32] There was a second, more successful, rebellion of Saxony in 870, when Paganism was restored for a while.

Despite the long existence of official Paganism among the Saxons, we know unfortunately little about their religion. We know that some of those who invaded Britain worshipped a divine ancestor Seaxnot, a totemic sword-god called after the single-edged cutting sword used by these people. The others traced their ancestry back to Woden, the storm-god. We can speculate that Irmin, the holy being of the continental Saxons, was a god of heaven whose name had developed from that of the mythical ancestor of the first-century Herminones. The German leader who beat back the Romans in the year 9 was also called Hermann (in Latin: Arminius). He might have been this same mythical ancestor, or he might have been named after the latter, as the Yngling dynasty of Scandinavia was named after the god Ingvi.

William A. Chaney has presented a closely argued case for the Anglo-Saxon kings being the mediators between heaven and earth, the bringers of 'luck' to their people.[33] When the kingdom's 'luck' disappeared, the king would be deposed or killed. One feature of this system is that any abuse of royal power would be extremely difficult, which recalls Tacitus' comment about the frankness and ingenuousness of the German tribes (*Germania* 22.4). The Anglo-Saxon kings also made a habit of marrying, on their accession, their predecessor's widow. Even the newly Christian King Canute did this as late as 1018. Since the Angles and Frisians who colonised what was to become England were originally among the worshippers of the goddess Nerthus, it has been suggested that this might be a matrilineal feature. Through such marriages the new kings might have been identifying themselves with a female power-holder, a representative of the kingdom's sovereignty like the goddesses of Ireland.[34]

Charlemagne's Franks were the Germans of the Low Countries and the Rhine. They had come into contact with Gallo-Roman civilisation in the first century BCE, and they occupied an uneasy border country which nevertheless contained the capital of all the Gallic provinces, Trèves or Trier. Their history as a nation begins in 446, when they captured Tournai, probably under the leadership of the semi-legendary (and semi-divine) Meroveus, literally, the 'sea-fighter'. Meroveus gave his name to the Merovingian dynasty, the so-called 'long-haired kings', who in the fashion of the late Roman Empire eventually became titular monarchs only, while their chief minister, the 'mayor of the Palace', had

*Plate 7.7* Wildberg image, possibly of a priest in ceremonial dress. Nigel Pennick.

executive power. Wearing long hair and a beard seems to have been a liturgical characteristic of the Pagan priesthood. An image of this exists in the Württembergische Landesmuseum at Stuttgart. It is a statue of a bearded Swabian Pagan priest, his vestments still bearing traces of red coloration, hair braided in ten waist-length pigtails. Found in a wall in Wildberg (near Calw, Baden-Württemberg) in 1698, the Wildberger Mann has been dated to the thirteenth century on stylistic grounds. A comparable figure from Ekaterinoslav, south Russia, exists in the Pitt-Rivers Museum in Oxford, the Kamene Baba. It, too, has the characteristic pigtailed hair, but lacks the beard of the Wildberger Mann, and so, despite lacking breasts, is described as female.

In 487 the Merovingian kings of the Franks were still leaders of their people. In that year Clovis conquered Syagrius, the last Gallo-Roman leader, at Soissons, and took over northern Gaul. At some time, traditionally in 496 but possibly as late as 503, Clovis converted to Catholic Christianity and so enlisted the support of the (Catholic) Roman Empire for his military ambitions. In 496 he defeated the Alemanni in the south-west of his territory and moved his capital to Paris. Then, with the Church's blessing, he took on the Arian Goths. In 507 he defeated Alaric II at Vouillé and confined the Goths to the French Pyrenees and to Spain. Clovis's battle with the Burgundians, who had settled in the Rhône valley, was won in 534, when they were incorporated in the Frankish Empire. One hundred years earlier, when this Baltic people had reached the city of Worms in their westerly migration, they had

*Plate 7.8* Images on the Gallehus Horn. Nigel Pennick.

129

been attacked by the marauding Huns and driven out in 436. The exiles settled in the Rhône valley and gave their name to the area, but after the victory of Clovis they disappeared as a nation. Their songs, however, did not. The story of the battle between the Burgundian king, Gundahar, and the Hunnish leader, Attila, together with various other historical figures such as Queen Brynhild, was commemorated in an epic which became the *Nibelungenlied*, the basis of Wagner's opera cycle *The Ring of the Nibelung*. The songs of the Germans, which had so distressed one Gallo-Roman poet living in Toulouse that he complained that his visitors' epic carousing put him off composing his hexameters, now survived to help form the new French language through the magnificent *chansons de geste*.[35]

The Germanic worship of the divine ancestor, living through his present representative, the king, was transformed into obedience to the Lord's anointed following the eclipse of the Merovingians during the early eighth century by their chief ministers. The latter, the Arnulfings and then the Carolingians, retained a hereditary hold on the rulership, and on taking power they were anointed by their bishops. At the coronation of Charlemagne in 800, the significance of this was extended. Just as in the eastern Church the Patriarch of Constantinople consecrated the emperor by acclaiming him at his coronation, so Charlemagne acquiesced in a similar procedure carried out by the Pope in Rome. During Mass on Christmas Day, the Pope placed a crown on Charlemagne's head, knelt before him and pronounced him *imperator et augustus*, the ancient titles of the victorious Roman emperor. Charlemagne's army was now an arm of the Roman Church, invaluable in the latter's territorial disputes with the eastern Empire. It also meant that Charlemagne was no longer merely the leader of a people or even of a territory, as the Anglo-Saxon kings were. He was the leader of western Christendom, and as such he could lead religious crusades. The myth of the Roman Empire, fighting for civilisation against barbarism, had now been amplified by the myth of the One True Faith which was co-terminous with the Empire. This would later be used to justify all kinds of territorial crusades. The Norman Conquest of England in 1066 was rationalised partly as an extension of the Roman Church to the semi-independent Church in England. The Norman invasion of Ireland a century later was presented as the bringing of Christian civilisation to people who were 'Christians only in name, Pagans in fact'.[36] And the Frankish crusades against the Pagans of eastern Europe, which we will consider in detail in chapter 9, were seen as the self-evidently justified colonisation of people whose religion made them barely human. However, Charlemagne's crusade was merely a dry run for these future developments, which did not crystallise fully until the accession of Otto I in 936 created the Holy Roman Empire.

In Britain, more than a century had passed since the 'dual faith' period, when King Rædwald of East Anglia (d. 625) had been able to have 'one altar to sacrifice to Christ, another to sacrifice to demons,'[37] and had later been buried, if it was he, in the magnificent Pagan burial mound at Sutton Hoo. The Synod of Whitby in 663 had amalgamated the Church in Britain with the hierarchy based in Rome, replacing the Irish pattern of individual hermits, travelling preachers, independent bishoprics and monastic communities which had been brought to northern Britain during the sixth and seventh centuries. Suddenly, Britain was once more part of an international community, and the kings and bishops played power politics accordingly. In 677 Bishop Wilfrid of York, on his way to appeal to Rome against a decision by King Ecgfrith of Northumbria, was shipwrecked on the coast of Frisia and took advantage of the opportunity to preach to the inhabitants. He was helped in his endeavours by the then chief minister of the Franks, Pippin the Arnulfing, and political and ecclesiastical ambition once more joined hands in an anti-Pagan crusade. Ironically, it was the Pagan Frisians who had been among the first 'Saxons' to invade Britain in the fifth century. They were still Pagan, and resolutely so. They fought back, regained the city of Utrecht from the Franks and expelled the new bishop. In 716 King Rêdbod led a Pagan campaign against the interlopers, but in 719 Wilfrid's successor, Boniface, returned and began to destroy Pagan sanctuaries and suppress Pagan teaching. In the year 722, the Frisian chieftains Detdic and Dierolf, 'although professing Christianity, were worshippers of idols',[38] and in Hessia and Thuringia in the 730s, 'the belief and practice of the converts [to Christianity] were still largely mixed with paganism'. In a letter to Pope Zacharias, Boniface even speaks of dual faith presbyters who offered sacrifices to the heathen gods as well as the Christian.[39]

Various Church councils held in Germany called for the suppression of heathen practices, including divination, the use of amulets, the need-fire and the offering of sacrifices, both to the old Pagan deities and to the saints who had taken their place.[40] But these had much less effect than the Church wanted, for there was continued resistance on a large scale. In 732, for example, it was reported to Pope Stephen that thirty churches had been burnt or demolished by Pagans in the Frankish territories.[41]

Boniface, no doubt rendering one favour for another, had in 731 consecrated Pippin as king of the Franks and thereby deposed the Merovingian dynasty with its strange Pagan taboos. But the Pagan rebellion the following year which destroyed thirty churches led to a further resurgence, and on 5 June 754 Boniface and fifty colleagues were killed in West Frisia by Pagans opposing conversion. Meanwhile, however, the Franks were attacking the Pagans in Saxony (see above p. 127), and in 785 the shrines of the god Fosite, including that on 'Holy Island' – Heligoland – were destroyed by the Christians. It looked as if the religious conflict in western Europe was over, until a new player arrived on the scene. The Viking Age had begun.

## THE VIKINGS

Scandinavia had played no part in western politics for 1,000 years, since the ancestors of the Goths had sailed over to the Vistula and set their course for the Crimea. Norwegian, Swedish and even Danish society was still based on small tribal groupings rather than on a larger national identity, and the ethics of cattle-raiding and clan warfare still prevailed over any possibility of advancement within a static social hierarchy. Unlike the Irish, who had a similar social structure but who also saw themselves as part of the international community of Christendom, the Scandinavians retained an outlook which western Europe had discarded some centuries before, and when their raiding parties arrived they appeared to mainstream Europe like uncanny visitors from another world. When Charlemagne's conquest of Frisia left the North Sea routes undefended (the Franks were no great sailors), the Norwegians and Danes set out in search of booty. Their tactics and attitudes were similar to those of the Celts who had swept down to plunder the Mediterranean lands 1,000 years before, and of the German raiding parties which had ventured across the Rhine five hundred years later to seize Romano-Celtic slaves and horses. But by the late eighth century most of Europe had forgotten these tactics and for a while was unable to fight back. The Vikings' nastiness was blamed on their religion rather than on their expansionism or their primitive social organisation, and the northern coasts of Europe quailed before the raids of 'the heathen'. Even modern commentators write of the Vikings as if the latter were conducting an unwarranted campaign against Christianity, having 'no respect for the sanctity of religious houses and the pacifism of their inmates'.[42] But there is no reason why they should have had. Churches and monasteries were full of rich pickings, and in the eyes of a warrior society, if their communities did not care for these enough to defend them, then why should strangers? In the ancient warrior

*Plate 7.9* Viking-age hogsback tombstone from Brampton, Yorkshire, England, with bear-cult and house of the dead imagery. Nigel Pennick.

societies, an attack on the deities of one's enemy was an attack on the enemy himself. The Goths destroyed the temple of Artemis at Ephesus in 250 BCE, the Romans destroyed the sacred groves of recalcitrant tribes, the rebellious Britons burned down the temple of the deified Claudius in Colchester, without these being specifically religious attacks. The eighth-century Christians and their modern apologists forget that their god was not the god of the Norsemen, and so he should expect no quarter. The two sides were playing by different rules.

Some earlier commentators argued that there might have been reason for specific religious bitterness.

> Many [of the raiders] were men who had suffered from the forcible means employed by Charlemagne for the conversion of pagans, or were the offspring of such men. Their enmity against Christianity was therefore fierce and unsparing; there was religious hatred, as well as the lust of spoil, in the rage which selected churches and monasteries as especial objects.[43]

Some or even many individuals might have found especial joy in revenging themselves against the god who himself had ordered atrocities against their shrines and their families. These Christian atrocities are, however, not condemned in the same tones that are used for Viking atrocities against Christian shrines and their guardians. Nevertheless, as the sagas record, religious hatred was not the main or even an important motive in the wave of invasions. The Vikings came for plunder.

They also became settlers. The last decade of the eighth century saw Norwegian Vikings colonising the Scottish islands, the Isle of Man and Ireland. On the islands, Christianity was tolerated but gradually died out, and Ireland became dual faith, although its literary culture, once fostered by the monasteries, collapsed into a fragmented vernacular form. Over the next three centuries the north-west fringe of Europe became one vast dynasty. The Scottish Lords of the Isles were Vikings. In the ninth century a Hebridean, a Christian lady called Aud the Deep-Minded, married the king of Dublin, was widowed, ruled with her son Thorstein the Red, and after his death sailed around the northern seas, 'with a crew of twenty free-born men', forging dynastic alliances and eventually settling in Iceland.[44] Further south, where political systems were more firmly established, things moved more slowly. The eastern half of England, from the Thames to the Tyne, was captured and re-Paganised in the 860s by the sons of the famous Viking, Ragnar Lodbrok. But Wessex was being stabilised under Alfred the Great (871–901), who had been taken to Rome as a boy and made an honorary consul by the Pope. Alfred united the south of England in one large and officially Christian confederation. He established a law code, he used the learning of the monks to bring literacy to his people, and he fostered the literary development of Anglo-Saxon. He also conquered and made treaties with the Danish earls who had settled to the east of him, most notably founding the initially Christian kingdom of East Anglia with its capital at Godmanchester (Guthrum's Camp), after defeating Earl Guthrum at the Battle of Wedmore and forcing him to convert. Northumbria, with its capital in York, was Scandinavian and dual faith for nearly a century (865–954) under Danish and Irish-Norse kings, with the connivance of various archbishops. Sometimes the kings were Pagan, sometimes Christian, but no religious persecutions took place. Eventually, King Canute (1016–1035), the Danish conqueror of Wessex and its English dependencies, adopted Christianity and brought England, Denmark, Norway and the Hebrides together in one empire.

Following Charlemagne's death in 814 Danish and then Norse Vikings sacked vast areas of France, including Bordeaux, Paris, Nantes, Toulouse and Orléans, and occupied Chartres (the old Druidic 'centre' of the country). They used French ports as bases for raids into the Mediterranean, including Spain, Morocco and perhaps Alexandria. Eventually, the French fought back, but in 911 King Charles the Simple bowed to necessity and invited one of the raiding parties to settle. One of the conditions was that the settlers should become Christian. The condition was accepted, the newcomers adopted Roman customs as the Franks had done before them, and in 1066 they invaded and conquered England.

Although the Normans – the 'men of the north' – were officially Christian, in the usual way dual faith practices prevailed. A resurgence of Thor worship in the tenth century turned the Christians into a minority within their own country,[45] and later the father of William the Conqueror became known as Robert the Devil because of his adherence to the old ways. Nevertheless, it was in Normandy that the future Christianiser of Norway, Olaf the Saint, was baptised in 1013, and it was with the approval of the Pope that Duke William invaded England in 1066.[46] The Normans had adopted centralised Roman-style administration from its contemporary guardian, the Church of Rome, and once more religion and politics went hand in hand.

In the homelands of the Vikings, dual faith was barely considered. Whereas in other communities, from Constantine's Rome to Alfred's Wessex, the Christian god had brought success to his followers, for the Scandinavians the opposite was the case. Their own gods had brought them success, and they were not going to turn their backs on these divine helpers to take a gamble with a new religion. Kings often tolerated Christian missionaries, but their earls tended to speak against them. In 963 King Håkon the Good attempted to Christianise Norway, but had to give up in the face of stiff opposition from his earls, who determined 'to make an end of the Christian faith in Norway . . . and compel the king to blood-offering', which they did.[47] When Håkon died, he was given a Pagan funeral in a howe at Sein, North Hordaland. His *skald*, Eyvind Scaldaspiller, composed a Pagan eulogy about how well the king, 'who had upheld the temples', was received with gladness in Valhalla by 'the high gods'.[48]

Later, the Christian sons of King Erik of Denmark came to Norway, smashed down the temples and abolished Pagan sacrifices, but they were deposed and executed by the nobles and the sacrifices restored. It was only in 998 that King Olaf Tryggvason, followed by Olaf Haraldson, canonised on his death in 1033, made Norway Christian by armed force, looting and burning Pagan temples and compelling community after community to be baptised or die, taking hostages to enforce continued Christian observance.[49] Nevertheless, many Pagans were willing to be tortured and to die a martyr's death rather than give up their beliefs. Olaf Tryggvason ordered that the Pagan seer, Thorleif the Wise, was to be blinded. He was captured by Olaf's agent, and bore his torture with such heroic composure that his attackers fled after tearing out one eye. Eyvind Kelde (drowned along with his comrades), Iron Skegge (killed defending the temple at Mæri), Eyvind Kinnrifi (tortured to death with hot coals), and Raud the Strong (tortured with a poisonous snake and red-hot iron), among others, died for the old faith. Also the Viking leader Ragnar Lodbrok, killed by Christians in Northumbria, was seen as a martyr, and is celebrated as such by contemporary followers of Ásatrú.

Norwegians had settled Iceland in the ninth century, escaping political unrest at home. Although some of the early settlers were Christian, the organisation of the island was basically Pagan, with the ritual hallowing of land, setting up of temples and regular attendance at the legal assembly held at the offering-tides. When Iceland adopted Christianity as the state religion in the year 1,000, it was not through persuasion or conversion but a substantial bribe that made the law-speaker Thorgeirr come down on the side of the Church against the faith of his forebears.[50] Surviving documents show that in the north, as elsewhere, Christian evangelists used every method available: trickery, bribery and armed force.

Following Biblical Jewish precedent, Christian writings report magic contests between Christian and Pagan priests, which the Christians win (e.g. the sanctified fires in *Njál's Saga*). But sometimes this ploy backfired. Writing about the twelfth-century Swedes, a contemporary English cleric stated:

> Swedes and Goths seem certainly, as long as everything goes well for them, to hold in name the Christian faith in honour. But when the storms of misfortune come over them, if the earth denies them her crops or heaven her rain, storms rage, or fire destroys, then they condemn (Christianity) . . . this happens not only in words but in actions, through pursuit of believing Christians whom they seek to drive from the country.[51]

Denmark likewise resisted Christianisation. In the early ninth century there were battles for and against Christianity, under Frankish pressure from the south. In Church architecture the northerly orientation, home of the deities in Scandinavian religion, clashed with the easterly orientation, which Christianity had adopted since the time of Constantine, the one-time sun-worshipper. 'In the east–west churches of the Frisians, who had recently been Christianized by Charlemagne, the Danish King Gotrik (c.800) had northern doors cut out and forced people to crawl through them.'[52] By the middle of the ninth century, Denmark collapsed into anarchy and Viking expansion began in earnest, leading to the creation of the English Danelaw and the Duchy of Normandy in what is now France. The Danish communities were united into one kingdom in about 950 under the formidable Harald Gormsson, who instituted the famous Jómsvíking community at the mouth of the Oder, brought Norway under his rule, and ruthlessly imposed Christianity on Denmark. This was enormously resented by the inhabitants, and in 988 Harald's son Swein drove his father from Denmark and reinstated the old religion. However, the pressures of international alliances proved too strong, and Swein ended as a reluctant patron of Christianity. His younger son Canute, who conquered England and established the Danish Empire, was, as we have seen, a keen Christian, but even so, in Denmark Pagan worship was carried out openly.

Sweden took little part in the Viking raids. Its ambitions lay eastwards. Swedish raiders and merchants travelled east to the Volga. They established trading posts at Riga, Novgorod and Kiev, and there, known as the Rus or Red Ones, gave their name to the country which they founded, Russia. They maintained their ancestral faith, and the report of an Arab traveller in 921 has left us an invaluable account of a northern ship-burial, providing details about which we could otherwise only conjecture (see below pp. 138–9). The Swedes of Kiev looked southwards to Constantinople, and in 860, 880, 907 and 914 they attacked the city. Eventually the authorities, in the time-honoured manner, employed their attackers as bodyguards and so a rich flow of commerce and diplomacy was set up between Russia and Byzantium. On the steppes, the Swedes also seem to have come into contact with the remnants of the Alans, who had arrived around 100 BCE and controlled the steppe from the Don to the Volga and southwards over the valley of the Kuban. The Greeks called the Alans As or Asii, from whom come both the name of Asia and the ruling dynasty of Norse gods, the Æsir. The area ruled by the Alans was a hub of trade and business, a centre of prosperity. This flourishing area seems to have been the Ásaheim of the later Norse writer Snorri Sturluson (1179–1241). It lay east of the Tanakvisl (River Don). Its capital city was Ásagarth (Asgard). It appears that certain elements of northern mythology, which we will describe in the next chapter, originate in the history of the Alan people in this period.

Sweden itself resisted Christianity, despite forced conversion. As a trading nation it was prosperous and comparatively settled, and the temple at Uppsala was famous throughout the northern world. Between 1000 and 1024, Olave Scotkonung imposed official Christianity on part of the country,

*Plate 7.10* The temple at Uppsala, Sweden, sixteenth-century engraving by Olaus Magnus. Nideck Picture Collection.

but there was a mass reversion to Paganism around 1060, when the bishops of Sigtuna and Skara were expelled. In 1080, King Inge the Elder was exiled from Uppsala for refusing to sacrifice at the temple there. Even after the destruction of the Uppsala temple in around 1100, Paganism continued openly until the 1120s, when the Christian Norwegian King Sigurd the Jerusalem-Traveller declared a crusade against the Pagans in Småland, south Sweden, and laid the country waste. The Swedes were the last Germanic people to adopt official Christianity.

# 8

# LATE GERMANIC RELIGION

Since the Scandinavian and Baltic countries remained for so long independent of the Roman organisation and Christian beliefs of the rest of Europe, their ancient religious practices contained many features from an earlier age. In the year 921 an Arab traveller, Ibn Fadlan, reported a full-scale ship-burial among the Rus of the Volga. His account gives the most remarkable insight into what might lie behind the great howe and barrow burials which litter the European landscape. First, the chieftain's body was buried for ten days in the semi-frozen ground while the preparations were made. Then the body was exhumed, blackened with the cold but otherwise not decayed, and dressed in the sumptuous clothes which had been made for it. It was laid on Byzantine silken cushions on a bench in the ship, and surrounded with food, drink and herbs before animals, including horses, cows, a dog, a cock and a hen, were cut to pieces and thrown onto the ship. One of the dead man's retainers, a slave girl, had volunteered to die with him. She had been treated like royalty meanwhile, as well as becoming thoroughly intoxicated through drinking, singing and having sex with as many men as she liked, 'for love of her master'. Before she went onto the ship she was lifted up three times to look over a structure that resembled a doorframe. She was looking into the Otherworld, where she said she saw first her parents, then her dead relatives, and finally her master, whom she wanted to join there. She then went onto the ship, singing two ceremonial farewell songs, and was led into the tent where the chieftain's body lay. A group of men banged their shields with sticks, to drown any screams, as she underwent a double death by simultaneous strangling and stabbing. Her executioner was the old woman in charge of the whole proceedings, a Hun known as the Angel of Death. Afterwards the chieftain's nearest kinsman approached the ship on its pyre of brush-wood. He was naked, and walked backwards with one hand on his anus. He picked up a brand, set fire to it and set the pyre alight. Other people added sticks and timber, and the whole structure went up in flames. In the opinion of the Rus, the Arabs and other inhumers were mad to bury their dead. 'We burn them up in an instant, so that they go to Paradise in that very hour.'[1]

It is impossible to imagine that this ceremony was exactly the same as those of the Bronze Age, or, indeed, that such ceremonies were ever identical throughout all of Europe. But it does show how at least one community interpreted barrow burials. It tells us that among them death was seen as the doorway into another world which could be seen from the present one by a person in a trance. It tells us that the funeral sacrifice was entered into willingly and was the occasion of a certain grim rejoicing. The double death of the chieftain's retainer recalls the double or triple deaths of the prehistoric bog-burials (stunning, strangling and stabbing or drowning) and the ceremonial triple deaths described in the Irish tales. Unfortunately, Ibn Fadlan had to speak to the Rus through an interpreter, so he did not pick up the meaning of other details such as the nature of the deities invoked, the reason for the carcasses of animals being thrown on the ship, the ritual sex of the followers and the slave girl, the reason for her manner of death, and the reason why the lighter of the pyre should be naked, walk backwards and have his hand on his anus.

The two horses that were sacrificed are part of a tradition which is one of the many that continued into modern times. Ceremonial horse slaughter for a sacral meal of horseflesh was part of northern European Paganism. The horse was the totemic beast of Woden/Odin, and part of the ceremonies used

*Plate 8.1* Reconstruction of a seventh-century horse sacrifice at Lejre, Denmark.
Nigel Pennick.

139

the stallion's penis (Volsi). Because of its sacral connotations, Pope Gregory III (731–741) forbade eating horseflesh as an 'unclean and execrable act'.[2] The Council of Celchyth (787) condemned the consumption of horseflesh as a stain on the character of British people.[3] This appears to be the origin of the continuing taboo on eating horseflesh in Britain. But the tradition did not die immediately. The monks of the Abbey of St Gall ate horse, and they gave thanks for it in a metrical grace written by the monk Ekkehard III (d. 1036).[4] Eating horseflesh was also banned at Paris in 1739.[5]

Pagan horse sacrifice continued in Denmark until the early eleventh century,[6] and it continued as a funeral rite of kings and knights. Horses were slaughtered at the funerals of King John of England,[7] the Emperor Karl IV in 1378 and Bertrand Duguesclin in 1389.[8] In 1499, the *Landsknechte* sacrificed a horse to celebrate the end of the Swabian Wars (*Schwabenkrieg*).[9] During the funeral of Cavalry General Friedrich Kasimir at Trier in the Rhineland in 1781, his horse was killed and thrown into his grave.[10] The archaic practice of divination by unbroken horses was used to honour the burial of an early saint. At the death of St Gall in Switzerland (seventh century), unbroken horses carried the coffin, and decided his burial place.[11]

Foundation-sacrifices continued to use horses. Just as burning a body allowed its spirit to escape quickly, so burying it may have imprisoned the spirit on the site. The *Saga of Olaf Tryggvason* (I, ch. 322) tells that the death of Frey, mythical ancestor of the Swedish kings, was kept secret for a while. When people found out that he was dead and buried in his howe, but that his kingly luck still protected the kingdom, 'they believed that it would be so as long as [he] remained in Sweden, and they would not burn him'. The animals sacrificed at the funeral of the chieftain of the Rus are therefore likely to have been seen as guardians of his grave. The practice continued into Christian times. When the monastery at Königsfelden in Germany was founded in 1318, a horse was sacrificed.[12] There are numerous examples of horse-skull burials in churches and special buildings. The church of St Botolph at Boston, Lincolnshire, had horse bones in the floor,[13] and that at Elsdon, Northumberland, in the belfry.[14] Eight horse skulls were found embedded in the pulpit at the Bristol Street Meeting House, Edinburgh, demolished in 1883,[15] and others at Llandaff Cathedral, Wales, where they were inside the choir stalls.[16] As late as 1897, a horse's head was buried in the foundations of a new Primitive Methodist chapel at Black Horse Drove, near Littleport in the Cambridgeshire Fens. A libation of beer was poured over it before bricks and mortar were shovelled on top. A workman described it as 'an old heathen custom to drive evil and witchcraft away'.[17] At Hahnenkan near Eichstadt, a horse was offered to St Willibald in the nineteenth century.[18] A minimal horse sacrifice is recorded from Holland in the eighteenth century, when Henrik Cannegeiter of Arnhem stated that the Dutch peasants drove away the Moirae (fates = bad luck) by throwing a horse skull upon the roof.[19]

The barrows of the dead were a link with the past and the ghosts of the ancestors in the same way that we have seen in all Pagan societies so far. They were seen as houses of the dead, and their inhabitants are often described as looking out of their houses or welcoming new inhabitants or even feasting within the mounds. In both Viking and Saxon barrows there are later interments of bodies and of ashes, and secondary interments of this sort also appear in Bronze-age barrows. In Iceland, the hill Helgafell (Holy Mountain), which looks like an enormous howe, was adopted as a symbolic burial place by the family of Thórólf Mosturbeard. These men were said to go 'into the mountains' when they died. In the Viking Age, we hear mostly of male burials, but barrows in Scandinavia include burials of women with rich grave-goods. In England one of the Sutton Hoo burials is of a middle-aged woman who has, among other ornaments, a small crystal ball suspended from her belt and what seems to be a libation spoon, with five holes pierced in it. We can guess that these implements were needed for priestly duties. When the Vikings captured Dublin in the 930s, Ota, the wife of the leader Turgeis, is said to have taken the Christian altar at Clonmacnoise as the altar of her own prophecies. In Germanic Europe as in Greece and Rome, it seems there was no full-time professional priesthood, and the political leaders also had religious duties to perform.

Continuity of site was practised. The moot hill, the meeting place of the tribal assembly, was sometimes a barrow, either that of a known ancestor or a prehistoric construction. Tynwald Hill on the Isle of Man is an artificial hill built specifically as a meeting place on the site of a Bronze-age barrow. The action of Ota in Dublin is usually presented as a desecration of a Christian holy place, but it might equally have been part of the reverent tradition of continuity. In Denmark the reverse happened. The Pagan burial site at Jellinge was taken over by the Christian religion at the time of Harald Gormsson (who was later expelled from Denmark by his Pagan subjects in 988). The stone of King Gorm, Harald's father and an assiduous worshipper of the old gods, was replaced by that of King Harald, and the Pagan *Hörgr* by a Christian stave church. Nevertheless, the layout of the site was kept intact and even added to by Harald, rather as Constantine used the old Etruscan discipline in laying out his Christian city of Constantinople. Similarly, the seventh-century Saxon palace of Yeavering in Northumberland was built on the site of a Bronze-age barrow, which was retained intact at the eastern end of the new enclosure. On top of it was put a tall post – a procedure identical with that carried out at the ship-burial on the Volga – and there were other ancient cremations and inhumations.[20] The Anglo-Saxon temple was built at the western end of the enclosure, beside a Bronze-age knoll which had been used for cremations. All the Anglo-Saxon buildings were aligned with the post on the barrow. Later, the barrow was to be enclosed in a Christian churchyard.

Part of the reason for using barrows as moot hills may have been that the

141

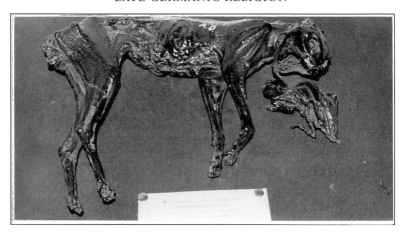

*Plate 8.2* Foundation-offering of a cat and rat, found in 1811 and preserved in W. Eaden Lilley's department store, Cambridge. The practice of making ceremonial offerings, usually of coins, papers and 'time capsules' under buildings continues all over Europe. © 1985 Nigel Pennick.

dead were supposed to be able to inspire the living at these sites, thus giving them wise counsel. The *Flateyjarbók* tells of a man who was inspired with the gift of poetry by a dead *skald* on whose howe he slept. The tradition of inspiration has persisted into modern times. The nineteenth-century mystic Richard Jeffries experienced a series of remarkable visions and transcendental states while lying on a tumulus on the Wiltshire Downs, which he recorded in his autobiography, *The Story of My Heart*. Barrows, then, were consecrated places, like the *loca sacra* and *loca religiosa* of the Romans, seen as gateways to the Otherworld under the guardianship of those who were buried there. This is the same situation as in Celtic myth, where, however, the deities and ancestors are disguised for a later age as the Little Folk.

## THE LATE GERMANIC DEITIES

Fortunately, we have a record of the Vikings' deities and their manner of worship. In the thirteenth century, the Icelandic diplomat and landowner Snorri Sturluson recorded many of the old sagas and poems and composed some of his own, including a thinly disguised introduction to Norse Pagan mythology, *The Deluding of Gylfi*. These stories, recorded after at least two centuries of official Christianity, were influenced by Classical as well as by Biblical models and so cannot be taken entirely at face value. But even allowing for the distortion of time and outlook, modern scholars generally agree that they offer us an invaluable record of a vanished world. The characters of Snorri's chief gods and goddesses are well known nowadays: Odin, the

*Plate 8.3* The Norse Pagan trinity of Frigg, Thor and Odin, sixteenth-century engraving by Olaus Magnus. Nideck Picture Collection.

leader of the gods and the god of battle; Thor, the thunder-god with his hammer; Freya, the radiant goddess and first chooser of the noble dead; her brother, Frey, the fertility god; Loki, the trickster; Odin's wife, Frigga; these and many others are familiar to today's schoolchildren. We tend to see them as a well-knit group defined by myth, like Homer's Olympians, but investigation of the deities' origins yields a more complex story, some outlines of which can be sketched here.

Snorri's introduction to the *Gylfaginning*, his account of the Norse-Icelandic pantheon of ancient times, gives these divinities a justified place within the world-view of his times. He traces the development of human-kind from Noah, in accordance with Christian teaching; he attributes different cosmologies to human beings' natural 'wisdom', exercised, however, 'without spiritual understanding'; and then he elaborates the Classical origin myth of Troy as the centre of the tripartite world, with its geomantic twelve-fold division, its chieftains and its population of monsters, dragons and a prophetess, the Sibyl of Europe. One of the twelve chieftains of Troy was, according to Snorri, the father of Thor, and Thor became duke of Thrace and married the Sibyl, one of their descendants being 'Vóden whom we call Odin', who, having the gift of prophecy, travelled north through Germany, Denmark, Sweden and Norway, where in accordance with the prophecy he founded the various Germanic races with their quasi-divine ancestors. Because of their origin Odin and his sons were called the Æsir, or 'race of Asia'.

The cult of Woden (in Norse: Odin) appears to have supplanted those of Tîwaz, the god of the sword and of justice described above (pp. 116–7, 119), and of Thunor, the god of thunder and of the protection of property. In the main part of the *Edda* the god Tyr (Tîwaz) loses his hand through a necessary bargain, and the god Thor is described as Odin's son, although in the introduction he was described as the latter's ancestor. These occurrences could be seen as disempowerment and takeover myths. As the god of battle, Odin is a fickle master, and he was known as a deceitful god. He was the ruler of the invisible world, of poetic inspiration, of battle-madness and of the written script – the runes – which we know were derived from North Italic script and which had reached Denmark by the third century CE. Odin is the god of trade, of living by one's wits, commemorated in the *interpretatio Romana* by inscriptions to Mercury. He is a suitable god for migrants, and by taking up residence (according to Snorri's introduction) in Sigtuna, Sweden, he may have supplanted the cult of Freya and Frey.

The kings of Sweden (Pliny's Ingaevones) derived their ancestry, according to Snorri in his introduction to the *Heimskringla*, from Yngvi, sometimes known as Yngvi-Frey. Yngvi shares his name with the rune Ing, signifying ancestry, but the name 'Frey' means simply 'lord'. Nobility based on aristocratic stock and 'good breeding' is here directly linked with the Germanic cult of the divine ancestor. Frey was a god of breeding. He was portrayed as ithyphallic, or if clothed, with some other token of his virility. He was invoked at weddings, and was thought to bring prosperity as well as many children. He had several descriptive bynames, one of which was *enn fróði*, the luxuriant. His sacred animals were the horse and the pig, itself a fertile creature, and he was said to travel around the Swedish countryside in a wagon, bringing prosperity to his worshippers.

Frey's sister Freya and Woden were the Pagan divinities most frequently alluded to in medieval German references to Paganism, and in the *Gylfaginning* Snorri tells us that Freya was the most renowned of the goddesses and that her worship survived to his own day. Indeed, during the twelfth century there had been a resurgence of Freya worship, and Schleswig cathedral has on its wall a mural from that time depicting Freya riding naked on a giant cat (in the sagas we are told that she rode in a chariot pulled by cats), alongside Frigga (Odin's wife), similarly unclad, riding on a distaff. It was an insult to Freya at the Althing (Parliament) which opened the final round in the battle over the Christianisation of Iceland. A Christian partisan called Freya a 'bitch goddess',[21] and the contest began. Freya seems once to have been an extremely important figure. The *Gylfaginning* tells us that each day after battle she chose half the slain, while Odin had the remainder. The story of how her golden necklace was stolen by Loki for Odin, like the story of Tyr's maiming by the wolf, also bears the classic hallmarks of a takeover myth. The golden necklace itself, like the tears of gold which Freya is said to weep, may link her with the sun-goddesses of the Baltic. Her brother Frey was connected with another solar figure, perhaps the spirit of the midnight Sun, the giantess Gerd. The *Gylfaginning* tells us that when Gerd went into her house on the northern horizon, she raised her arms to open the door, and 'they illumined the sky and sea, and the whole world grew bright from her'.

*Plate 8.4* Twelfth-century mural of the goddess Frigga riding a distaff, in the cathedral at Schleswig, Schleswig-Holstein, Germany. Nigel Pennick.

Freya and Frey were said to be the children of Njörd, a god of the sea whose home is known as the 'Boatyard', and his unnamed sister. Frey was said in the sagas to have a magic ship, *Skiðblaðnir* (Skate-blade), which could be folded up and kept in a pouch when not needed. Freya was not connected with a ship in the literature of the Viking Age, although from Roman times we know of the ship as an attribute of Sequana, goddess of the Seine, and of the unnamed goddess of the Suebi reported by Tacitus. Modern commentators have been quick to see Njörd as a later form, perhaps the brother, of Nerthus, the goddess of Tacitus' Danish tribes. Nerthus, like Frey, travelled in a wagon, bringing happiness and prosperity to her worshippers. Prosperity, good harvests and peace are what are said in the prologue to the *Gylfaginning* to have been brought by Odin and the Æsir when they reached Sweden: another indication of their taking over an earlier cult of the Vanir there. Nerthus was connected with water: her home was on an island and her slave attendants were drowned after seeing her. We do not know of ritual drowning associated with Frey, but *Víga-Glúm's Saga* tells us that Frey's sanctuary was defiled by having blood shed in it. Weapons were not allowed in Frey's temple, which recalls the cult of Nerthus, when all weapons had to be put away. Freya and Frey, Njörd and the other deities called by Snorri the Vanir seem originally to have been bringers of peace, prosperity and

145

continuity, and their worship seems to have included a ban on weapons. The association of Freya with battle is said in the fourteenth-century *Flateyjarbók* to have been the price she paid for the return of her necklace from Odin. A complex set of origins is indicated here.

Deities in wagons seem to have been an ancient part of north European religion, perhaps to do with the migratory habits of the Celts and, especially, the Germans. Pliny (IV.80) includes among his Sarmatians the Aorsi, or Wagon-Dwellers. The various *Lives* of St Martin of Tours indicate that in fourth-century CE Gaul, images said to be of Kybele, shielded by white curtains, were carried around the fields. Gregory of Tours records that at Autun the image of the goddess Berencyntia was carried on a wagon for the protection of the vines and other crops.[22] When the Gothic King Athaneric decided to reimpose Paganism on his subjects he sent the image of a god around in a covered wagon and demanded that the inhabitants of each village sacrifice to it. Much later, the *Flateyjarbók* (I.467) tells of the Swedish King Erik consulting the god Lytir, whose presence came into a wagon. The presence was felt by the additional weight of the wagon, which was drawn then into the king's hall. In the same way, Tacitus tells us, the priest of Nerthus 'felt' when the goddess was present and led her wagon forth amid great rejoicing.

Archaeological finds of sacred wagons include small models and full-size vehicles, covering a 2,000-year period. These include several small wagons which may be models of full-size vehicles that were drawn along sacred road-ways. Many of them include representations of horses. The best known is the vehicle found in a peat bog at Trundholm, Denmark, deposited around 1200 BCE, which carries a bronze horse and what is thought to be a solar disc. (Much later *The Deluding of Gylfi* tells us that the Sun and Moon are drawn across the sky on chariots.) A 12-cm-high late Bronze-age (c.1000 BCE) vehicle from a burial at Alcolshausen, Landkreis Würzburg, Germany, now in the Mainfränkisches Museum at Würzburg, carries a cauldron-like vessel. A seventh-century BCE Celtic bronze sacred wagon from Strettweg, near Graz, Austria, depicts a goddess surrounded by male and female attendants holding stags.[23] She holds a vessel above her head. A similar cauldron-holding female figure on a wheeled vehicle surrounded by animal and human attendants was among the Etruscan exhibits at the Franco-German exhibition held in Paris and Berlin in 1992. A boar-hunting horse-man is depicted on a small Celtic wagon from Merida in Spain (second–first century BCE). Full-sized wagons include that from the Celtic tumulus-burial at Hochdorf, Baden-Württemberg, Germany (sixth century BCE); two found at Dejbjerg Mose, Ringkøbing, West Jutland, Denmark; and the ninth-century CE wagon buried with a ship at Oseberg, Norway, which accompanied the body of a noblewoman. We can only assume that the cult of the Vanir had some connection with this ancient symbolism, whatever it meant.

Another important god in the sagas was Thor. He is thought to be a later form of the god known to Tacitus and equated with Hercules, who was said to have appeared to some of the Rhineland tribes.[24] Hercules with his club was also a common equivalent of Taranis the Gaulish thunder-god. Later, the Saxon thunder-god Thunor was equated with Jupiter and gave his name to Jupiter's day: Thursday. Many settlements throughout Scandinavia, Germany and Britain are named after Thor, but we do not know of any royal houses who traced their lineage from him. According to the *Edda* he was not a god of the nobility. The Norse Vikings who settled Ireland were his worshippers, and their temple of the Black Thor in Dublin was renowned throughout the Viking world. When in 994 the Irish King Mæl Seachlainn conquered Dublin and took the Sword of Charles (said to have been owned by Charlemagne) and the holy ring of Thor from the great temple, it must have seemed that the end had come for the Norsemen. Thor was a god of great vitality and zest for life: strong, greedy, bombastic and lacking in subtlety, he was no mysterious god of the shadow realm. The thunder was said to be Thor's hammer striking in heaven, and lightning the sparks as the hammer hit the ground. His sacred tree was the oak, his animal was the goat – greedy, determined and unsubtle – and two goats pulled his chariot across the sky. In Snorri's *Edda* he is a figure of some ridicule, but in everyday worship two hundred years before he was clearly seen as honourable and highly venerated.

Thor seems to have had a connection with the land, because his worshippers in Iceland would often take the soil from beneath their temple pillars with them when they settled. They also took the high-seat pillars themselves, which were sometimes carved with an image of the god and with the 'god's nail'. Thor was connected with the oaks of the forest, which the pillars may have represented,[25] as well as with the axis of the heavens, the source of thunderstorms, which was also represented by a tree.[26] In this the cult of his predecessor in the Rhineland may have been signalled by the Jupiter columns described in the previous chapter. A newcomer to Iceland would cast his high-seat pillars overboard within sight of land and would then settle wherever the pillars were washed up. Helgi the Lean, a descendant of Froði (Frey), by contrast, cast a boar and a sow overboard to determine where he should settle. Thor, like Jupiter, also held the guardianship of oaths, which were sworn on his temple-ring, usually an arm-ring. The priest of Thor wore this ring only and always during temple ceremonies. The three Danish kings of East Anglia whom King Alfred forced to terms in 876 likewise took their oath on 'the holy armlet of Thor'. Thursday – Thor's Day in the seven-day week as used by the Scandinavians – was the first day of the week and a holy day. The Althing of Iceland always began on a Thursday, and both Summer's Day and Winter's Day were Thursdays, of variable date. By contrast with the *Edda*, the historical records show Thor as an honourable figure, an enforcer of law and of oaths. He not only protected the community, but in a sense he held it together, a paradoxical achievement for such a violent, irascible figure.

## RELIGIOUS ORGANISATION

History, by contrast with Snorri's *Edda*, indicates that the polytheistic pantheon was held together not so much by a chief deity, as in official Graeco-Roman religion, nor even by a deity of place, as in archaic Graeco-Roman religion, but by the cult of the divine ancestor. In the early tribal days the divine ancestor of the king was the deity of the tribe, and we see the last appearance of this among the Anglo-Saxons. (It is not clear whether the mainland Saxons, Pliny's Herminones, defeated by Charlemagne in 772, worshipped a divine ancestor or a more abstract sky-god.) The temples had many altars, however, from that of King Rædwald of East Anglia with his altar for Christ and his altar for 'demons', to that of the great temple at Uppsala with its images of Thor, Odin and Frey, and individuals were free, as in all Pagan societies, to offer their special allegiance to whichever deity suited them best. If one deity seriously failed them, they would transfer their allegiance to another, as, for example, the Icelander Víga-Glúm, who transferred from Frey to Odin.

Iceland, colonised from Scandinavia in the ninth century, showed Pagan democratic principles in action. Uniquely among the Scandinavian lands, it was governed by a kind of theocratic oligarchy, ruled by hereditary Goðar. Originally, the Goði was a priest of a tribe or clan which had the same temple in common. In the settlement times, there was no full-time priesthood (if there ever had been), and the chieftain or landowner had the duty of upkeep of his temple. Temples could be private or public. *Vápnfirðinga Saga* records that a public temple (*Höfuð-hof*) was owned by a woman named Steinvör.[27] The Icelandic Law Book states that a woman who inherited a chieftaincy had to delegate her authority to a man in the district. The testimony of *Vápnfirðinga Saga* indicates that she may have been able to retain its priestly duties for herself.[28] Sometimes, whole wooden temples were transported from Norway. *Erbyggja Saga* tells how Thórólf Mostrarskegg dismantled his temple of Thor in Norway and transported it, including the sacred soil beneath the god's image, to Iceland. Other temples were built new in Iceland. As tribalism declined, the office of Goði became progressively more secularised. In Iceland, the Goði became an official of the commonwealth, with sovereign power over his liegemen, hallowing and presiding over courts. The Goði of the temple at Kialarnes, descendant of the first settler of Iceland, Ingulf Arnarson, bore the title *alsherjargoði*. His temple was the oldest in the land, and its priest had precedence over the others. Hence he would hallow the Althing each year.

The Goðar were the nucleus of the law-making assembly (*lögrétta*). The Goðar also settled prices of goods. Iceland was divided geomantically into four quarters, which contained three jurisdictions (Things). Each Thing was divided into three Goðorð, each presided over by a Goði. There were thus thirty-six Goðar in all. Later, another jurisdiction was added to the northern quarter, bringing the total to thirty-nine. The original thirty-six Goðorð were called *full oc forn*, 'full and ancient'. The Althing contained other men: nine elected Lögrettamaðr, making forty-eight. Each member was accompanied by two assessors or counsellors, making the whole body number 144. In 1056 and 1106 respectively, the bishops of Skalholt and Holar were added to the *ex officio* members of the Althing.[29]

Northern Paganism included the regular use of seership, both to discover the present or future state of things and the will of the spiritual beings, the goddesses and gods. Runic techniques are well attested, and in the tenth chapter of Tacitus' *Germania*, as we have already seen, he describes the German diviners making lots using twigs marked with sigils: proto-runes. According to legend, the runes had been given to humankind by Odin, and they were empowered with sacred magic, enabling the user to gain access to other levels of consciousness. It is clear from the sagas and the Icelandic Settlement Book that it was common for people to have second sight or to work magic to see into the future. Even the Christian Queen Dowager Aud of Dublin, a late settler in Iceland, knew when she was going to die. She held a feast, which she declared would be her funeral feast, correctly predicting

*Plate 8.5* Shepherd saluting the setting moon, from a German shepherds' calendar of 1560. Nigel Pennick.

her death three days later.[30] Seership seems to have become desacralised with the growth of Christianity. Originally, the Pagan offering-tides were also occasions of foretelling the future, as is made clear in the sagas. The *Orkneyinga Saga* shows this progression clearly.[31] The mythical ancestor of the Norwegians, Thorri, is described in chapter 1 as holding a feast after the main midwinter sacrifice 'with the aim of finding out what had happened to' his missing daughter Goa. By Christian times, in the late eleventh century (ch. 36), the earl's heir Håkon was in Sweden when he 'got to hear of a certain wise man who could see into the future, though it is not known whether he used sorcery or other means'. Håkon consults the seer, who places himself ironically outside Christianity by saying: 'I'm glad you feel you can place so much trust in me, more than you and your kin give to your professed faith.' By the mid-twelfth century (ch. 77), we have the merely laconic description of one of the earl's followers as 'a shrewd man [with] a talent for seeing into the future, but . . . ruthless and violent'.

Norse mythology, as recorded by Snorri, has its three spirits of Fate, the Norns. It is quite likely that these figures were influenced by the literary tradition of the three Fates from Classical sources, but we must also remember the native tradition of the three goddesses, the Matres, from the Rhineland. In Snorri's account the first Norn is Urd, 'that which was', who parallels Clotho from Greek tradition. Verdandi, 'that which is becoming', is the equivalent of Lachesis; and Skuld, 'that which is to come', is identified with Atropos. Like the three Greek Fates, the first Norn spins the thread of existence. She passes the spun thread on to Verdandi, who weaves it into the present pattern of existence. In Anglo-Saxon this fabric was known as the Web of Wyrd. The woven web then passes to Skuld, who tears it apart and disperses it. The Norns' Web of Wyrd was envisaged as a woven fabric composed of myriad strands or threads. This concept occurs in an Old English expression, 'woven by the decrees of fate'. Saxo Grammaticus, describing Denmark around the year 1200, stated that in his time, it was customary for the Pagans, wishing to know their children's future, to consult the threefold goddess. 'Three maidens sitting on three seats', three priestesses (their setting reminiscent of that of the three Matres), served as oracles for the three Fates. In medieval England, they were called The Weird Sisters. Writing around 1385, in *The Legend of Good Women*, Geoffrey Chaucer spoke of 'the Werdys that we clepen Destiné' (the Wyrds that we call destiny). Later, the three Fates reappear as the three witches in William Shakespeare's *Macbeth*. The story of Macbeth came from Holinshed's *Chronicles* of 1577, which tells of 'three women in wild apparel resembling creatures from an elder world'. Further on in the work, Holinshed states that these were none other than the 'Weird Sisters, that is . . . the goddesses of destinie'.

In Scandinavia and Iceland, women performed ceremonies of trance seership known as *seiðr*. As far as is known, this was not used for healing, as in

*Plate 8.6* The Weird Sisters, from the story of Macbeth in Holinshed's *Chronicles*, 1577. This is the sixteenth-century manifestation of the three goddesses of time that are acknowledged throughout European Paganism. Nideck Picture Collection.

Lappish shamanism, but served an oracular function. It was ruled by the goddess Freya, who is also said to have taught it to Odin, but men in general did not practise this technique as for them it was considered shameful. The Nordic sibyl was called *spákonr* or *Vǫlva*. The reverence felt for sibyls is implicit in the Icelandic text *Vǫluspá* (The Sibyl's Vision), believed to date from the tenth century. The poem describes northern cosmology and beliefs in the form of a question-and-answer session with a seeress. The characteristic practice of the sibyl was *útiseta*, 'sitting out', where she would sit on a raised seat or platform, upon which she would go into a trance. Often, she had a considerable congregation, and was accompanied by helpers. *Orvar-Odds Saga* (2), for example, records that a sibyl was accompanied by a choir of fifteen maidens and fifteen youths. The *Saga of Erik the Red* tells of *seiðr* being practised in the nominally Christianised Westviking community of Greenland. The practice of sitting out continued with the Dutch Witta Wijven of Drenthe Province until the mid-seventeenth century.[32] In earlier times, the Dutch wise women were called Hagadissae. They gave their name to the capital city of the Netherlands, Den Haag.

The practice of magic was also widespread in the Norse settlements. *Seiðr* had its magical applications, apparently including the raising of corpses and the 'hag-riding' of unfortunate living beings through the 'night-mare'. Male sorcerers, too, are included in the *Landnámabók*. One was Lodmund, who, failing to find his high-seat pillars after they had been cast overboard, settled in a place of his own choice. When the news reached him that the high-seat pillars had been discovered, Lodmund hurriedly loaded all his possessions into his ship, set sail and, instructing his crew not to speak to him or even to say his name, lay motionless, wrapped in his cloak. As the ship drew away a huge landslide engulfed the house, and Lodmund then pronounced a formal curse on all seagoing vessels which attempted to put into its harbour. Later in life, when blind in old age, Lodmund was magically attacked by a neighbour. The neighbour, also a sorcerer, diverted a stream to overrun Lodmund's property, saying it was the sea, but when his servant came to tell him, Lodmund dipped his staff in the water, pronounced it fresh, and magically diverted it back. Eventually, the two neighbours directed the stream to form a boundary between their properties.[33]

In battle, followers of Odin not only aroused themselves into battle-madness, but attempted to affect their enemies by placing the 'war-fetter' on them. This was an unaccountable paralysis which made the enemy unable to fight back. It might have been a sonic technique as practised nowadays in the Japanese martial art of kiai-jitsu, stunning the nervous system into paralysis. The Roman writers report a more psychological technique by waiting troops: for example the Germans who shouted into their shields to create an echo, and not only terrified the enemy but divined the outcome of the battle from the quality of sound produced.[34] The Celtic army opposing Suetonius Paulinus on Anglesey used similar tactics to reduce the Roman troops to shocked immobility.[35] On the other hand, the war-fetter might simply have been magic of the normal kind, affecting its victim without any identifiable cause.

The Icelandic pattern of freelance magic is probably unusual, a by-product of the individualism and self-sufficiency of the early settlers. In organised Pagan societies magic, like any other source of individual power, has always been strictly regulated. It is accepted in that its effectiveness is taken for granted, but any hint of its abuse is generally severely punished, and scapegoating with its usual misogyny is rife. The Haliarunnos, the Gothic women necromancers expelled by King Filimer in the fifth century, were blamed for the arrival of the Huns. The Goths thought that these women had mated with monsters in the desert and given birth to this terrifyingly warlike race – thereby neatly shifting the blame for King Ermenrich's inability to withstand the Hunnish invasion. The early Christian laws actually lift some of the threats against magicians, e.g. the Edict of Rothari, the Lombard king of Italy, published in 643. Chapter 376 enjoins: 'Let no man presume to kill another man's slave-woman or servant on the ground that she is a witch (or *masca* as we say); for Christian minds refuse to believe it possible that a woman could eat a living man from inside him.'[36] Organised magic, contained within the communally sanctioned limitations of the cult, was, however, normal, and this also was denied as a 'delusion' by the laws of the newly Christian Germanic kings. The Pagan view of nature as a theophany, a showing-forth of the divine essence, leads naturally to a belief in magic and foreknowledge. Interestingly, under both Pagan and Christian regimes, seers and seeresses, those with passive foreknowledge of the future, were generally respected and exempt from persecution, whereas sorcerers with their active use of the unseen powers were feared and often persecuted.

Viking society seems to have been a relatively egalitarian place for women, who could own and administer their own property and are often described in the sagas as independent agents rather than simply as junior members of someone else's household. In 845 the Arab scholar and diplomat Al-Ghazali visited the stronghold of the Vikings, who had been raiding his territory. There he met the queen, called Noud, who talked to him freely and informed him that among her people husbands were not jealous and their wives were free to change them if they wished.[37] One queen did exactly that in the late tenth century. Sigrid the Proud, the wife of King Erik of Sweden, left him and married Swein of Denmark because she did not want to die with Erik as the price of joining him in Valhalla.[38]

Women owned and commanded ships, as we know from the example of Aud. In the *Song of Atli* we read that King Hniflungr courted Gudrun because she was 'a woman of deeds', and later in the poem she tells how she, her brothers and her husband went a-viking, each commanding their own ship.[39] A documented example of a woman warrior occurs in chapter 9 of *Sögubrot*, which recounts the battle fought at Bravoll in eastern Jutland around the year 700 between the army of Harald Hilditonn (king of Denmark, Sweden and part of England) and that of the pretender, Sigurd Hring. One of Harald's champions was a woman, Vébjorg:

> The Shield-Maiden Vébjorg, made fierce attacks on the Swedes and the Goths; she attacked the champion Soknarskoti; she had trained herself so well to use the helmet, mail-shirt and sword, that she was one of the foremost in knighthood [*Riddarskap*], as Storkold the Old says: she dealt the champion heavy blows and attacked him for a long time, and with a heavy blow at his cheek cut through his jaw and chin; he put his beard into his mouth and bit it, thus holding up his chin. She performed many great feats of arms. Later, Thorkel the Stubborn, a champion of Hring, met her and they attacked each other fiercely. Finally, with great courage, she fell, covered with wounds.

The lays and sagas also describe women as using the runic script. Although brought by Odin, this was evidently not seen as a male mystery. In chapter 3 of the *Song of Atli*, Gudrun sends a runic message to Kostbera, wife of Hogni, who recognises that the message has been tampered with by the messenger. A fragment of wood, part of a loom found at Neudingen in Germany in 1979, shows unequivocally the existence of rune-mistresses in ancient times. There, incised in runes on a woman's tool, are the words 'Blithgund wrait runa' – 'Blithgund [a woman's name] wrote these runes'.

## NORTHERN MARTIAL ARTS

The northern warrior tradition appears to have originated in hunting magic.[40] In the heroic period, it had developed into a form of physical-spiritual martial arts activity comparable to the later Japanese Samurai Shinto code of *Bushido*. At all times, warriors had to exercise self-reliance and always be willing to die selflessly for family and comrades. In order to be capable of feats of arms, a strict training in self-control was necessary, and this was essentially religious. Later, the religious element seems to have been taken over by Christianity, transforming the northern martial arts into the knightly arts of chivalry, and the totemic animals into heraldic devices.

There were three main animal-cults in the northern martial arts: those of the bear, wolf and boar. The wearing of a bearskin shirt was the mark of the Berserker, a practitioner of the martial arts who went without normal chain-mail armour, yet who was so strong and ferocious that he was feared by his opponents. Bear-warriors 'went without mail byrnies, as ferocious as dogs or wolves', records the *Ynglingasaga*; 'they bit their shields and were as strong as bears or boars; they killed men, but neither fire nor iron could hurt them. This is called "running berserk"'.

The bearskin shirt was a totemic sign that, in battle, the Berserker could draw upon the strength of the bear. The Berserkers were devotees of the cult of the bear, widespread throughout the northern hemisphere.[41] The power of the bear was gained at the Berserker's initiation. *Hrolfs Saga Kraki* tells us that, among the tests, the would-be Berserker had to kill the image of a beast set up in *Hof*, then to drink its blood, when the power of the beast would be assimilated with the warrior's power. The power of the bear was also called upon in times of trouble. When he was marooned with his crew on an island in the Baltic, Orvar-Odd set up the head and skin of a bear, supported on a staff, as an offering (*Orvar-Odd's Saga* 5). In the *Færeyinga Saga*, a dead bear is propped up with a piece of wood between its jaws. The bodies of dead Berserkers were laid on a bearskin prior to the funeral rites.[42]

Because of their renowned martial prowess, tested in battle, Berserkers were valued fighting men in the armies of Pagan kings. Harald Fairhair, Norwegian king in the ninth century, had Berserkers as his personal body-guard, as did Hrolf, king of Denmark. The bear-warrior symbolism survives in the present day in the bearskin hats worn by the guards of the Danish and British monarchs. But despite their fighting prowess, their religious duties were still observed. For example, *Svarfdoela Saga* (12) records that a Berserker postponed a single combat until three days after Yule so that he would not violate the sanctity of the gods.

The Úlfheðnar wore wolf-skins instead of mail byrnies (*Vatnsdoela Saga* 9). Unlike the Berserkers, who fought in squads, the Úlfheðnar entered combat singly as guerrilla fighters. A wolf-warrior is shown on a helmet-maker's die from Torslinda on the Baltic island of Öland. In Britain, there

NP.88.

*Plate 8.7* Sixth-century helmet panels from Torslinda, Öland, Sweden, with scenes showing Berserkers, Úlfheðnar and Svínfylking warriors from the northern martial arts tradition, and the binding of the Fenris-Wolf by Tíwaz/Tyr. Nigel Pennick.

is a carving on the eleventh-century church at Kilpeck in Herefordshire showing a wolf-mask with a human head looking out from beneath it. This may be a stone copy of the usable masks hung up on Pagan temples, worn in time of ceremony or war. Similar masks, used by shamans, serve as spirit receptacles when they are not being worn. In his *Life* of Caius Marius, Plutarch describes the helmets of the Cimbri as the open jaws of terrible predatory beasts and strange animal masks.

The boar was a sacred animal in the cult of the Vanir. 'The Lady', Freya, had a wild pig called Hildisvín (battle-swine), and her brother Frey owned the golden-bristled boar Gullinbursti, which could outrun any horse. Hilda Ellis Davidson speculates that priests of the Vanir may have worn swine-masks, claiming protection from Frey and Freya.[43] In Vendel-period Sweden and early Anglo-Saxon England, the image of the boar appears on many ceremonial items, such as the Benty Grange (Derbyshire) helmet. The Swedish King Athils had a helmet named Hildigoltr (battle-pig). He captured another boar helmet, Hildisvín, from his enemy, King Ali.[44] The Boar-Warriors fought in the battle-formation known as Svínfylking, the Boar's Head. This was in the shape of a wedge, led by two champions known as the Rani (snout). Boar-Warriors were masters of disguise and escape, having an intimate knowledge of terrain. Like the Berserkers and Úlfheðnar, the Boar-Warriors used the strength of their animal the boar as the basis of their martial arts.[45]

## 'DUAL FAITH' AND VERNACULAR PAGANISM

The arrival of official Christianity was marked in Germanic communities as elsewhere by the usual prohibitions of continuing Pagan practices. These give us some idea of what everyday Pagan worship was like. For example, the *Punishments for Pagans and Others who turn from the Church of God*, ordained around the year 690, lists:

2: If anyone eats or drinks unknowingly at a heathen shrine,
5: If any keep feasts at the abominable places of the heathen,
15: If any burn grain where a man has died for the wellbeing of the living or for the house . . . [46]

It would appear that at the end of the seventh century, there were still 'heathen shrines' in England, recognised as such. Another prohibition, from half a century later, states:

Anyone who practises divination or evocation at a spring or a stone or a tree, except in the name of God . . . [47]

The prohibitions were intensified at the time of the Viking invasions. We have already seen how the Scandinavian countries adopted Christianity unwillingly, under bloodthirsty coercion. Countries such as England which had already taken Christianity as their official religion adopted a missionary zeal against the resurgence of Paganism under the influence of the invaders. The English King Edgar (959–975) explicitly forbade toleration or assimilation:

[We enjoin] that every priest zealously promote Christianity, and totally extinguish every heathendom; and forbid well worshippings and necromancies, and divinations, and enchantments, and man worshippings, and the vain practices which are carried on with various spells, and with frith-splots [sanctuaries], and with elders and with various other trees, and with stones, and with many various delusions, with which men do much of what they should not . . . And we enjoin, that on feast days there be complete abstinence from heathen songs and devil's games.[48]

Later, the newly Christian King Canute, the Danish ruler of an England which had been officially Christian for nearly four hundred years, added (1020–1023):

> Heathendom is, that men worship idols; that is, that they worship heathen gods, and the sun or moon, fire or rivers, water-wells or stones, or forest-trees of any kind; or love witch-craft, or promote morth-work [death spells] in any wise; either by sacrifice, or divining, or perform anything pertaining to such delusions.[49]

Julius Caesar had said that the Germanic tribes worshipped the Sun and Moon. Although we can assign solar and lunar attributes to various deities mentioned by later observers and practitioners, we have no evidence for the worship of those two celestial bodies as such. Canute's decrees were drawn up by Archbishop Wulfstan of York, but presumably the king, of Danish upbringing and the son of a Pagan father, would be unlikely to legislate about practices which he knew to be fictitious. His decree leaves us with a tantalising hint of unrecorded practice.

Following the official conversion of the Scandinavian lands and their raiders, within the Germanic European states many Pagan practices were assimilated into Christianity or persisted as folk-

*Plate 8.8* The Saxon lunar god, from R. Verstigan, *A Restitution of Decayed Intelligence*, Antwerp, 1605. Nideck Picture Collection. This follows the Germanic tradition of the 'Man in the Moon' and Celto-Germanic-Baltic hare totemism.

traditions alongside the new religion in the usual way. At Cologne in 1333, Petrarch saw women conjuring the Rhine as a rite of the people.[50] Cologne was the site of an important Pagan temple.[51] When 'three great fires in the air' came down to rest on the Horselberg, a holy mountain in Thuringia (better known as the Venusberg of *Tannhäuser*), in 1398, the phenomenon was interpreted as an apparition of the goddess Horsel.[52] Sometimes priests took part in adapted Pagan rituals which were part and parcel of community life. The ritual perambulation of parish boundaries ('beating the bounds'), the 'wassailing' of cider apple trees by pouring a libation over them and firing shotguns into the air, the annual blessing of a plough in the parish on a day specially named after the occasion (Plough Monday, the first Monday after Twelfth Night), are all ceremonies which persist to this day in Britain. In Germany and Scandinavia, where the urbanisation of the population at the time of the Industrial Revolution was not so drastic, even more ceremonies for honouring the land and the seasons have remained. Midsummer bonfires and sunwheels persist in Denmark and Norway, midsummer fairs throughout northern Europe. In Germany and the Netherlands, the fourth Sunday in Lent is known as 'Rejoicing Day' and attributed to the Biblical Book of Isaiah 66.10, but in fact it seems to be the old Summer's Day, when mummers and marchers celebrate the victory of summer over winter.[53] Most towns and villages still have their Maypoles or May trees, and local festivals such as the Shepherds' Race in Markgröningen, Baden-Württemberg, are well attended. What Caesar of Arles, in the sixth century, called 'devilish, erotic and wicked songs' (*cantica diabolica, amatoria et turpia*), or 'obscene and wicked songs *with choruses of women*' developed into carols as we know them: songs to celebrate midwinter and spring in their Christianised form. In his book, *The Anatomie of Abuses* (1583), the English Christian fundamentalist Stubbes recorded the Pagan ceremonies of his time:

> Then march these heathen company towards the church and church-yard, their pipers piping, their drummers thundering, their stumps

*Plate 8.9* Horn Dancers at Abbots Bromley, Staffordshire, England, 1897. The horns are said to date from Anglo-Saxon times, a direct continuity of Pagan ceremonial. From the *Strand Magazine*, 1897. Nideck Picture Collection.

dancing, their bells jingling, their handkerchiefs swinging about their heads like madmen, their hobby-horses and other monsters skirmishing amongst the throng; and in this sort they go to the church (I say) and into the church (though the minister be at prayer or preaching) dancing and swinging their handkerchiefs, over their heads in the church . . . Then, after this, about the church they go again and again, and so forth into the church-yard, where they have commonly their summer halls, their bowers, arbours, and banqueting-houses set up, wherein they feast, banquet and dance all that day and (peradventure) all the night too.

Dancing no longer takes place in the churchyard or in the choir, but at Abbots Bromley, Staffordshire, the reindeer antlers for the traditional 'Horn Dance' are ceremoniously kept in the church. The antlers have been carbondated to the eleventh century, a time when reindeer were already extinct in the British Isles, and it is thought that they were brought in by Norwegian settlers.[54]

*Plate 8.10* Serpent-labyrinth village dance at Ostmarsum, the Netherlands, 1939. Collective ceremonies assert and maintain the continuity of village life, commemorating local deities, the ancestors and the cycle of the year. Nideck Picture Collection.

Some of the deities of the old pantheon persisted under the new order. Jacob Grimm reports that in seventeenth-century Scandinavia, offerings were made to Thor against toothache.[55] Until 1814, when it was destroyed by a farmer, the Odin Stone, a holed stone at Croft Odin, Orkney, was used for oath-taking.[56] In 1791, a young man was arraigned by the Elders of Orkney for 'breaking the promise to Odin', an oath sworn on this stone.[57] When visiting the stone, it was customary to leave an offering of bread, cheese, a piece of cloth or a stone. An 1823 woodcut of standing stones in Orkney shows the Ring of Stenness, known as The Temple of the Moon, where a woman is invoking Odin to hallow her promise of betrothal.[58] Even in the twentieth century the Swiss psychiatrist C.J. Jung explained a dream of his own by reference to the still-current imagery of the Wild Hunt led by the Green-Hatted One, Wotan.[59] O.S. Reuter identified what seems to be an early reference to the Wild Hunt in a passage from the (Christian) Old Norse visionary poem *Draumakvädi*: 'The horde of demons arrives from the north with splendour and ornament, and old Greybeard [Odin] at their head.'[60] In medieval and modern folklore, the Wild Hunt was a supposed troop of spirits which rode the storm, sometimes thought, as Jung reports, to carry souls away to somewhere other than the Christian heaven. In Germanic culture, it was often thought to be led by Woden, although churchmen elsewhere seem to have envisioned it as led by a goddess, Herodias or Diana, as for example in the tenth-century *Canon Episcopi*.

Quite apart from direct survivals, over a long period Christian images were added to Pagan shrines, or Pagan images actually renamed as those of saints or prophets. Many of the Pagan deities were simply renamed by Christian priests. Beneficial deities became saints: Freya became Maria; Baldur, St Michael; Thor, St Olaf; Tónn, St Antonius, etc., whilst demons and destructive deities were identified with the Christian Devil. We have already seen the polytheistic outlook of King Rædwald of East Anglia, with his personal shrine in which he worshipped both Pagan and Christian deities. It was sacred places in the landscape, such as holy wells, hills and caves, which suffered the least alteration. Certain churches on old Pagan sites in German-speaking lands, dedicated to Verena and Walburga, were known as *Heidenkirchen* (Pagan churches).[61] A hill in Alsace bearing a church of St Maternus was known as *Heidenkanzel* (Pagan pulpit).[62] In Saarland, there was the *Heidenkirche* on the Halberg.[63] In the Tyrol there is a sacred hill called *Heidenbühel*. It was surmounted by a chapel inside a cemetery called *Heidenfriedhof* (Pagan cemetery). Elsewhere there were churches called *Heidentempel*.[64]

Sometimes the local deity was simply called a saint, e.g. Thor's holy well at Thorsås in Sweden was known as Saint Thor's Spring.[65] Other Pagan places were revered well into the medieval period: among the more notable examples are the fane of the Swabian goddess Zisa at the Zisenburg in Augsburg; the sacred places of Jutta at Heidelberg; the prophetic holy well of Mons Noricus,

*Plate 8.11* Twelfth-century carving of Woden, his ravens Hugin and Munin, and swastikas, symbol of Thunor, in the church at Great Canfield, Essex, England.
© 1992 Nigel Pennick.

Nuremberg; and the labyrinth dance-place of Libussa at Prague. The tenth-century stone cross at Gosforth, Cumbria, has images from both Norse and Christian mythology. Thirteenth-century murals in Schleswig Cathedral, Germany, depict the goddesses Frigga and Freya.[66] There is an image of Woden, complete with ravens and fylfots, in the church at Great Canfield, Essex, England. The church at Belsen, Kreis Tübingen, Baden-Württemberg, Germany, has two images of the god Béél. A fifteenth-century wall-painting of the Goddess in the Labyrinth exists in the church at Sibbo, Nyland, Finland.[67] At the time of the conversions, images could serve both Christian and Pagan worshippers. Axe-carrying statues of King Olaf the Saint, slain at the Battle of Stiklastad in 1030, were set up in Norwegian churches, where they were worshipped as images of Thor by Pagans.[68] In more recent times, an ancient Buryat sacred image in a monastery at Lake Baikal was transformed into an image of St Nicholas and worshipped with equal zeal by Pagan and Christian devotees.[69] Pagan pillars were erected in north Germany under the name *Rolandseulen*, and in the fifteenth century, there was a temple of Jupiter Christus at Istein, Germany.[70]

In the Pagan tradition, where each deity has its place, the Christian deities took their place in the Pagan pantheon. The Icelandic settler Helgi the Lean is said to have believed in Christ, calling upon Thor for seafaring and adventurous acts.[71] Pagan prayers and invocations were modified by the addition (and sometimes the substitution) of the names of Christian divinities. The second *Merseburg Charm*, dating from the tenth century, mentions Phol, Woden, Frigga and Volla. The *Canterbury Charm* against sickness (1073) contains the words 'Thor hallow you'. An Icelandic leechbook from the late thirteenth century contains the names of Odin, Fjölnir, Thor, Frigg and Freya along with Judaeo-Christian names of power.[72] The runic Healing Stick from Ribe in Denmark (*c.*1300) is a classic example of a dual faith holy object. This 30-cm-long pine stave bears a runic spell to exorcise pain in the shape of *The Trembler* (probably malaria): 'I pray, guard Earth and High Heaven; Sól and St Maria; and God the King; that he grant me healing hand, and words of remedy, for healing of pain when relief is needed'.[73]

Following the Norman conquest in 1066, official Christianity in England retained a separatist outlook. The king reserved the right to appoint bishops, and the Pope campaigned against this. The tension surfaced during the reign of the particularly separatist King Henry II (1154–1189) with the popularity of the Grail myth, which told of Joseph of Arimathea, the uncle of Jesus, setting up an independent church in England at Glastonbury. The myth of the English apostolic succession served a convenient political purpose, but the vehicle which carried it incidentally perpetuated an older Celtic Pagan tradition in the stories of the miraculous food-producing vessel, the Grail, and its female priestess or guardian. The popularity of the Grail stories, which were favoured in England, Wales, Germany and France, arose at a time when the importance of the Christian communion (a miraculous meal) was growing, as was the cult of the Virgin Mary. Pagan stories were used here to carry the symbolism of a development within Christianity.

England remained at odds with the Roman Church. In 1208, the Pope put an interdict on the country because King John refused to submit to him. All consecration was stopped: churches closed, bells were not rung, weddings celebrated without clergy, and the dead buried in ground not consecrated by the Church. In 1209, things were taken further, and England as a whole was excommunicated. King John ordered all priests to leave the country, and expropriated the property of the Church. Then came a period of remarkable prosperity and vitality. John's Yule court at Windsor was particularly sumptuous, attended by all the nobles of the realm. At this time, Richard of Devizes was amazed to visit London, where he found a vibrant pluralism of lifestyles: 'Actors, jesters, smooth-skinned youths, Moors, flatterers, pretty boys, effeminates, pederasts, singing-girls, quack doctors, belly-dancers, sorceresses, extortioners, night-wanderers, magicians, mimes, beggars, buffoons: all this tribe fill all the houses.'

Some curious relics of indigenous tradition remained or were renewed in medieval England. In her *English Society in the Middle Ages*, Lady Stenton describes how, in 1255, a company of thirteen people hunted all day illegally in Rockingham Forest. They cut off the head of a buck and put it on a stake in the middle of a certain clearing. They put a spindle in its mouth, making

*Plate 8.12* Decorated poplar tree at Aston-on-Clun, Shropshire, England, the last surviving commemorative tree in memory of King Charles II, whose 'Royal Oak' traditions continued the Pagan belief in the Lord of the Forest. © 1991 Nigel Pennick.

it gape towards the Sun, 'in great contempt of the King and his foresters'. The symbolism of this is obscure. Over one hundred years later, following the death of Queen Philippa in 1369, King Edward III's lady friend Alice Piers appears to have had great influence. She sat herself with the judges, and directed justice. In 1374, she appeared in the guise of 'The Lady of the Sun', the personification of the goddess Sól. She sat by the king's side in a chariot, attended by a train of nobles and knights, each of which was led by a richly dressed damsel. They rode from the Tower of London to Smithfield, where a week-long tournament was held in honour of the Lady of the Sun. Being very unpopular at court, she was forced to leave, but the king recalled her. Significantly, Alice attended him on his deathbed, where she refused the priests access to him. When he died, he had no last rites of the Church. She took the rings from his hands, and left.

In Germany, anti-Pagan activities were fostered. The custom of *Heidenwerfen* was encouraged by the Church. An image representing a Pagan deity was set up, stoned, smashed and burnt. *Heidenwerfen* are recorded from Hildesheim (from the thirteenth century), Halberstadt (sixteenth century) and Trier. At Hildesheim, a wooden post was set up in front of the church. A crown and mantle were put on it, and it was called Jupiter. Then it was stoned and burnt.[74] Until 1811, a torso of a Roman Venus Victrix was kept at the monastic church of St Matthias near Trier. Occasionally it was set up, and the parishioners were encouraged to stone it.[75] Here it was Roman rather than German deities which were attacked, just as the temple of Jupiter Christus at Istein honoured a Roman deity. Classical texts had been trickling into northern Europe since the reconquest of Spain which began in 1086, and monastic teaching was also full of examples couched in the language of the New Testament, with its image of embattled Christians pitted against the deities of the ancient world. Classical names and attributes were thus available to the clergy of the Middle Ages, and it would seem that these were used freely. The people, however, clung to the traditional names of their indigenous deities.

# 9

# THE BALTIC LANDS

The area between the Elbe and the Gulf of Finland emerged from prehistory and travellers' tales comparatively recently. It was never part of the ancient Roman Empire, and it joined the Holy Roman Empire only between the tenth and fourteenth centuries. Hence information from ancient chronicles and from the day-to-day observations of letter-writers, diarists and satirists is lacking until late in the history of the area. Until recently, historical accounts have tended to be biased. The imperial powers – Church, Germans, Scandinavians, Russians – who fought to control the area overlooked the independent history of its inhabitants, and later nationalistic movements among the once-colonised peoples tended to exaggerate their own achievements. With the weakening and collapse of the Soviet empire in the 1980s, independent historical investigation has once more become possible, and we write at an early stage in that process.

The ancient history of the area is sketchy but uncontroversial. In the fifth century BCE Herodotus reported the existence of 'Scythians' who lived around the rivers Dnieper and Don, nomads and hunters (IV.17ff.). He describes a tribe called the Geloni, originally Greeks, who were driven out of their cities on the Black Sea and travelled north to the Don, where they built a wooden city, supported by an agrarian economy and containing temples to the Greek divinities, and spoke a language that was half Scythian, half Greek (277). Six hundred years later, Tacitus reported the existence of the mysterious Aestii on the eastern shore of the Baltic, who spoke a language akin to British, and who gathered amber, worshipped the mother of the gods and took as her emblem the wild boar. The geographer Ptolemy, writing in the middle of the second century CE, described the Venedi (Wends), the Finni, the Ossi (Osilians) and other dwellers on the Baltic shore.[1] The Lithuanian tribes of the Galindae and Sudini lived inland, 'to the east' of the Finnic peoples on the shore. In the sixth century CE the Gothic historians Procopius and Jordanes added to the picture. When the Rus arrived from Sweden in the ninth century and settled on the Volga, dominating the Slavic tribes, they seem to have employed the Estonian Chud as mercenaries.[2]

The Rus (the Swedish Vikings described in chapter 8) carved out an empire corresponding to the modern states of Belarus and the Ukraine, dominating the Slavic-speaking inhabitants of the area, and extended their influence down the eastern boundary of Europe to the Black Sea and Constantinople. The lands around the Baltic seaboard were, however, left alone.

It seems that the Balts had been seafaring, piratical people. Johannes (1488–1544), the brother of the famous Bishop Olaus Magnus, wrote the *History of All the Kings of Gotland and Sweden*. He gives several examples of eastern Baltic naval warfare, dating from the fifth century CE. For instance, in the year 410, Tordo, the thirty-third king of Sweden, armed his country against a mighty fleet of Estonians, Curonians and Ulmigeri (Prussians), whom he forced to retreat.[3] Meanwhile, the Saxons took their turn to ravage Gotland, Holstein, Denmark, Pomerania, Curonia and Estonia.[4] The migration of the Goths from Gautland (southern Sweden) and the island of Gotland began, according to Johannes Magnus, after a series of particularly severe raids by the peoples of the eastern Baltic.[5] The future Visigoths under Götrijk landed in Rügen and Pomerania. One group of them then migrated south to the Alps. A second group set off under the leadership of their king to conquer the Prussians, Curonians, Samogytians and Estonians, after which Götrijk handed over command to his son, Filimer, and returned to Gautland where he re-established his kingdom. The third group, under Ermanerik, conquered the Vandals and then the Estonians.[6] Much later, the Swedish King Erik the Victorious (940–944) beat off an invasion of Estonians and invaded them in his turn, forcing them to become his vassals. However, the victory does not seem to have outlasted its author. Adam of Bremen[7] records the existence of pirates called the Ascomanni or Wichingi (Vikings) who ravaged the coast of Frisia in the year 994 and sailed up the Elbe. Their name suggests that they came from the Estonian province of Askala, the 'land of wizards'.[8] The famous Norwegian King Olaf Tryggvason was captured by Estonian Vikings and enslaved when he was a boy, in about 970.[9] Saxo Grammaticus, writing in the late twelfth century, and Henry of Livonia, writing in 1227, both describe Estonian pirate ships and tactics.[10]

Most of the Baltic lands in the first millennium CE seem to have been inhabited by people who were neither nomads nor settled agriculturalists, but raiders. The ethics of a raiding society are an extension of the hunter-gatherer outlook. Just as animals are there to be killed and eaten, so other human settlements are there to raid and pillage. The successful raider would bring home piles of loot and defend his settlement against other human predators. Raiding here is not an outbreak of lawlessness, but a normal and, indeed, central occupation of adult male life. This was also the outlook of the ancient Irish (sc. *The Cattle Raid of Cooley*), the Norse and Danish Vikings, and the people of the mainland of eastern Europe in early medieval times. In the Treaty of Christburg (1249) it was reported that the Prussians had a special class of priest who attended funerals, 'praising the dead for their thefts and

*Plate 9.1* Wooden images of Baltic divinities, late medieval. Nigel Pennick.

predations, the filthiness, robbery and other vices and sins they committed while alive'.[11] Anyone who reads the Viking sagas will recognise a similar glorification going on. The Viking *skaldar*, the epic poets, were never described as priests, but in Ireland the *fili* and before that the bards certainly were. In these pre-literate societies an individual's fame had to be reaffirmed and re-earned at regular intervals. Acts of what we (and the ancient civilisations) would call boastfulness and self-exhibition were normal, and a warrior's good name would simply die without the efforts of his bard.

At the end of the tenth century the Holy Roman Empire cast its crusading eyes eastwards. Following the missionary activities of Willibrord and his Northumbrian monks in Frisia in the 690s, Christian campaigners in the Frankish Empire had treated the Elbe as the eastern limit of their activity. In 831–834, however, a see was established at Hamburg by Pepin I of Aquitaine, grandson of Charlemagne, and a century later (946–949) the Holy Roman Emperor Otto I used it and other new foundations as outposts in his sustained campaign to conquer for Christendom the West Slavs, the inhabitants of the Pagan lands of the east. His only success in the north was in Poland. Poland was set up as a Catholic state between 962 and 992 by Prince Mieszco I. But between it and the Catholic rulers of Saxony lay Pagan territory, the land of the ancient Venedi or, as they were now called, the Wends. The Wends ejected the missionaries and their land-hungry followers in 1018 and 1066, and the Holy Roman Empire waited fifty years before trying again.

167

'The Slavs', so runs a proclamation [of 1108] of the leading bishops and princes of Saxony, 'are an abominable people, but their land is very rich in flesh, honey, grain, birds, and abounding in all produce of fertility of the earth when cultivated so that none can be compared with it. So say they who know. Wherefore O Saxons, Franks, Lotharingians, men of Flanders most famous, here you can both save your souls and if it please you acquire the best of land to live in.'[12]

This was an incitement to a crusade, following the spirit aroused in the western empire by the first Crusade of 1096. The peoples east of the Elbe did not submit easily, and some in the far eastern corner of Europe never did. In 983 the great Slav uprising in Brandenburg ejected the Ottonian conquerors, but in 1047 the kingdom of Wends was established by the Christian Gottschalk, stretching from the Elbe to the Oder. In 1066 both Gottschalk and the bishop of Mecklenburg were killed by the Pagan resistance.[13]

Reconquest began with the Wendish Crusade in 1147. The western part of Wendland, between the Oder and the Vistula, was known as Pomerania (the land of the 'dwellers on the shore'), and was the first target of the eastern crusade, but as late as 1153 the god Triglav was being worshipped by Slavs and Saxons at Brandenburg. One thousand years previously this area had been the centre of Germanic Paganism, where the Semnones worshipped their supreme god in their sacred grove.[14] In the High Middle Ages, Svantovit, revered by Balts and Slavs alike, still had his main cult-centre at the north of this area, on the holy island of Rügen in the Baltic. The island itself was sacred to the god Rugevit, whose sacred rowan trees grew there in abundance. At Karentia (Garz), at the southern end of the island, there was a shrine containing the multi-headed images of Porevit and Rugevit. In the temple of Svantovit, on the northernmost promontory of Rügen, there was a carved pillar depicting the four aspects of Svantovit. One aspect held a horn of precious metal which was filled with wine annually as an oracle, when the whole nation assembled at the harvest festival and the high priest decided whether the nation should go to war or not. The high priest was the only Wendish man allowed to grow his hair long. He was given his own estates and all the bullion taken in war; in addition, he had his own army of three hundred cavalry.[15] The temple itself was a square building, like many Celto-Roman temples and that at Uppsala.[16] The images of the deities were considered so sacred that only the priests were allowed to see them in the inner sanctum where they were kept. Other sacred objects were kept in the temples. At Arcona were a holy saddle and bridle of Svantovit, used on the sacred horses during ceremonies. A major cult-object was Svantovit's sword. At Wolgast, the temple held the sacred shield of Gerovit, and at Stettin were aurochs horns decorated with gold and jewels. A sacred white horse was kept in the *Temenos* at Arcona. Others were kept at the shrine of Zuarasiz (Radegost) at Rethra. Triglav's shrine at Stettin, which included an oak tree

and a holy well, had black horses. Stettin itself contained four temples as well
as halls where the nobles met for sacred feasts using gold and silver dishes.[17]

At Rethra, during a rebellion, the bishop was executed and his head offered
to Radegost. Triglav was being worshipped at Brandenburg by Slavs and
Saxons around 1153, at a time when Duke Nyklot of the Abotrites (who lived
near Mecklenburg in Pomerania) was reasserting Paganism in the wake of the
official conversion in 1128. Svantovit's temple was destroyed by Archbishop
Absolom and King Valdemar I of Denmark in 1168, and the temple
at Karentia in 1169. But a granite slab built into the wall of the church at
Altenkirchen bears a carving of a beardless man holding horns.[18] It is still
known as Svantovit.[19]

The Pomeranians converted to Christianity in 1128 under the influence
of the missionary Bishop Otto of Bamberg. Amid great debate and organised Pagan resistance, the upper classes of Pomerania were persuaded by the
advantages of a culture shared with their trading partners. An active Pagan
faction remained after the conversion, as we have seen, and the temples on

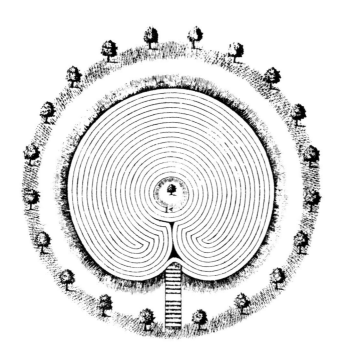

*Plate 9.2* Shoemakers' Guild labyrinth dancing-place at Stolp, Pomerania (Słupsk,
Poland), from the *Pommeranische Archive* III, 1784. Nideck Picture Collection.

Rügen remained active until 1168–1169, after the death of their defender Duke Nyklot in 1160. The peasants, as usual, remained Pagan for a great deal longer than the aristocracy, and nowhere did they accept Christianity without coercion and often armed resistance.[20] Pomerania was absorbed into Poland in 1294, and here, too, the old traditions have lingered. When the ashes of a Polish freedom fighter and his wife were reinterred in their native village in 1993, two young birch trees, sacred trees in Baltic Paganism, had been planted by the grave. An observer noted that this seemed to be a uniquely Polish mixture of 'Christian faith, militant patriotism and ancestor worship'. The remains of the general, he thought, were reinterred as if to guard the village and remind its inhabitants of their identity, as ancestral burials always do.[21]

## OLD PRUSSIA AND THE BALTIC SHORE

East of the Gulf of Gdansk was Old Prussia, and on the eastern shore of the Baltic were Lithuania, Livonia and Estonia. The languages of Old Prussia, Lithuania and the southern part of Livonia (modern Latvia) are an archaic branch of Indo-European, on a par with such old languages as Sanskrit, Ancient Greek and Gothic. Until the twentieth century the Baltic languages were seen as a branch of Slavic, but nowadays they are placed in their own category. Most scholars think that the people of this linguistic group arrived in their present home some 4,000 years ago, although it may be that the Finno-Ugric speakers who are now confined to Estonia and points north lived further south than they do now.[22] As documents from the first 1,300 years of the Common Era make quite clear, all of these Finnic peoples were known to themselves, to the ancient world and to Germanic speakers as the Aestii, to the Scandinavians as Sembi, and to the Slavs (Wends and Poles) as Pruzi (Prussians).[23] The Highland Lithuanians, who lived inland,[24] moved in, according to this view, to settle in the coastal areas between the Vistula and the Dvina after incursions of Christian crusaders had destabilised the area.[25]

The identities of the Baltic states and their boundaries, unclear from pre-history, also shifted radically following the Frankish incursions of the tenth century, but their attitude to religion did not. These countries retained official Paganism well into the medieval period. The tribes of Old Prussia were devoutly Pagan. It was only through wars of extermination at the behest of Christian prelates that official Paganism was ended. The genocide of the Old Prussians was not accomplished easily. They took part with the Wends in the Baltic rebellion of 983, considering Christianity to be the worship of the *Teutonicus deus*.[26] In 997, Adalbert, bishop of Prague, was killed in his attempt to Christianise Old Prussia. He was followed by Bruno of Magdeburg, who was killed by the Yatvegians (southern Lithuanians/East Prussians, around the river Niemen) in 1009, when Christianity was extirpated from the country.

Because of these failures, Bishop Bertold asserted that only the conquest of Old Prussia and the Baltic lands would end Paganism. He died in battle in 1198, but his call was taken up by the founding of Christian military orders. In 1200, the Livs were subdued by Bishop Albert of Bremen, which led to the foundation of Riga, and in 1202, the establishment of the Fratres Militiae Christi, the 'Order of the Sword'. These knights attempted to impose Christianity by force, but they were resisted strongly. In 1225, the Teutonic Order (The Order of St Mary's Hospital of the Germans at Jerusalem, founded at Acre in 1190) were expelled from their feudal lands in Transylvania by the Pagan Kumans, and went to Prussia to take Baltic lands for their order.[27] Then began a sixty-year war, which was by no means a one-sided affair. The Knights of the Sword were defeated in battle by a Pagan army of Lithuanians at Saule near Bauska in 1236. In 1260 the 'Great Apostasy' in Old Prussia led the Teutonic Knights to institute the same test of loyalty as the Romans had when faced with the Christian menace twelve hundred years before. All inhabitants of the country were made to swear allegiance to the national deity, in this case the Christian god. Those who did so were rewarded with civil privileges.[28] Between 1270 and 1273, an official campaign of extermination was waged by the Christian military orders – the Teutonic Knights, the Knights of the Cross and the Knights of the Sword – against the Pagan Sambian nation of Old Prussia. A few years later (1280–1283), the crusade reached Sudovia, east of Old Prussia. The country was reduced to desolation, its inhabitants massacred or expelled. Until 1525, Prussia was an *Ordenstaat*, a country owned by a Christian military order, and it gave its name and its militaristic reputation to its successor state, Brandenburg.

Lithuania, by contrast, actually came into being as a Pagan state to counteract the dual threat from the Christianising military orders to the west and the Tartar invaders from the east. By the mid-fourteenth century it had become the largest state in Europe, fully modern, fully bureaucratic and possessed of a flourishing Pagan religion which was organised with all the political advantages that the Christian religion offered its own host states.[29] The fragmentation of the old local deities and allegiances was overcome by national celebrations of victory and the state funerals of heroes, in which the deities common to all the Lithuanians were invoked. Like the Scandinavians in the Viking Age, the Lithuanians had nothing tangible to gain by adopting Christianity, but unlike them, they were able to transform local Paganism, the worship of the spirits of place, into state Paganism, the worship of the tutelary spirits of the nation, in the same way as the Romans and other Mediterranean civilisations had done. In 1251, the Lithuanian King Mindaugas, the architect of this reconstruction, actually became Christian, but this did not lead to compulsory conversion for all his subjects, and Paganism remained during his reign and afterwards. In fact, it was thought that Mindaugas' conversion was only nominal. The *Galician-Livonian Chronicle* states that:

*Plate 9.3* The Lithuanian deities Perkūnas and Perkūnatele (Zemyna), as envisioned in the sixteenth century. Nigel Pennick.

Secretly he made sacrifices to the gods – to Nenadey [god of ill fortune], Telyavel [protector of the dead], Diveriks the hare-god [sky-god], and Meidein [forest-goddess]. When Mindaugas rode out into the field, and a hare ran across his path, then he would not go into the grove, nor dared he break a twig. He made sacrifices to his god, burnt corpses and conducted pagan rites in public.[30]

The Samogytians nevertheless warned Mindaugas against the political yoke which accompanied Christianity. They resisted the new religion to the end. Attempts by the Knights of the Sword to Christianise Samogytia (Lowland Lithuania) had met with a decisive defeat in 1259, and the Samogytians continued to offer their support to the Livonian tribes fighting against the Knights of the Sword based in Riga. Meanwhile, the main government in Vilnius was following an expansionist path. In 1315, Lithuania under Gudimin formally annexed Little Russia, the original home of the Rus, into which it had been expanding since Kiev was sacked by the Tartars in 1240. This move re-Paganised Little Russia. The inhabitants soon called themselves Lithuanians, but the official language was Belorussian.[31] Pagan Lithuania displayed religious tolerance: religion was a matter of individual conscience. After 1312, when Christian priests entered Lithuania, official Pagan shrines and monasteries of the Catholic and Orthodox sects existed side by side in the capital, Vilnius, whilst Muslim scribes were employed in the Royal-Ducal Chancery.[32] Highland Lithuania was officially Christianised in 1387, in return for the crown of Poland. Samogytia, a district which had tirelessly battled against the Frankish crusaders, did not accept official

Christianity until 1414. After the union of Poland and Lithuania had been made permanent in 1569, Poland began to be seen as the dominant partner in the relationship, and the state language became Polish. The political importance of Lithuania from the thirteenth to the sixteenth centuries has thus remained one of the best-kept secrets of European history. The ruling classes of Lithuania became Polonised, but the peasants kept their language and folk-customs, even under persecution after Lithuania passed to Russia in 1795. The movement in favour of popular culture, which grew in all the Baltic countries during the late nineteenth century, encouraged the collection and reaffirmation of the old practices, and a Lithuanian Pagan movement has grown steadily throughout the twentieth century.[33]

The Lithuanian temples, like those in the other parts of Pagan Europe, were originally funded and maintained independently, not as part of a larger national or transnational religious organisation. Medieval stories of centralised Paganism, based on a central temple, Romowe (Romuva), under the jurisdiction of a High Priest, *Kriwe Kriwejto*, were considered fanciful by some researchers,[34] but more recent commentators have tended to give them credence,[35] and modern Lithuanian Paganism, formally restored in 1967, repressed by the Soviets in 1971, and tolerated since 1988, has taken the name Romuva. Since 1988, the shrine-site at Romuva, in the Russian enclave of Kaliningrad (formerly in East Prussia), has been restored as a place of pilgrimage and celebration. According to a legend reported by Maciej Styjokowski,[36] the site of the present capital, Vilnius, was chosen by one Duke Sventaragis, who, when out hunting, came across an oak grove. Its beauty so enchanted him that he gave orders for his body to be cremated there, in the fashion of the Germans and Scandinavians which we have already seen:

> According to the custom of his forebears, the duke was cremated wear-
> ing his finest armor, arms, and his most beautiful raiment. Consumed
> by fire together with the remains of the duke were his beloved hunting
> dogs, hawk, falcon, steed, and manservant.

Afterwards the spot became the cremation ground of the Lithuanian dukes, and today it is the site of the cathedral square.

Although official Baltic Paganism was abolished in the fifteenth century, as in other parts of Europe popular Paganism continued. Largely, the medieval Estonian and Latvian peasantry did not accept Christianity. The language of the Church was Latin or German, and the Latvians preserved their own Pagan culture in their folk-songs and home religious practices. The oral tradition of Latvian Paganism, the *Latviju Dainas*, was published in six volumes between 1894 and 1915 by the Imperial Academy of Sciences in St Petersburg. The restoration of Dievturi came from Brastinu Ernests, who collected and commentated on traditional Latvian sacred folk-songs (1928).[37] It is fortunate that these have been preserved, because they contain an invaluable legacy of folk-culture and popular religion dating from the eleventh to the nineteenth century.[38] The more southerly lands, Curonia and Old Prussia, had their languages stamped out by the colonial powers and so much of their oral tradition was lost.

## DEITIES OF THE BALTIC PANTHEON

Despite the differences in language, many deities of the Baltic pantheon are shared by the Slavs. Saule, the sun-goddess (otherwise Saule Motul, Mother Sun) and her daughters reside in a castle beyond *dausos*, the hill of heaven, abode of the dead. She is depicted riding across the hill of the sky in a copper-wheeled chariot; at eventide, she stops to wash her horses in the sea. The Sun itself is a jug or spoon from which light is poured. Saule is another example of the deity in the wagon. Her festival, Kaledos, is held at mid-winter; images of the Sun are carried through fields and villages to bring prosperity in the coming year. The Scandinavian–British festival of Yule is paralleled at Kaledos by guising in the form of cranes, goats, horses, bears and bulls, burning the *Blukis* (Yule log) and feasting on pork. Saule also has a festival at midsummer, Ligo, at which a bonfire is lit at the top of a pole in a high place. (The pole or tree as a symbol of the World Tree, the celestial axis of the Earth's rotation, is well attested in Baltic tradition.) The site is decorated with wreaths of flowers, there are dances and hymns, and a special meal of cheese and mead is prepared. In the Baltic lands there are wayside shrines on poles which are sometimes topped with a solar emblem, and Saule is described in colloquial speech as perching on top of a tree, especially a birch or rowan. She is symbolised by wheels, eggs and golden apples, and the flax is sacred to her.[39] Saule is also the hearth fire, and the house-snake, Zaltys, which lives by the fire, is said to be beloved of her.[40] Latvia, too, enjoys midsummer festivities and lyrical poetry. The Soviet authorities banned the ligo songs and abolished Midsummer Day as a national holiday as late as 1960.[41] The folklore tradition with its record of Pagan deities was being used for nationalistic purposes, and now in the post-Soviet era a renewal of national interest in indigenous practices is taking place for the same reason.

Mehnesis (Lithuanian: Mènuo) the moon-god, travels the sky in a chariot drawn by grey horses. He was married to Saule, but later fell in love with Auseklis (Lithuanian: Ausrinè), the morning/evening-star goddess, and was punished by Perkunas, who broke him into halves. The god of light is Svaixtix ('Star'). Perkunas (Pehrkons, Perun, Varpulis) is the axe-carrying thunder-god (like the Thracian Lycurgos and the West African Yoruba god Shango). He is the opponent of evil spirits, riding, like Thor, in a goat-drawn chariot. Other weather-deities include Lytuvonis, the rain-god. The sea is ruled by the goddess Juras Mate. Metalworking and construction is under the tutelage of Kalvaitis, the divine smith, whilst destruction is personified in Jods, the spirit of wrongdoing.

*Plate 9.4* German greeting card, *c.*1925, showing the Pagan sun-tree. Spilkammaret, K. Frank Jensen.

Zemyna (otherwise Zemlja or Perkunatelé) is the earth-goddess and psychopomp of the dead. Her name is the linguistic equivalent of that of Semele, mother of Dionysos, in the Greek and Thracian traditions. She has a brother, Majas Kungs (Lithuanian: Zemepatis, Zeminkas), ruler of the home, except for the hearth, which is guarded by the fire-goddess Gabija. The sky-god is Dievs (Lithuanian: Dievas). Dievs is depicted as a handsome king, wearing a belted silver robe and cap, and carrying a sword. His domain is beyond the sky's hill, *dausos*, the realm of the dead, a country entered by three silver gates. Modern Latvian Paganism is called Dievturi, after Dievs, and the movement, Dievturiba. 'To live in harmony with Nature and other members of society and to follow the will of the Gods' is the stated objective.[42] In association with Laima, goddess of life, Dievs determines the fate of humans. Mara, the goddess of the material world, giver, preserver and, finally, taker of life, was worshipped in southern Poland as Marzanna, whose special area is fruit.[43]

## SHRINES AND TEMPLES

Temples existed in the large settlements, but as elsewhere in Europe, much worship was conducted out of doors at sacred places in the countryside. Pigs were sacrificed at rivers to Upinis, god of clean water. In Prussia, Antrimpas, god of lakes and the sea, was revered similarly. In Lithuania, specific sacred places were called *Alkas*: they included groves which could not be cut; holy wells that could not be fished; and sacred fields that could not be ploughed. Cremations took place in or beside them, and offerings were made there on altars (*Aukuras*). Dittmar, bishop of Merseburg (976–1018), wrote of the sacred wood at Zutibure (Svantibor), containing images of the gods. A mountain near the river Nawassa was sacred to the Samogytians (Lowland Lithuanians). There, a perpetual sacred fire was kept, attended by a priest.

In Baltic Paganism, it is believed that there is a component of the human being, the *Siela*, that does not depart with the *Vele* (soul), but becomes reincarnate on Earth in animals and plants, especially trees. In Pagan times, no abuse of tree or animal was tolerated. Individual sacred trees were revered also: Laima was venerated aniconically in linden trees, and Puskaitis, god who rules over the spirits of the Underworld (the *barstukai* – elves or fairies), was honoured by offerings left at elder trees. As in the west, the last sheaf of the corn harvest is venerated as the Rugiu Boba (The Old One of the Rye). Thirteenth-century texts refer to Medeine, goddess of the forest, whilst in the eighteenth century there are references to Giraitis, god of forests, and Silniets.

Lasicius (Bishop Ján Lasicki, 1534–1602), writing in his *De Diis Samagitarum* (Basle, 1580, 1615), and *Religio Borussorum* (1582), tells of the Pagan religion practised among the Borussians, Samogytians, Lithuanians, Ruthenians and Livonians of his day. He recounts the gods worshipped and the agricultural festivals officiated over by Vurschayten (priests). These include Pergrubius, god of flowers, plants and all growing things, whose festival was on 23 April. This is, of course, St George's Day in the Church calendar, and the Baltic festival of Pergrubius echoes the Green Man festivities of England on that day, and may also indicate a religious significance in the date of the 1343 St George's Night Rebellion in Estonia (see below, p. 178). In Poland, the cult of Pergrubius was assimilated with St Florian, guardian of 'St George's Flower Month'. Other festivals were Zazinck, the beginning of harvest, and O Zinck, the harvest home, when a goat was sacrificed. A later festival, Waizganthos (Vaizgautis), was held to augur well for the crop of flax and hemp in the forthcoming year, and this, as we know from other sources, was sacred to the Sun.

Patriarchally, Lasicius assumed that all of these deities were male, latinising them with masculine endings. However, from other sources we know that some of these 'gods' were goddesses, for he ascribes the harvest thanksgiving among the Samogytians to the earth-god Zemiennik, who is clearly the earth-goddess Zemyna. Among the Prussians, he tells of the worship in 1582 of Occopirnus, god of heaven and earth, and his counterpart Pocclus, god of the Underworld and death; Pilvitis (Pluto), god of riches; Pargnus, the thunder-god; Ausceutus (Asklepios), god of health; Potrympus, god of rivers and springs; Antrimpus, god of the sea; and Marcoppolus, god of the noble class. In addition to gods, he tells of lesser demigods and sprites, including the air-spirits, under the rulership of Pacollus, and the Barstuccae (*Erdmännchen*), Elves. Lasicius also tells of a custom which has persisted, deprived of its guardian-deity, until the present day.

> In addition these same people have amongst themselves seers, who in the Rutenican [Belorussian] language are called Burty, who invoking Potrimpus cast wax into water and from the signs or the images described in the molten wax, describe and foretell the nature of any situation which has been enquired about. I myself met one little woman who, having waited in vain for a long time for news of the return of her son, who had left Prussia for Denmark, consulted the seer, from whom she learned that her son had perished in a shipwreck. For the wax had melted in the water to form the shape of a broken ship and the effigy of a man on his back, floating next to the ship.

In the 1990s in the English Midlands, a visitor to an expatriate Latvian household on New Year's Eve was invited with great delight to take part in 'our ancient traditional custom'. Each guest heated up a small nugget of lead in an old pan on the stove, then poured the lead into a bucket of cold water, where it solidified, so allowing the lady of the house to read the guest's fortune for the coming year.

In the late seventeenth century, Matthäus Praetorius tells us in his *Delictae Prussicae oder Preussische Schaubühne* that at the harvest feast, black sucking-pigs were offered by priestesses to Zemyna, goddess of the Earth. The meat was made into sandwiches with the first bread of the harvest, and a portion of meat was taken to a barn, where the goddess was invoked in private. Rites of Zemyna also accompanied the planting of crops: for example, a loaf from the previous year would be ploughed into the Earth at the commencement of ploughing. As with trees and animals, Baltic Pagans revered the Earth, often kissing her on starting work or going to bed. It was considered sacrilegious to hit the Earth, spit on her or otherwise abuse her. The grass-snake, Zaltys, was revered and kept as a living guardian at sacred places and around the stoves of farmhouses. Lasicius had reported that in his day once a year

*Plate 9.5* Lithuanian Pagan worship, showing fire altar and sacred snake (Zaltys), sixteenth-century engraving by Olaus Magnus. Nideck Picture Collection.

the domestic snakes were charmed out of their hiding places by the Pagan priests and offered the best of human food to eat, in order to ensure a prosperous year ahead.

## FINNO-UGRIAN PAGANISM

Most of the languages of Europe, including Slavic, form one vast family, the Indo-European, with a common basic vocabulary and grammatical structure. The northernmost countries of the Baltic region, however, fall into a completely different linguistic grouping, that of the Finno-Ugrian languages. These include Finnish, Lappish (Saami), Estonian, Livonian and Karelian. In addition, there are some smaller groupings in Russia west of the Urals: the Erza, Komi, Mari, Moksha and Udmurt peoples, some of whom remain Pagan to this day. In Russia, the Mari and some Udmurt resisted both Islamicisation and Christianisation. During the 1870s, the Kugu Sorta (Great Candle) movement successfully resisted Church attempts to convert the Mari.[44] In Lapland, repeated attempts by the Church between 1389 and 1603 to suppress Paganism resulted in dual faith practices. When Saami were forcibly baptised, they washed off the effects of baptism with chewed alderbark, sacred to Leib-Olmai, the reindeer-god. Johannes Schefferus, who recorded Pagan practices in seventeenth-century Lapland, wrote that it was an 'alloy of heathenism and Christianity, visible to all, seemingly condemned by none'.[45] His picture of an altar to Thor reveals a lively Paganism which was still actively practised. But there were also Pagan martyrs, like a *noid* (shaman) burnt alive along with his drum at Arjeplog in 1693.[46] In Estonia during the battle against Danish colonisation, the Pagan rebels of the 1343 Jüriöö Mäss (St George's Night) Rebellion destroyed all churches and

178

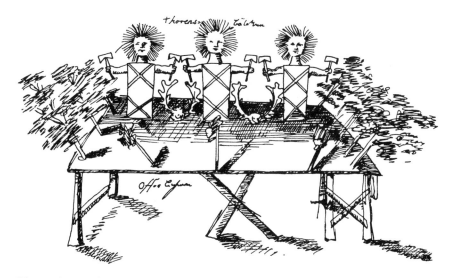

*Plate 9.6* Lappish altar with images of Thor, offerings of reindeer skulls and vegetation, from Johannes Schefferus, 1671. Nideck Picture Collection.

manors, and drowned or otherwise killed all priests and lay brothers, but the Teutonic Knights were called in to slaughter many thousands of rebels in revenge.[47]

The Estonians, according to the fifth-century Roman historian Cassiodorus (*Variae* 546), were the people known to Tacitus as the Aestii. The extent of their territory in early medieval times is disputed, as we have seen, but the nature of their religion is not. Their religion was individualistic and included magical practices. They were known to the Scandinavians as experts in wind-magic, as were the Lapps (known at the time as Finns) on the north of the peninsula. The *Saga of Olaf Tryggvason* includes the story of Raud, 'a man much given to making sacrifices and a great sorcerer, [whom] a great number of Finns followed whenever he needed them'. Raud, whose name is the Finnish for 'iron', 'red' and 'strong',[48] prevented the Christianising King Olaf from entering the fjord in which he lived by raising squalls and a storm. The king arranged for his bishop to perform Christian counter-magic to calm the storm, and then sailed into the bay and killed Raud and his followers.[49] One northern province of Estonia was known as Askala: 'land of wizards'. In 1070, reports Adam of Bremen, the land of Curonia (on the south side of the Dvina basin) was inhabited by 'a primitive race, shunned by all because of its great cult of idols . . . Every house is full of diviners, augurs and magicians. People from all over the world come to ask questions of them, especially the Spaniards and the Greeks'.[50] Between the Baltic and the Mediterranean stretched the so-called 'amber routes', along which this valuable fossilised resin was transported. Some sources even say that the amber was transported by maidens to the shrine of Apollo at Delphi. The maidens were originally given safe passage, but after they had been attacked they used to deposit their amber at the border and it was taken in relays to the temple.[51] Amber, as a gold-coloured jewel, would presumably be sacred to Apollo in his capacity as sun-god. Diodorus Siculus reported that in about 500 BCE, beyond the land of the Celts there was an island containing a circular temple of Apollo, whose people spoke a unique language of their own and who had enjoyed friendly relations with the Greeks from 'most ancient times'.[52] The island might have been Rügen, or it might have been Samland on the east coast, which at the time was cut off by the sea from the mainland. The respect shown to the holy maidens in Pliny's account recalls Tacitus' observation that the Aestii worshipped the mother of the gods, and that the people beyond them were even ruled by women. As we shall see, the cult of the sun-goddess was also honoured north of the Dvina.

A traveller called Wulfstan reported to the court of King Alfred the Great (871–901) about the situation on the eastern Baltic. He said that the Wends held the country up to the Vistula, and beyond that were the 'Estum' or Estonians, who had a large country with a king in every town. The poor drank mead rather than ale, and the nobles drank mares' milk mixed with blood. Their burial customs, according to Wulfstan, included leaving the dead uncremated in the house of their relatives and friends, who then had a wake with drinking and sports until the day of the cremation. The richer the deceased, the longer the wake. The dead did not putrefy, however, because the Estonians had a way of making ice to preserve them. On the day of the funeral, the wealth that remained was divided into five or six piles which were deposited in increasing order of size at increasing distances from the property to a distance of about one mile. The local men with the fastest horses then assembled together and raced towards the dead man's house. The swiftest rider would reach the largest pile of property first, which he would claim, and so on in decreasing order of success. After the contest, the dead man was taken out and burned with his clothes and weapons. This story not only indicates the pugnacious nature and the horse-based economy of eastern Baltic society, but also recalls the tenth-century Rus funeral described by Ibn Fadlan (above, chapter 8). Just as a Rus warrior mocked the Arab for leaving his dead unburned, so, according to Wulfstan, the Estonians insisted that 'the people of every language' should be cremated, and anyone who left a bone unburnt should pay a large fine.[53]

Presumably the rite of cremation speeded the dead person's journey to join the dead beyond the 'hill of heaven', as it did for the Rus merchant interviewed by Ibn Fadlan. The dead would then not become earthbound spirits, which are usually thought to be dangerous to the living. The importance of burning even corpses of foreigners might have come from a fear of such spirits. Henry of Livonia records that as late as 1222 the Estonians disinterred

Christian dead and burned them.[54] By contrast with the Pagans of the time, the Christians thought it was important to preserve dead bodies because these would be resurrected at the end of time, and so it is tempting to see the action of the victorious Estonians as a deliberate attack on their enemy's sacred places. But in the light of what we now know, it is equally likely that this was primarily an act of psychic hygiene, ridding the place of ghouls. Interestingly, when conquered, the Estonians gleefully adopted the Christian feast day of All Saints (1 November). Syncretistically, they saw it as a continuation of their own veneration of the dead and the deities in the sky.

Like much of Pagan northern and eastern Europe, there was no written scripture among the Finno-Ugrian peoples, religious traditions being transmitted orally. Much later, they were written down as the Finnish poems of the *Kalevala*, and the Estonian *Kalevipoeg*. Runes were in use for calendars until much later than in Sweden. In Estonia, they were still being made at the end of the eighteenth century (one from Hiiumaa is dated 1796).[55] Thursday was the holy day, upon which the food was better than during the rest of the week – meat and butter were eaten then. The Pagan calendar divided the year into four quarters: Künnipäev (Plough Day, 14 April, equivalent to the Nordic Summer's Day); Karuspäev (Bear's Day, 13 July); Kolletamisepäev (Withering Day, 14 October, equivalent to the Nordic Winter's Day); and Korjusep (Collection Day, 14 January, the late Nordic midwinter feast).

Finno-Ugrian Pagan deities include a sky-god known by local names, e.g. Jumala in Finnish, Taevataat ('Sky Grandfather') in Estonian, Jumo (Mari), Inmar (Udmurt) and Ibmel (Saami). In Lapland, Pieve, the (feminine) Sun and Mano (Aske) the (masculine) Moon were deities who were never anthropomorphised. Pieve appears as a lozenge or circle with four rays, and Mano appears as a crescent.[56] Akko became the chief god of the Finns. His consort Akka guarded the harvest and fertility. Akka was known as Maan-Emo (Earth Mother) among the Estonians, and Muzem-mumi by the Udmurts. The thunder-god appears to the Saami under the name Horagalles (Old Man Thor), Tooru/Taara in Estonia, and as Torym to the Ostyaks. Rota, the national god of the Saami, is identified with Odin. Trade and settlement contacts between Scandinavia and these northern Finno-Ugric lands seem to have led to a partial assimilation of names and attributes. The Scandinavians of the Viking Age also saw the Lapps and Finns as miracle-workers, experts in the craft of magic. Living in small bands following a hunter-gatherer culture, the Lapps and, to a lesser extent, the more settled Finns preserved the role of the shaman, the expert who journeys in trance between the everyday world and the Otherworld, returning with information to benefit the tribe. Two Lapps were sent on a shamanic astral journey, a 'magic ride to Iceland', by the Norwegian Viking Ingimund the Old. He had lost a silver image of Frey, and the Lapps returned from their 'magic journey' to describe where it was to be found in Iceland. According to the story, told in the

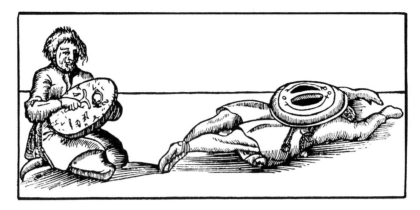

*Plate 9.7* Lappish shaman in trance, from Johannes Schefferus, 1673. Nideck Picture Collection.

*Landnámabók* (179), their description was entirely accurate, and when he went there Ingimund found his silver image exactly where the Lapps had predicted.

As in other parts of Europe, Finno-Ugrian religion honours the ancestors, the spirits of the land and elements, which are important in shamanic practices. The Saami venerate Radien-ahttje, their ancestral deity, accompanied by his consort Radien-akka, and the son and daughter, Radien-pardne and Rana-neida (patroness of springtime). Consecrated spindles were set up to Rana-neida at sacred places.[57] The cults of the guardian-spirits Metsik and Tónn were powerful in Estonia. Among a myriad of beings are the Estonian Ukus (house-spirit), the Saami Biegg-Olbmai (the wind-master), Väralden-Olmai (the man of the world, god of reindeer and hunting), the Udmurt spirits of the water, Obin-murt (rain-man), Vu-Murt (water-man) and Vu-nuna (water-uncle). The bear-cult, too, played an important role in many tribes.[58] Bronze amulets depicting a human figure with the head of a moose have also been found in the graves of the Chud (Estonians) at Lake Ladoga, and the Saami god Radien Kiedde is portrayed with antlers.

As with the Celts and Baltic peoples, sacred groves play an important role in Finno-Ugrian religion. The Mari *Jumon oto* was used for services in honour of the beneficial deities, whilst dangerous deities were propitiated in the *keremet*, a grove surrounded by a fence, equivalent to the Norse *Vébond*. At the end of the nineteenth century, at least sixty-four groves were in use by the Mari. The Udmurts also had groves (*lud*), and built sacred structures (*kvala*), basic windowless wooden buildings that were shrines of the family and clan gods. Inside was kept a wooden vessel containing images of the family or tribal ancestor. In common with European Paganism in general, sacred trees were decked with images and symbolic ornament.

*Plate 9.8* The Norse god Ulli (Ullr), deity of winter hunting. Seventeenth-century Swedish print. Nideck Picture Collection.

One Finno-Ugrian people, the On-Ugri, migrated south and set up home in the Crimea. They became the Hungarians, and will be described in the next chapter.

# 10

# RUSSIA AND THE BALKANS

The lands north of the Black Sea were settled around 700 BCE by the Scythians from central Asia. They were a mixed horde of people whose ruling element was Iranian. Eventually, their Empire encompassed the entire steppe, from the Volga and Kuban on the east to the Dniester in the west. Between the Don and Danube, thousands of burial mounds have been excavated. Among the most impressive are the royal burials containing, in addition to the deceased ruler, slaves and wives, horses, harness, weapons, utensils and wheeled vehicles. The Scythians' chief deity was Tabiti (Hestia in the *interpretatio graeca*), consort of Papaeus (Zeus). Other deities were Api (Mother Earth), Argimpasa (the Celestial Aphrodite) and Oetosyrus (Apollo). Thagimasadas (Poseidon) was the god of the Royal dynasty, which was said to be descended from Targitaus, son of Papaeus. The Scythian Empire lasted around four hundred years, but pressure from the Persian Empire late in the fourth century BCE, Celtic advances from the west and Sarmatian advances from the east fatally weakened it. During the third century, the Celts advanced eastwards from Galicia into the Dnieper Valley, but were forced to retreat. The first Sarmatians to reach the steppe from the east were the Iazygians, who settled on the north-west shore of the Black Sea. Later, the Roxalans, another Sarmatian tribe, settled the land east of the Iazygians. The Sarmatians finally gained complete control of the steppe during the second century. Around 100 BCE, the Alans, the last Sarmatian tribe to arrive, controlled the steppe from the Don to the Volga and south-wards over the valley of the Kuban. Meanwhile, the Scythians had fled northwards, as their burial mounds show, and pressed the Slavs north into what is now Russia.[1]

There were Greek colonies on the Black Sea from 400 BCE. The shores of what are now Bulgaria, Romania and the Crimea were richly populated and integrated with the great Asian and Levantine civilisations of the time. The Greeks called the Alans As or Asii, from whom come both the name of Asia and the ruling dynasty of Norse gods, the Æsir, as already described in chapter 8. The area of the Alans was a flourishing hub of trade and business. It lay east of the Tanakvisl (River Don). The Alans were such excellent warriors that they served as mercenaries with other tribal armies. During the second half of the second century CE, Sarmatian and Teutonic forces crossed the Danube and attacked Dacia (modern Romania). Later, around 450, Alan forces served in the Hunnish army under Attila. Finally, the Alans were overrun by the migrating Goths, who after being overrun by the Huns in 376 left their language in the area, where it was last recorded in the sixteenth century.

This western shore of the Black Sea was held by Constantinople as part of the Roman Empire and will be discussed below. The north-east of our area, roughly 30° east from Greenwich, was contacted (as we have already seen) by Swedish Vikings in 859, when they imposed tribute on the inhabitants of the area around what was to become Novgorod. In 862 they were invited back by the inhabitants to impose order amongst them. Ruric and his Swedish warriors were to protect the trading cities on the Neva and the Dnieper. They and their descendants set up bases at Novgorod and Kiev, established a trading empire, attacked the Byzantine Empire several times as well as serving as mercenaries in the Varangian (Swedish) Guard in the imperial capital, and attempted to conquer Bulgaria. The Vikings retained close contact with their Scandinavian homeland, and although they inter-married with the indigenous ruling families, the latter and their peoples remained essentially Slavic.

In 988 Prince Vladimir (980–1015) imposed Christianity on the Russians. He summoned a council of boyars to discuss the possible adoption of Judaism, Islam, Christianity or some other politically aligned religion, which would gain him useful political and trading contacts with the wider world of adherents to that faith.[2] The council was attended by priests and missionaries of various faiths. It was decided that Russia should become Orthodox Christian, but in a form based on a nationalist Russian Church. The union of Church and state in the eastern Roman Empire was so strong that a nation which adopted Christianity was also expected to accept the emperor as over-lord. Political parties in Russia followed religious lines: the nationalist party was Pagan, whilst the Imperial party was Christian. Vladimir blackmailed the Byzantine emperor into giving him his sister in marriage as the price of mercenary help in the Byzantine civil war, then returned to Kiev and began the work of Christianisation. Pagan temples were demolished, and churches built on their sites. The Kievan great image of Perun was first flogged by twelve strong men and then thrown into the river, to which the entire population of the city was then marched to be forcibly baptised. Byzantine influence gave the Russians a developed system of law, art and literature, which made up for its comparative dormancy during the centuries when its western allies had been part of the Roman Empire.

In 1169, Kiev was sacked and the capital removed to Vladimir by Prince Andrew Bogliouski. Next, external politics intervened. In 1224, the Tartar invasion began. The Russian defences were routed, as were those of Moravia,

Silesia, Cracow and Pest. The Tartar forces failed to take Vienna but set up the khanate of the Golden Horde with its capital Sarai on the Lower Volga. The Russians among others were reduced to tributaries, paying a heavy poll tax from which monks and priests were, however, exempt. As a result the Russian Orthodox Church became wealthy and influential. The Tartars converted to Islam and ruled the area for two hundred years, from 1264 until the rise of Muscovy and the Turkish Empire. In 1328, the Russian Ivan Kalita (Moneybag), Grand Prince of the township of Moscow, began to act as a tax-farmer for the Tartars. He acquired a monopoly and Moscow grew strong. Kiev lost importance and the main power passed to Moscow. However, from 1315 to 1377, Kiev became Pagan again, under the Baltic pantheon. The Lithuanian leaders Gudimin and his son Olgerd conquered the area and ruled from Vilnius.[3] When in 1386 Jagellon I of Lithuania converted to Catholic Christianity in order to unite Lithuania with Poland, Lithuanian Russia, centred on what is now the Ukraine, became known as Little Russia, Baltic Russia, or White Russia.[4] Moscow saw the Poles and Lithuanians, like the Muslim Tartars, as heretics. The Tartars remained an influential power in Russia, exacting tribute well into the sixteenth century. Bishop Ján Lasicius reported attending a Tartar prayer meeting near Vilnius in 1582.[5] When Constantinople fell to the Islamic Turks in 1453, Moscow took on the role of Imperial Holy City. Ivan the Great (1462–1505) later adopted the title of Caesar (Tsar) and added the two-headed eagle of the Roman Empire to the Russian national arms.[6]

The Slavonic deities are related closely to the Baltic ones. The sky-god is Svarog. His son is the fire-deity Svarozhitsch (Svarogitch) (the holy light), sometimes identified with the sun-deity, Khors or Dazhdbog, consort of the moon-deity Myesyats and father of the stars. To the Russians, Myesyats is a goddess, but in the Ukraine (as in the Baltic), he is a god, husband of the sun-goddess. Svarog was also known as Svantovit, and was later worshipped under the guise of St Vitus. Bielbog (Byelobog), the white, bright god, is opposed by Tschernobog (Chernobog), the black god of evil. In addition, there is a god of war, Jarovit, and Domovoi (Domovik), the god of the ancestors. Perun was assimilated with the Jewish prophet Elijah. He was associated with the weather-god, Erisvorsh, and the wind-gods Stribog, Varpulis (the storm-wind) and Dogoda (the gentle west wind). In the Ukraine and Belarus, Perun is the deity of summer, contrasted with Kolyada, the god of wintertime. Krukis is the patronal deity of blacksmiths and domestic animals, whilst judgement of wrongdoing is overseen by Proven.

Janet McCrickard lists evidence for a lost solar goddess in Russian and South Slavic folklore.[7] In Russian, the name for the Sun is neuter but verbs associated with it are always conjugated in the feminine form. In traditional songs the Sun appears as a bride or maiden, the Moon as a youth, father or grandfather. McCrickard also tells a Russian story which is exactly like that of the Scandinavian god Frey and the giantess Gerd, described above in chapter 8. A young man wanders to the world's end, where there is a cottage. A young girl of dazzling radiance comes to the cottage, takes off her dress and covers herself with a sheet. Darkness falls. In the morning she gets up, puts on her shining dress and flies into the sky. Her mother calls her 'Solntse': Sun.

The three Fates (Norns, Weird Sisters) are represented in Slav religion by the Zorya: Utrennyaya, goddess of dawn; Zorya Verchernyaya, warrior-goddess of dusk; and the Goddess of Midnight. They watch the demonic god chained to the wagon of the polar night; when he escapes, the world will end. The goddess of the dead is Baba-Yaga, who resides in a hut surrounded by a bone fence with skulls on top. This reflects the bone-strewn earth-lodges of the wise women in Drenthe province, Holland, which existed until the seventeenth century, and Siberian shamanic buildings made from mammoth tusks and bones. The Russian *volkhv* (shaman) dealt with other spirits, including the Domovoi (house-sprites), Leshy (wood-spirits who lead travellers astray) and Vodanyoi, malevolent water-sprites.

The fertility goddess Kupala was revered at midsummer by ritual bathing in sacred rivers, offerings of garlands to the waters, jumping through bonfires and the erection of a birch pole decked with ribbons. Until well into the eighteenth century, Yarilo, god of erotic sexuality, was revered. Cattle were guarded by the god Walgino. The Slav and Czech goddess Devana (Serbian Diiwica, Polish Dziewona) is, like Diana, the goddess of the hunt. The natural world is recognised in the south Russian goddess Polevoi (Polevik), the field-spirit, whose hair is green; and the related Poludnitsa, a white-clad goddess of the fields. In Poland, three gods, Datan, Lawkapatim and Tawals, guard the fields. Ovinnik, the spirit of the barn, is worshipped as a black cat.[8]

In Slovakia, the chief god was Praboh, closely associated with the goddess of life, Zivena. She was counterposed with a death-goddess, Morena. Agriculture was the realm of Uroda, goddess of the fields, and Lada, goddess of beauty. As in the rest of Europe, the thunder-god Parom was revered universally. The Bieloknazi (White Priests) served and invoked the white gods, whilst the Black Priests practised magic.[9] The Slovaks have their imagery of light and darkness in common with the Russians, whose white god and black god have already been mentioned. A similar opposition of light and darkness occurs in the contrast of the light elves and dark elves in late Scandinavian mythology, although such a stark contrast is generally foreign to Pagan pantheons, which see all forces as having their place in the natural order. The imagery of light and darkness might well be one remnant of Iranian influences which were current among the Scythian inhabitants of Russia during the last five hundred years BCE.

One branch of Finno-Ugrian speakers drove a wedge between the South Slavs of the Balkans and their kinsfolk in the north. These were the Magyars, who had been driven from their home in the Volga area to the Black Sea

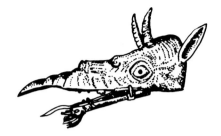

*Plate 10.1* Guising animal heads (*Perchtenmasken*) for midwinter ceremonies, eighteenth century, Salzburg, Austria (cf. medieval English guising). Nigel Pennick.

steppes, where they mingled with the Turks. Between the fifth and the ninth centuries they confederated as the On-Ugri (the People of the Ten Arrows), and eventually became known as the Hungarians. Boundary disputes in the Byzantine Empire in the ninth century forced them west across the steppe to the Danube provinces which had once been Dacia and Pannonia. (The old provinces of Noricum and west Pannonia had been conquered by Charlemagne from the Avars and Lombards in 799 and made into the Ostmark: Austria, the eastern boundary of the Roman Catholic dominion.) In 890 the Magyars invaded the area under their king, Arpad. Holding fast to their tribal shamanism, they made incursions into the Western Empire as far as Alsace. They were repulsed by Henry the Fowler (919–936) at Merseburg in 933 and by Otto I at Augsburg in 955, and then fell back to settle in what is now Hungary, which under them returned to Paganism.

The official conversion of the Hungarians by Frankish missionaries occurred in 997, with the first bishopric being set up in 1001 at Estergom. In 1236 King Béla IV re-established contact with the ethnic Hungarians who lived in Bashkira, near the Udmurts and Mari. Their territory was known as Greater Hungary and they were still Pagan, eating horse- and wolfmeat. The Kumans (or Pechenegs), Turkic nomads who had settled in western Siberia, arrived in Hungary in the late tenth century, after ejecting the Magyars from the latter's earlier home on the north-west shore of the Black Sea. They formed a Pagan ethnic enclave known as Little Kumania, and were taken up by the Hungarian King Ladislas IV (1272–1290) to such an extent that the Pope preached a crusade against him for favouring Paganism. Shamanic practices persisted among the Hungarians, and the traditions of the *táltos* (shaman) are recorded until the 1940s.[10] Hungary, too, is the home of a highly sophisticated Pagan art revival, far removed from the tribal shamanism of the nomads. In the year 188 an Iseum was built at Szombathely, on what was then the Norican–Pannonian border. It was enlarged in the third century, and then rebuilt in the 1950s, complete with a frieze of Isis riding on Sothis. An annual Mozart festival is held there at

188

which *The Magic Flute* is performed. This opera, as is well known, is based on Masonic symbolism, but more generally it includes the light-and-darkness imagery of Iranian dualism, the source of the Mithraism which was so popular in this area during the last years of official Roman Paganism. Zoroastrian dualism and Egyptian syncretism lie at opposite ends of the Pagan spectrum, and yet here there is a continuity of practice, if not exactly of belief, in the preservation of a Pagan Mystery-cult.

## THE BALKAN STATES

The countries south of the Danube had been part of the Hellenistic Empire of Alexander the Great and his successors. The Thracians, for example, were viewed by the Greeks rather as the late Scandinavians viewed the Lapps: as experts in atavistic magic. According to Herodotus (V.7), the only deities worshipped by the Thracians were Artemis, Dionysos and Ares. With the epithet *basilea* (queen), Artemis was worshipped by Thracian and Paionian women who brought offerings wrapped in wheat straw.[11] In fact, the Thracians worshipped other goddesses as well. Bendis was shown dressed like Artemis, as a hunting-goddess. She was honoured at Athens in the Bendideia, being described by Aristophanes as the Great Goddess, *Megalē Thea*, the Thracian Bendis, related to Artemis Brauronia, whose female devotees performed her ritual bear-dance. Devotees of the Thracian goddess Kotyto were received into her fold through baptism. Tereia, another mother-goddess, was associated with the Phrygian Kybele, and Kabyle in Thrace was one of the cult-places of Kybele.

Thracia, Moesia, Macedonia and part of Dalmatia, later to become Illyria and Dacia Ripiensis, were the Balkan provinces of the Roman Empire. As the buffer zone of the vulnerable Danube frontier they were from the third century subject to invasion by migrating Goths, Huns and others. The depredations of Alaric, the Christian Gothic leader who sacked Rome in 410, devastated the economy of northern Greece and destroyed many of its old Pagan shrines, but the Balkans proper suffered even more than Greece from nomadic invaders, both Christian and Pagan. In the sixth or seventh century this area, together with a large part of Greece, was settled by the Slavonic-speaking peoples described above, most of whom were converted to Greek Orthodox Christianity in the ninth century. Between the pressures of nomadic invasions, political machinations by the eastern and western Empires, and the subsequent occupation by the Islamic Turks, which lasted from the fifteenth to the nineteenth centuries, the Balkan states had little chance to evolve organically as nation-states. The Turks were, however, tolerant of other religions, while the leaders of these lacked the political power to enforce systematic orthodoxy among their followers, and so a varied mixture of Christian and Slavic Pagan practices has continued throughout the area until the present, as we describe below. Dual faith practices were also observed before the Turkish conquest. In 1331, in the upper Isonzo valley, on the borders of modern Slovenia and Italy, around Caporetto, the Christian Church mounted a crusade against the Slavs who retained their Paganism.[12] Later, the pan-Slavic movement in the nineteenth century, promoted by Russia in order to extend her influence in the eastern Mediterranean, actually encouraged the retrieval of the folk-practices and Pagan survivals described above.

Romania, north of the eastern Danube, was resettled after the Slavic invasion by the old Roman colonists who had fled across the river centuries before to form the province of Dacia Ripiensis. To this day Romania retains a Latin-based language. Its Pagan tradition is, however, similar to that of the West Slavs. Before communism attempted to stamp out all rural traditions during the twentieth century, the moon was venerated in Romania as the goddess Ileana Sânziana, 'queen of flowers', 'sister of the Sun'. There were spells addressed to the moon, and each new moon was hailed with the prayer:

> Moon, new moon,
> Cut the bread in two,
> And give us
> half to Thee,
> Health to me.

At certain times of year, troupes of ceremonial dancers undertook a nine-day ceremony. They visited nine boundary-points, filled a ceremonial vessel with water from nine springs, and prayed to their patron goddess Irodeasa. (Her name is presumably not original but a version of 'Herodias', the name of the wickedest woman in the Bible, often used for Pagan goddesses by Christian prelates who preached against them.) The dancers carried swords and clubs, some wore masks or blacked their faces, and they were accompanied by a hobby-horse. At the close of the ceremony on the ninth day, a sacred pole made for the duration of the rite was cast into a river.[13] The lyrical folk-songs of Romania are called *doinas*, like the Latvian *dainas*, although the bulk of Romanian language is descended from Latin.

Bulgaria, too, followed a different path from its Slavic neighbours. It had been settled after the fall of Rome by the Huns, but later invaded by Slavic migrants, who intermingled with the Hunnic inhabitants and created an aggressive, expansionist nation-state which challenged the eastern Empire based on Constantinople. In 613 Kurt, king of the Bulgars, became Christian, but the bulk of his people remained Pagan. At the beginning of the ninth century, when the Greeks were recapturing their peninsula from the Arabs, the Bulgarian King Krum, a Slavic Pagan, played one side off against the other. Eventually, in 811, he killed the eastern Emperor Nicophorus in battle, displayed the latter's head in the usual fashion, and then had the skull plated with silver and used as a drinking vessel. Krum died in 814, and the Bulgarians adopted Christianity some fifty years later, after a naval blockade by the Greeks. Between 889 and 893, King Vladimir of Bulgaria returned to Paganism, but afterwards his brother Simeon the Great restored Christianity as part of his programme to establish Bulgaria as an up-to-date civilised state which could (and did) challenge Constantinople. It was due to Simeon's machinations that the Magyars were driven westwards to found Hungary.

Initially, the Balkan states had adopted official Christianity in the seventh century, at the same time as the other barbarian-invaded extremities of the Roman Empire. Bulgaria was joined in 640 by Serbia which adopted the Orthodox rite, but Slavonia (part of what is now Croatia) was only converted in 864, after the Slavs had replaced the Avar conquerors of the sixth century. In that year the missionaries Cyril and Methodius arrived from Constantinople and created an alphabet that was adequate to the Slavonic languages in order to translate the Bible. This became known as the Cyrillic script and spread throughout the Slavonic Orthodox churches. Moravia was converted by Cyril and Methodius in 863 and Bulgaria once again in 864. Cyril and Methodius had arrived in Constantinople as emissaries of Rome to the eastern Empire, since the schism between the two was foreshadowed in that decade. They were sent initially to convert the Turkic Khazars of the Crimea, so that religious ties would bind these more closely to the Empire than the political ties of pure self-interest which were at the time being undermined by their newly arrived neighbours, the Pagan Rus of Kiev. Once more, religious change was a by-product of political manoeuvring. The conversion of Little Russia in 988 can likewise be seen as a move in the game between Kiev and Constantinople for influence over Bulgaria and the mouth of the Hellespont.

## THE BYZANTINE EMPIRE

In Constantinople itself, the process of Christianisation had from the start been heavily influenced by Pagan philosophical thought. Among the governing classes, Pagan ideals of human virtue and public duty remained operative, and among the educated classes, open Paganism continued in places until the end of the sixth century.[14] The Greek *paideia* (education) was as essential a part of a young person's upbringing as education is today, and rather as, say, the modern Icelandic literary corpus contains the ancient tales of the Norse divinities and their Pagan followers, so the *paideia* of early Christian society contained the myths, history and philosophy of a Pagan age. At the same time, uneducated working people still believed in wonder-workers and demigods, and the cult of saints was easily grafted onto this outlook.[15] A transcendental, mystical outlook which had much in common with Neo-platonism was adopted into Christian theology, and the doctrine of theosis, 'that God was made man so that man might become God [by mystical contemplation]', became a central part of Orthodox belief and practice. In the fourth century, Saints Basil and Gregory rejected the conception of (what they rather unfairly called) 'a narrow Jewish godhead' and allowed the divine presence to be celebrated in a wealth of art and ceremony. Mystical schemata such as the *Celestial Hierarchies*, attributed to St Paul's disciple Dionysius the Areopagite but actually written in the early sixth century, became part of official doctrine at a time when the analogous system of Jewish Cabbala, itself probably derived from Neoplatonism (see above, p.51), was still the pursuit of a heretical minority.[16]

Indeed, some Pagan ceremonies seem to have been retained in Greece with little or no alteration. The ninth-century patriarch Photius described one such at Thebes, the Daphnephoria:

> They wreathe a pole of live wood with laurel and various flowers. On the top is fitted a bronze globe, from which they suspend smaller ones. Midway down the pole they place a smaller globe, binding it with purple fillets – but the end of the pole is decked with saffron. By the topmost globe they mean the sun, which they actually compare with Apollo. The globe beneath is the moon: the smaller globes hung on are the stars and constellations, and the fillets are the course of the year – for they make them 365 in number . . . The *Daphnephorus* himself holds onto the laurel, he has his hair hanging loose, he wears a golden wreath and is dressed out in a splendid robe to his feet and he wears light shoes. There follow him a chorus of maidens, holding out boughs before them to enforce the supplication of the hymns.[17]

At the time of the attacks by Islamic invaders, however, the Christian Church in Constantinople went through an iconoclastic period. From 726 to 787 and from 813 to 843, the eastern Empire was officially without graven images, and some orgies of puritanical destruction followed. The images, together with the cults of the saints and the Virgin, had previously been accepted rather ambivalently by the Church authorities as the ill-fitting relic of Paganism which, of course, they were. During the iconoclastic controversies, the opposing camps were renamed and the iconoclasts, the one-time party of Christian orthodoxy, became dismissed as 'Saracen-minded', those in favour of icons being known as 'Hellenophiles'. The restoration of the images in 843 was accompanied by great Christian rejoicing and was marked by an annual celebration, the Feast of Orthodoxy. Thus, ironically, Pagan practices were reintroduced in order to distinguish Christianity from Islam.

J.C. Robertson, in volume V of his *A History of the Christian Church*, reported an actual Pagan reconversion by a professor at the court of the Emperor Alexius Comnenus (acc. 1081). An Italian called John, a professor of Classical literature at Constantinople, began to teach the transmigration of souls, and the Platonic doctrine of Ideas. One of his disciples, according to Robertson, is said to have thrown himself into the sea, exclaiming 'Receive me, O Poseidon!'. The professor himself was eventually persuaded to 'renounce his errors', and Christian order was restored.

The Byzantine Empire reached its widest extent in 1023. It encompassed all of Asia Minor, Cyprus, Crete, half of the Levant, the southern Crimea, Greece and the mainland from the rivers Danube to Drava, plus eastern Sicily and southern Italy, that is, the old Magna Graecia. Shortly afterwards the western Church separated itself doctrinally from the eastern Church, and the two Empires should have gone their separate ways. However, the first Crusade, in 1096, reunited them against the Arabic conquerors of the old Roman province of Palestine. Nevertheless, the fourth Crusade of 1204, which was diverted by the western forces to conquer Constantinople, conveniently for Venetian trading interests, eventually consolidated the breach between the two halves of the old Empire. Meanwhile, a new enemy had arisen in the east. In the last decade of the tenth century, the Turks moved out from Turkestan in search of conquest. They embraced Islam and so added a religious crusade to their territorial ambitions. By 1360 they had north-west Asia Minor, or Turkey as it now became, and a toehold on the mainland at Gallipoli. They consolidated, expanded and, in 1453, captured Constantinople itself. The eastern Christian Empire passed to Moscow, and by 1648 Turkey had all of North Africa, the Levant, Mesopotamia, Asia Minor, Greece and the Balkans, part of Austria, Hungary, Romania and the Crimea. The old eastern Roman Empire had been captured and even extended (north of the Danube) by the new Ottoman Empire. The Crimean territories were eventually lost to Muscovite Russia in the late eighteenth century, and Greece became independent in 1832. In the late nineteenth century, with the pan-Slavic movement, the territories either side of the Danube were lost, followed by north Africa and the southern Balkans. After the First World War, Mesopotamia and the Levant became independent, leaving Turkey in possession only of Asia Minor, Constantinople and the latter's hinterland.

The centuries of Turkish rule had frozen south-eastern Europe in a pre-industrial but ideologically neutral state, where Pagan traditions were preserved in Christian belief and accommodated to the *realpolitik* of a tolerant but officially Islamic state. In 1892, when Greece and the Balkans were independent, a British officer in Greece, Renell Rodd, described many Pagan survivals which were actively continued at the time. He described how each household in even the rudest peasant village had its icon shrine, often with a perpetual flame burning before it: 'It will be solemnly borne away to the new dwelling if the family change quarters, like the household gods of the olden time; and should the little lamp go out upon the road, it would be held to forbode some grave misfortune.'[18] The renaming of ancient deities as saints has continued in Greece as elsewhere in Europe. Cults of St Eleutherios replace that of Eileithyia, goddess of childbirth, and at least one church of the

Virgin of Fecundity is built on the site of an ancient temple of this goddess.[19] Shrines of Demeter are replaced by churches of St Demetrios, and the twelve Apostles are invoked in ancient temples of the Twelve Gods. It was St Dionysios to whom the nineteenth-century Cretans ascribed the introduction of the grape, and St Paul who was credited with Herakles' ancient achievement of expelling the snakes from Crete. Votive offerings are given to the Christian icons of the domestic shrines as they were once given to the ancient deities in their public temples, and as late as the 1890s, the sacrifice of a lamb or a fowl would be blessed by the local Christian priest at the foundation ceremony of any new building.[20]

The local saint's day in each Greek village or city was called a *paneguris*, the same word as the ancient *panegyria*, a solemn coming together of all the people. In Athens the ancient Anthestereia, the so-called 'flower festival' which was actually a feast of the dead, was replaced by the medieval and modern 'feast of roses', the Rousalia, held on Easter Tuesday. Rodd reports that the modern Rousalia was also celebrated elsewhere in Greece at the feast of All Souls, this time explicitly in memory of the dead.[21] At the ancient Anthestereia, the casks of new wine were broached; interestingly, the Greek word *anthos* (flower), like the modern Spanish word *flor*, also refers to the yeast that forms on the top of weak or old wine. The feast could thus be seen as a celebration of the flowering of new life from the detritus of decay. In the modern rose festival, Renell Rodd reports, a song was sung, wishing goodwill to the community's children, and the male children were then lifted three times into the air with prayers that, in the words of another flower metaphor, they should flourish. This strange continuation of an ancient festival, itself apparently a garbled form of an even earlier original, was already dying out by Renell Rodd's time.[22]

In ancient times, the sky-god Zeus was seen as the cause of rain. In modern times, '[The] god is raining' is still a common turn of phrase. Old Poseidon, known as 'Earth-shaker', a principal god of the Minoan-Mycenean pantheon, seems to survive in the saying on the island of Zante, describing an earthquake: '[The] god is shaking his hair'. In ancient times the Furies were propitiated as the Eumenides, the Kindly Ones; in the nineteenth century it was smallpox which was personified as 'Eulogia': 'the kindly spoken one'. Charon, the mythical boatman who in ancient times was thought to carry souls across the River Styx, metamorphosed in modern Greece into Charos, an ill-wishing herald of death similar in function to the Etruscan Charun. But, unlike the latter, Charos appears as a grave and dignified old man dressed in black, and even, in a fresco on Mount Athos, as a skeleton with a scythe over his shoulder, like the Anglo-Saxon Old Father Time.[23] A widespread fear of vampires and the unquiet dead in modern popular culture might be attributed to Slavic influences, but as we saw in chapter 1, such a belief and the expiatory sacrifices which went with it were also present in ancient times. In the nineteenth century, most places still had their *stoikheion* or *genius loci* (such as the one that was propitiated by foundation-sacrifice). In particular, large or ancient trees had their spirit-guardian, which would be ceremonially shunned at the moment of felling the tree. And as in other parts of Europe, household snakes were venerated until modern times. In present-day Istanbul, the ancient Constantinople, Pierre Chuvin reports continuing widespread veneration of the spirit of place. Holy spots such as tombs and trees are surreptitiously decorated with ribbons or honoured with candles; springs have coins thrown into them and votive plaques are attached to structures above ground, despite notices at the sites explicitly forbidding these practices in the name of Islam.[24]

Many archaic Greek folk-beliefs and domestic practices thus seem to have survived in surprisingly unchanged form into the modern age. Public religion, too, has persisted by translation into the cult of saints, the persistence of festival dates and practices, and the continuity of sacred sites. Some of the ancient beliefs themselves passed at an early stage into the form of Christianity which took root in the eastern Empire, and the mystical inheritance of Neoplatonism in particular distinguishes Orthodox belief from its Catholic neighbour. But quite apart from the unacknowledged or discreetly assimilated survivals of Paganism which we have now seen from all over Europe, the articulated and explicit legacy of the ancient civilisations has also passed into mainstream European culture. It is to this reawakening that we now turn in the final chapter.

# 11

# PAGANISM REAFFIRMED

The High Medieval period (950–1350), as we have seen in the earlier chapters, saw the militant monotheistic religions, Christianity and Islam, imposing their influence on the rulers of Europe, so that the official religions of the emerging kingdoms and empires became monotheistic and in practice androtheistic, referring to their supreme deity only in the masculine gender. We have also seen Pagan practices and beliefs continuing here and there, unnoticed by official sanctions, and also being incorporated into Christian practice as this developed. In that sense the Pagan outlook and deities remained, shaped the form of Christian society which overlay them, and were available as a living tradition to be recognised and reclaimed by later investigators in an age of independent thought. In Islamic areas of Europe, the situation was different. Islamic doctrine did not compromise with Pagan values (indeed, the famous 'Satanic verses' of the Koran were almost immediately repudiated by Mohammed as an attempt by the Devil to incorporate the three goddesses of Mecca in the celestial hierarchy), and Islam remained militantly anti-polytheist.

In Christian lands, the High Middle Ages were the crusading years. Christian dualism, never far beneath the surface of its official monotheism, was first turned against the Islamic conquerors of Palestine, then against its Pagan neighbours in the Baltic, and then against alleged heretics, infidels and apostates within its own jurisdiction. The persecution of the Jews in Europe intensified noticeably in extent after the eleventh century,[1] but its origins stem from the formative age of the Christian religion, in which early Church leaders regularly defamed Jews, Pagans and Christians of other sects. The prototypical defamer is St John the Divine, who wrote of Jesus telling those Jews who did not believe in him: 'Ye are of your father the devil' (John 8.44). In his *Expository Treatise against the Jews*, Hippolytus (170–236) wrote that the Jews were 'darkened, unable to see the true light'. Origen (185–254) called the Jews 'a most wicked nation', and said that they had suffered rightly through rejecting Jesus of Nazareth. Gregory of Nyssa (331–396) called Jews 'slayers of the Lord', 'advocates of the Devil' and 'haters of righteousness'. Chrysostom's *Eight Homilies against the Jews* claimed that 'The Jews sacrifice

*Plate 11.1* Medieval dancers in animal guise. Folk-dance all over Europe continues this and similar traditions of Pagan sacred dance. Victorian engraving after MS. Bodl. 264, Fl. 21 V. Nideck Picture Collection.

their children to Satan . . . they are worse than wild beasts . . . The synagogue is a curse'. His most notorious piece of anti-Semitism continued: 'I hate the Jews, because they violate the Law. I hate the synagogue, because it has the Law and the Prophets. It is a duty of all Christians to hate the Jews.' In the year 414, the Patriarch Cyril instigated religious riots in Alexandria which led to the murder of all Jews who could not escape. The defamatory propaganda of those early times was institutionalised in the Church, periodically being brought out to attack Jews and Pagans. The purpose of this book is not to detail the history of the Witch-, Jew- and Gypsy-hunts, but their contemporary justification was given in these doctrines promulgated by the polemicists of late antiquity.

By the mid-fourteenth century, a small but significant Pagan influence was entering Europe from abroad. The modern Gypsies appear to be the descendants of people who migrated westwards from India at some time in the twelfth century. In 1322, two Franciscan priests on pilgrimage to Palestine reported cave-dwelling Gypsies near Candia, Crete. By 1348, *Cingarije* were in Serbia. Gypsies entered central Europe in the early fifteenth century; they were in Hildesheim, Germany, in 1407, at Zürich in 1419, and in France in 1421. Like the Jews, the Gypsies suffered appalling persecution for racial–religious reasons. They were persecuted wherever they went in Europe, often being killed, or sold into slavery. In 1370, forty Gypsy families in Wallachia, Romania, were taken prisoner and given as slaves to the monastery of St Anthony at Voditza.[2] In 1530, it was a capital offence to be a Gypsy in England, and in 1665 Gypsies were deported from Edinburgh to be slaves in the West Indies.[3] In Romania, they suffered slavery until 1856.

In addition to the racist fear of their dark skins, their Pagan beliefs and practices made the Gypsies the butt of persecution. Signs were erected on the roads into Bohemia, showing Gypsies being tortured and hanged, with the slogan, *Straff die Heiden* ('Punish the Pagans'). In Holland, Gypsies were also called *Heiden*, and *Heidenjachten* (Pagan-hunts) were instituted to exterminate them. Until the eighteenth century, periodic *Heidenjachten* were conducted as joint operations using infantry, cavalry and police. In sixteenth- and seventeenth-century Switzerland, laws sought to exterminate the Gypsies. They were made outlaws, so that anyone encountering them should kill them. Gypsy-hunts were instituted, and a 1646 Ordinance of the city of Berne gave anyone the right to 'personally kill or liquidate by bastinado or firearms' Gypsies and *Heiden*. In 1661, the Elector Georg II passed the death penalty on all Gypsies in Saxony, and hunted them with cavalry. Later, in 1721 the Emperor Charles VI ordered the extermination of the Gypsies, and in 1725 Frederick William I condemned any Gypsy over eighteen caught in his lands to be hanged. Gypsy-hunting continued in Denmark until 1835. The twentieth century has seen no end to their perse-cution. Early in the Second World War, all Gypsies in England and France were arrested and put into prison camps,[4] where they remained until 1948. All Gypsies in the Third Reich were taken to Auschwitz in 1943, where, it is estimated, between 250,000 and 300,000 of them died. Internal passports for Gypsies were compulsory in France until 1970.[5]

Many internal crusades were preached and practised within Christendom, some of which we have already seen, but one other deserves mention here. In 1208 Pope Innocent II, a ruthless and efficient systematiser, preached a crusade against the Cathars of southern France, a group of Christians who held overtly dualist beliefs and who were more influential in the politics of the area than the officials of the Roman Church. As a result of the crusade, the economic and cultural infrastructure of this prosperous and civilised area, which had preserved a version of the Roman way of life from five hun-dred years before despite the alternation of Catholic, Arian and eventually Saracen rulers, was destroyed. At the same time, the Inquisition was created. In 1233, one Dominic Guzman was given charge of an order of monks to inquire into the remnants of heretical belief in the area. His order, the Dominicans, soon took over all the other 'inquisitions' in the Papal juris-diction, and the perennial search for doctrinal correctness found itself with teeth. Over the next two centuries, the Inquisition gradually gained the power to suspend many of the normal processes of law, with the result that it became difficult for a suspect, once accused, to be acquitted. At this time, the beginning of the modern age, the western Church was desperately trying to standardise belief against the background of an increasing influx of information from different cultures and from the processes of rational thought itself. People who, to modern eyes, are as varied as scientists, sorcerers and freethinking reformers of Christianity itself, all fell under suspicion as opponents of true belief.

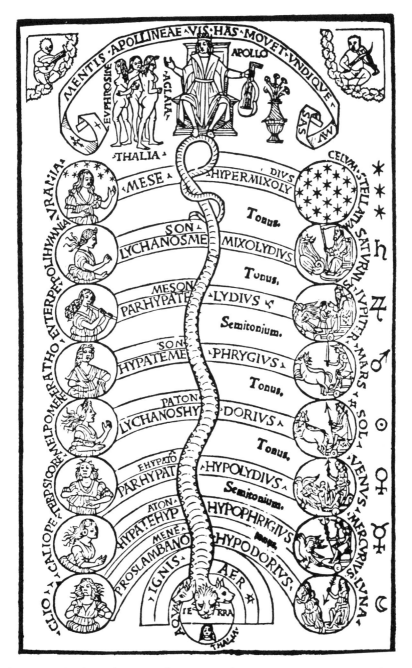

*Plate 11.2* The divine harmony, from Luc Gafurius' *Practica musice*, 1496, showing Pagan divinities and cosmology in a Renaissance context. Nideck Picture Collection.

## RENAISSANCE REASSERTION OF PAGAN VALUES

At the same time that doctrinaire Christianity was being enforced, however patchily, in the west, a resurgence of humanist classicism began to reinstate the Pagan goddesses and gods of European antiquity. The influx of Greek philosophy from Arab sources in Spain had already revolutionised academic thought in the universities, and many clerics were overawed by the art as well as the learning of the ancient world. Most notoriously, the pursuit of 'reason', argument from first principles, was opposed to that of 'authority', the literal adherence to the writings of the Church fathers, by the twelfth century. A different application of independent thought, the development of experimental method, was pursued by Roger Bacon and the Franciscans of Oxford a century later, although it became a casualty of the reimposition of theological dogma at Oxford following the anathematisation of Lollardy (John Wyclif, 1324–1384). In Italy, however, the rich laity had wealth and peace enough to take up the pursuit of letters, and Classical texts began to be re-examined in abundance. Symbolic goddesses and gods reasserted their place, for example Minerva, the goddess of crafts and learning, who replaced the medieval abstraction Sapientia. Christine de Pizan (1365–c.1430), the feminist author, began her heraldic treatise with an invocation to Minerva:

> O Minerva, goddess of arms and chivalry, who by virtue of understanding far surpassing other women discovered and established the use of forging iron and steel among other noble arts . . . Adored lady and high goddess, do not be displeased that I, a simple little woman, who am as nothing compared to the greatness of your famed learning, should undertake now to speak of such a magnificent enterprise as that of arms.[6]

The Tempietto Malatestiano at Rimini was designed by Leon Battista Alberti, and built in 1450 as a temple of victory for Sigismondo Malatesta, soldier, patron of the arts and enemy of the Pope. At the court of Rimini, 'recourse to Pagan gods', quite openly, was noted.[7] The Pagan iconography, probably devised by Basinio da Parma and Roberto Valturio, and executed by Agostino di Duccio and others, is expressed in several thematic chapels inspired by 'the most hidden secrets of philosophy'.[8] The Cappella dei Pianeti contains the planetary deities and the signs of the zodiac. The Cappella delle Arti Liberali enshrines Greek divinities, whilst in the Cappella degli Antenati, Jewish and Sibylline forerunners of Christianity are presented. Finally, in the Cappella di Sigismondo, the radiant Sun is thematic, representing the Apollo/Christ concept. It was condemned by Pope Pius II as full of Pagan images, and for this, Malatesta was excommunicated.[9] At Pienza, town improvements by Federico de Montefelto after the year 1455 included a church and a temple. This temple, the Tempietto delle Muse (Chapel of the Muses) reflected the church, providing equal veneration for the Christian and Pagan world-views.

In 1453 the capital of the eastern Roman Empire, Constantinople, fell to the Ottoman Turks, who then placed Greece, the Balkans and the Danube area under Islamic rule. (Internal strife within Christianity had ensured that the Catholics in the west refused to support their Orthodox co-religionists in the east.) Fleeing scholars brought Classical texts to the west, and later on the Ottomans set up a trade in these manuscripts with western scholars. One cardinal is said to have returned from a trip with nine hundred codices. The philosophical thought of the ancient world began to exert an influence on western ethics, with Ciceronian *humanitas*, civilised, humane behaviour, competing with Christian humility as a personal ideal, and the Pagan appreciation of beauty and excellence in the manifest world challenging the Christian contempt for the flesh. Lorenzo de Medici, ruler of Florence, even set up a Platonic Academy with philosophical discussion, art and music. The Renaissance ideal of the gentleman as a cultivated person, skilled in the arts and in letters, grew up in Italy at this time, as a deliberate continuation of the outlook of antiquity. It had nothing to do with Christianity, and it was seen by most people as something independent of and transcending religious affiliation. Hence atheism and humanism were also fruits of the Renaissance, although in antiquity, as we have seen, the corresponding outlooks were understood simply as philosophical refinements of the religion followed more crudely by the masses.

Representations of Classical antiquity referred to the accumulated wisdom of the ancient Pagan world, of which the Renaissance was the heir. Pagan themes appeared in art. Raphael's *The School of Athens* (1508–1511) in the Vatican is a prime example. Images of Pagan gods and goddesses began to reappear in public, especially as bronzes on fountains. Between 1567 and 1570, the doyen of bronze-masters, Giovanni de Bologna, created several fine Pagan deities, including the Hercules fountain at Bologna, Oceanus at the Boboli gardens and a fine Neptune in Florence. Soon, images of Pagan divinities spread outside Italy. An early example is the Hercules fountain in Augsburg made in 1602 by Bologna's disciple Adriaen de Vries. In central Europe, Pagan deities replaced the earlier popular figures of St George as a presiding spirit of fountains. The re-emergence of goddesses and, less emphatically, gods, was universal, in areas both under Catholic and Protestant rule. For example, at the restoration of King Charles II in 1660, the new coinage bore images of Britannia, goddess of Britain, as had not been done since Roman times. Later, the patriotic hymn, *Rule, Britannia*, was written, invoking goddess/nation. Elsewhere, other images of national goddesses emerged. A statue of the goddess of the land, Virtembergia, stood on top of Schloss Solitude, near Stuttgart, built in 1767 as a residence of the rulers of Württemberg.

In addition to their reappearance on a national level, Pagan deities began to adorn the gardens of private palaces and mansions. Some owners even added overtly Pagan temples, which often are ignored by students

*Plate 11.3* Poseidon-fountain, Heidelberg, Germany. © 1993 Nigel Pennick.

of religion. The prime example of this is at Schwetzingen near Worms in Germany. Whenever a Christian chapel was erected by a landowner, then it is assumed to be authentic. Yet comparable Pagan temples are not. Space does not allow an analysis of the literature of this period, yet from it we can be certain that the ancient Pagan spirit of temple-in-landscape was understood and used properly by the landscape gardeners of the period. In his *Ichnographica Rustica* (1718–1742), the gardener Stephen Switzer (*c.*1682–1745) gave the rules for the location of images of the Pagan deities in gardens:

> *Jupiter* and *Mars* should possess the largest Open Centres and Lawns of a grand Design, elevated upon Pedestal Columnial, and other Architectonical Works . . . *Neptune* should possess the Centre of the greatest Body of Water . . . *Venus* ought to be placed among the *Graces, Cupid, &c.* And in all the lesser Centres of a Polygonar Circumscription, it would be proper to place *Apollo* with the *Muses* in the Niches . . . Then *Vulcan* with the *Cyclops* in a Centre of less note, and all the Deities dispers'd in their particular Places and Order.

Often, as at Stuttgart, the divinity was envisioned as guardian of the landscape. An enormous Hercules stands on top of a hill near Kassel, approached by a straight road that serves as the axis for the palace of the Elector, and one of the main streets of the city. The re-emergence of Pagan deities was not confined to those of the Classical pantheon. John Michael Rysbrack carved a set of the seven Saxon deities of the days of the week, commissioned by Lord Cobham in the late 1720s for his gardens at Stowe.

## THE REFORMATION AND ITS EFFECTS

The reform movements within Catholicism which crystallised into the Protestant Reformation in the early sixteenth century brought about a desire for simplicity of ritual and belief which rejected many of the compromises which the Church had made with Pagan practice. The veneration of the Virgin Mary and of the saints, the use of images and of incense, and the marking of holy sites (cf. the Roman *loca sacra* and *loca religiosa*) with crosses and

Iouis fiue Panos Hierogly-
phica repræfentatio.

A Facies rubicunda, caloris vis in Mundo.
B Radiorum cœleftium in fublunària vir-
C Elementa mafculina.                    (tus.
D Poteftas in annû omnefq; reuolutiones.
E Virtute eius omnia fulciuntur.
F Dominium in firmamentùm, feu fixa-
    rum ftellarum fphœràm.
G Terra (elementum fœmin.) hifpida
    plantis, fatis, arboribufque.
H Aquæ & liquoris fons (elem. fœm.) ri-
    gatione fœcundans terram.
I Agri, fegetes, aliaque vegetabilia.
K Harmonia 7. Planetarum.
L Afpera & inæqualia montes indicant.
M Vis fœcunditatiua.
N Stabile fundamentum.
O Vis ventorum, & celeritas in agendo.

*Plate 11.4* The Great God Pan, from Athanasius Kircher. A Renaissance image of Pan as the embodiment of Nature. Nideck Picture Collection.

wayside shrines, disappeared under Protestant influence. Traditional practices such as Maying, carolling, wassailing, and the many Pagan practices incorporated into Christmas celebrations, were also attacked. Under the Puritan rule of the Long Parliament in England and Wales (1642–1653), most of the permanent Maypoles in the towns and villages were destroyed. Not all of these sites and practices were restored when a more tolerant attitude returned towards the end of the seventeenth century.

The Reformation did, however, have one unexpectedly helpful effect on the preservation of Pagan continuity. By insisting on the use of the vernacular language in religious practice, Protestant missionaries preserved languages which had been on the verge of dying out, especially in the Baltic lands, and so unintentionally allowed the preservation of traditional tales and songs, which remained alive as part of the corpus of vernacular usage. These were reclaimed from time to time as part of nationalist movements, and the great nineteenth-century movement of nationalist revival saw them collected and recited by educated people in an effort to arouse a spirit of national identity. If the native languages had not been revivified by Protestant reformers in the sixteenth century, most of the information in their oral traditions would have been lost for ever.

## A FALSE TRAIL: THE GREAT WITCH-HUNT

It has become a commonplace in modern Paganism that the hunting of alleged witches, which became widespread between about 1480 and about 1650, was a deliberate persecution of surviving Pagans and that it claimed some eight or nine million victims. The figure of nine million appears to have been suggested in the 1950s by Cecil Williamson, proprietor of the witchcraft museum on the Isle of Man, who erected a monument to that effect.[10] Modern estimates from careful archival research put the number at a maximum of 100,000 executions,[11] and some estimates are considerably lower.[12] The accused witches were victims of a new belief about a satanic conspiracy to subvert Christendom, prevalent among the intellectuals of the time. When unsophisticated folk accused their neighbours, as they occasionally did, of harmful magic and ill-wishing, the lawyers and clerics were all too ready to step in and transform the proceedings into an investigation into the supposed satanic conspiracy. Confessions and accusations were obtained by torture, and at times scores of people were executed. 'The place of execution looked like a small wood from the number of the stakes', wrote one observer of a trial at Wolfenbüttel in Brunswick in 1590.[13] Yet the trials were unevenly distributed both in time and in location. Communities could go for years without disturbance and then suddenly succumb to a bout of witch mania. Some countries were barely touched by the persecution at all, but others, such as Scotland and Germany, executed thousands of presumably innocent victims. The research so far indicates that few of the accused witches were practising harmful magic and that none of them at all were practising diabolic anti-Christianity.[14] However, in some of the cases in Scandinavia and in the eastern German territories, where magical Pagan religion had continued, such magical practices may well have been the cause of the initial accusations. In Iceland this was certainly the case. The use of runes was defined as witchcraft and made illegal in 1639,[15] and the surviving Icelandic grimoires show a mixture of Pagan and Christian terminologies, used with the classical magical intention of commanding the spirits invoked rather than of becoming the servant of the Devil in the way imagined by the Inquisitorial theorists of the mainland.[16] Cases on the mainland, however, involved accusations of diabolic pact and were generally levelled against innocent people. Only on the fringes of Europe did the Great Witch-hunt attack Pagan magic as such.

As we have already seen, the western Church stepped up its attacks on unorthodox thought by increasing the powers of the Inquisition. Until 1480, everyday magic of the sort we have seen prohibited by the early Christian bishops and the Anglo-Saxon kings, and described in the Norse sagas, was seen as outside the remit of the Inquisition. It was seen as foolishness, not heresy. But in 1480, a papal bull specifically stated that harmful magic, *maleficium* or witchcraft, was now to be seen as heresy and thus to come under the scrutiny of the Inquisition. This was because it was now said to involve a pact with the Devil. The increased practice of learned magic among the intelligentsia, sparked off by texts coming from the eastern Mediterranean via the Arabs in Spain, in Palestine and on the Mediterranean islands, had alerted the attention of the western Church hierarchy to what seemed to be deliberate commerce with demons. The image of magic as a diabolic pact spread down the social scale, until even the simplest peasant curse or baleful glance could be interpreted as an expression of satanic power.[17] The nature of the pact changed, too, in the eyes of the accusers. The Christian ceremonial magicians of the thirteenth century claimed (and were perceived) to be compelling fallen and inferior spirits by the power of their magical art. But by the fifteenth century they were deemed to have sold their souls to the Devil in exchange for material benefits and latterly for none at all: that is, to have sold themselves into slavery.[18] The diabolic witch, as imagined by the inquisitors, had sold herself into the Devil's power for no particular benefit. This may give a clue as to why it was women more than men who were accused of the new-style diabolic conspiracy. Not only are women more often accused (in all communities, worldwide) of spontaneous harmful magic, but in the misogynistic view of the early modern Church, only women would be stupid or weak or naturally slavish enough to give their power away to a malign spirit in exchange for no benefit to themselves. The fact that the Great Witch-hunt was primarily a hunting of women seems not to have been an expression but a result of the misogyny of the time. It was not a deliberate attack on women as such, but an attack on devils, with the assumption that the only human beings stupid enough to be taken in by these enemies of humankind were, naturally, women.

So much for the conclusions of modern research. The modern Pagan myth which is challenged by them stems from the romantic perceptions of the nineteenth century. This is when the arts and crafts movement began, together with the collection of folk-tales, traditional songs and dances, as well as nationalistic political movements fuelled by images of ethnic purity. The educated, newly emancipated middle classes saw the old vernacular ways disappearing around them and romanticised their significance, filled with nostalgia for a certainty (previously seen, pejoratively, as simplicity) which was rapidly fading. For some reason which has not been satisfactorily explained, some commentators saw the indigenous European religion as persisting among those accused of witchcraft three hundred years before. 'The witches' sabbath may be explained as an esoteric form of those pagan fertility rites which survived in Western Europe centuries after the official introduction of Christianity', wrote Arno Runeberg in 1947.[19] Runeberg, like two of the nineteenth-century theorists, in fact came from the north-east of Europe, where, as we have seen, the local religion took a more overtly magical form than elsewhere and was influential long after it had been assimilated into Christianity, relegated to folk-tradition, or reasserted as an aristocratic enthusiasm in the rest of Europe. Karl-Ernst Jarcke, professor of criminal law at the University of Berlin, argued in 1828 that the people accused in a local witch-trial had actually been followers of the old Germanic religion. In 1839, the archivist Franz-Joseph Mone of Baden proposed that the orgiastic features of the alleged witch-cult had in fact been part of an underground religion derived from Dionysiac worship in the Greek colonies on the Black Sea and brought back to Germany by the returning Goths. A version of the theory even reached popular culture. Mendelssohn's choral work *Die Erste Walpurgisnacht* (1832) described a traditional May Eve (30 April) celebration, where the village folk, under attack from local Christians, pretended to be witches in order to frighten their opponents away. And Runeberg, of Helsinki, produced in the twentieth century a wonderfully detailed study of Norse, Finnic and more distant magical religions, arguing that the supposed witch-cult was in fact a mutation of heretical Catharism and indigenous folk-magic. These thinkers drew attention to their regional heritage, but unfortunately failed to demonstrate by reference to contemporary records that any of the people accused had actually taken part in either 'witchcraft' ceremonies or ceremonies of a continuing Pagan religion. As we have seen, modern research tends to argue against these conclusions.

The most famous interpreter of diabolic witchcraft as a Pagan survival was, however, Professor Margaret Murray (1863–1963), an Egyptologist who first became interested in the European witch-trials when she was over sixty. Her conclusions, published in *The Witch Cult in Western Europe* (1921) and *The God of the Witches* (1933), were criticised at the time by archivists such as

C. L'Estrange Ewen, who had actually looked at the evidence of the trials, but it was not until Norman Cohn's definitive study, published in 1975 as *Europe's Inner Demons*, that the soundness of her arguments was generally questioned. Murray had quoted from evidence taken from defendants at the witch-trials, cutting out what she presumably thought was the irrelevant accreta, invented under torture, and leaving in what she thought was the bare bones of truthful evidence, the description of ritual celebrations and feasts presided over by a man known as the Devil. But as Cohn demonstrates, the passages omitted contain fantastic details such as shape-shifting, flying through the air, making rideable horses out of straw and so on, which cast doubt on the truth of anything else claimed in those confessions. Now these are the sort of feats which were and are claimed by sorcerers in shamanic Pagan communities, e.g. the Lapps' 'magic ride to Iceland' on behalf of the Norwegian, Ingimund, and it is quite possible that people who really followed a magical religion might have confessed to such apparent impossibilities and thought they were telling the truth. Arno Runeberg, for example, takes such 'fantasticall detailes' in his stride. Why did Margaret Murray leave them out? The most plausible answer is that she deliberately distorted her evidence.

Why should she have done so? Norman Cohn argues that Murray, together with the other authors mentioned, was driven simply by a deep personal need to believe in the continuation of Pagan religion, or perhaps more in its persecution by representatives of a hated modernity, and so created 'evidence' to prove their case. But in fact, no more evidence was needed to prove the continuation of Pagan customs and attitudes. The work of Sir James Frazer, which influenced Margaret Murray and Arno Runeberg deeply, as well as that of the many other nineteenth-century researchers, had already provided that. What Runeberg wrongly assumed and what Murray seems to have selected her evidence to 'prove', was the existence of a priesthood, a Pagan ministry which actively opposed the official religion of Christianity. And this the alleged witches never were. After the Baltic crusades, there was no organised Pagan resistance to Christianity in the west. What did remain was a continuation of Pagan attitudes and of local objects of veneration, and what arose independently was an affirmation among educated people of ancient Pagan civilisation and, among some, of its presiding deities. The witch-hunt was succeeded by the age of rationality, and during that intellectually secure period, the Pagan priesthoods began to be reinstated.

## THE AGE OF REASON AND THE RE-EMERGENCE OF THE PRIESTHOODS

The witch persecution nevertheless marked a watershed in western European history. It coincided with the Reformation and has been seen as a side-effect of the latter, but perhaps more significantly it coincided with the emergence of rationalism, the freeing of the human spirit from the 'uncanny bonds' of superstition which, so it was thought, had held it in check. The freethinking of the Reformation can itself be seen as an expression of the independence of rational thought. The witch-hunt was seen by rationalist thinkers, probably correctly, as a last outburst of irrationality, both on the part of Protestant-inclined zealots who wanted to abolish the second component of the 'popery-and-superstition' complex, and also of Catholic-inclined ones who wanted to affirm its first component. The ordinary people who habitually accused their neighbours of ill-wishing were simply freed by changes in the law from the swingeing penalties which until the late fifteenth century had threatened accusers who failed to prove their case,[20] and so denunciation was able to proceed unhindered. The persecution died down at the end of the seventeenth century because rational society no longer believed in witchcraft, and many countries passed laws which declared as much.

The rise of the mathematical sciences in the sixteenth and seventeenth centuries led to a new and self-confident belief in humankind's power over Nature. No longer did gamblers have to doff their caps to the caprices of Dame Fortune. They could now calculate their chances through the mathematical calculus of probability. Astronomers could calculate eclipses and planetary positions, ballistics experts could predict the fall of shot, physicists could demonstrate that colour was merely a 'spectre' (i.e. spectrum) caused by the refraction of light. The old belief in a symbolic universe, ordained by divine providence (for the Christians), or expressing the nature of the indwelling divinity (for the Neoplatonists), gave way to a new belief in a meaningless, mechanical universe which was deterministically ruled by

*Plate 11.5* The goddess Luna. A Renaissance drawing of the Roman goddess.

mathematical laws. These produced exact and predictable results which both prayer and magic were unable to match. The universe became less animated, but human self-confidence grew enormously.

These changes were most marked in the old western Empire. In the east, the Muscovite state used these same technical developments when Ivan the Terrible (1533–1584) set his sights on the Baltic coast, claiming for Muscovy the name of the original Kievan state: Russia. In the last years of the seventeenth century, Peter the Great succeeded in extending the Empire to the coast, where he founded a new capital, a centre of culture and commerce, in St Petersburg, near the old Ladoga trading station. The Kievan Russians had in fact been amalgamated into Lithuania-Poland in 1386, but rebelled and joined Moscow in 1648. Their territory became known as the Ukraine, or 'outermost area', in a neat reversal of its historical primacy. In 1795 ethnic Lithuania itself was ceded to Russia, following Estonia and Livonia (1721). The countries whose state religion was Eastern Orthodox did not suffer from the Great Witch-hunt, although there were accusations of simple ill-wishing (without diabolic overtones) in Russia in the eighteenth century, in which ninety-nine people, only one-third of whom were women, were accused.[21] In all of these countries the native languages were encouraged by Protestant reformers, who used them to preach the gospel in the vernacular, and they were later kept alive or even revived under the various colonising empires by nationalistic movements.

In the territory of the South Slavs the Empire of the Ottoman Turks expanded until, in 1683, they were beaten back from the gates of Vienna. In 1699 the Turkish portion of Hungary as well as Transylvania was ceded to the Austrians, and the Ukraine and Podolia to Poland. In 1774 Catherine the Great extended the Russian domain south to the Black Sea, annexing the Crimea. Thereafter, the Ottoman Empire in Europe remained fairly stable until the mid-nineteenth century, when Russia's pan-Slavic policies encouraged insurrections which gradually turned the Balkans from the world of official Islam to the world of official Christianity. Architecture, art and literature drew their inspiration from national folklore traditions, and when Paganism re-emerged in such places as Lithuania it was linked to nationalistic awareness.

In north-west Europe, antiquarian studies of megalithic sites became popular in the late seventeenth century, leading to a new awareness of Paganism among the learned. In 1676, in his *Britannia Antiqua Illustrata*, Aylett Sammes wrote that the Druids believed in 'the Immortality of the Soul, to which they added the Transmigration of it, according to the opinion of Pythagoras' (p. 101). In his *The Description of the Western Islands of Scotland* (1703), Martin Martin wrote of the Orkney stone circles at Stenness and Brodgar as: 'believed to have been Places design'd to offer Sacrifice in time of Pagan Idolatry; and for this reason the People called them the Ancient temples of the Gods' (p. 365). In Germany, Johann G. Keysler wrote *Antiquitates Selectae Septentrionales et Celticae* (Hanover, 1720), describing the remains of ancient Paganism at places in Germany and the Netherlands as well as Britain.

During the eighteenth century, there was a growing awareness of Britain's ancestral heritage, which was seen as Druidic. According to the architect John Wood the Elder (1704–1754), his native Bath was the Metropolitan Seat of the Druids, where Apollo was worshipped. Wood made a close study of megalithic sites, including Stonehenge, whose sacred geometry he reproduced in the Circus at Bath, in order to restore to it its antique Pagan grandeur. In his *Choir Gaure*, published in 1747, he wrote that Stonehenge was 'a temple erected by the British Druids'. In the eighteenth century, Druidic awareness penetrated many areas. A statue of a Druid was erected at the entrance of Penicuik House, Midlothian, Scotland, by Sir James Clerk in 1763. Copper penny tokens issued by the Parys Mine Company on the island of Anglesey in 1787 depicted the head of a Druid surrounded by a garland of oak leaves. It alluded to Anglesey's sacred heritage of the Druidic holy island.[22]

In Wales, there arose a renewed national awareness of the Druidic heritage, resulting in several influential books. The Reverend Henry Rowlands of Anglesey published *Mona Antiqua Restaurata* in 1723. Druidic Paganism was viewed not as harmful, but as a benign awareness of harmony with Nature. For example, in 1733, Pope wrote:

> Nor think in Nature's state they blindly trod;
> The State of Nature was the Reign of God.

The Druid John Toland's *Christianity not Mysterious* denied the necessity for believing in the uniqueness of Judaeo-Christian revelation, and later William Blake wrote: 'The antiquities of every Nation under Heaven is no less sacred than that of the Jews. They are the same thing.'

Druidism became nationally known in 1792, when a Bardic assembly was held in London. In October that year, *The Gentleman's Magazine* reported: 'This being the day on which the autumnal equinox occurred, some Welsh Bards, resident in London, assembled in congress on Primrose Hill, according to ancient usage.' The instigator of this Druidic event was Iolo Morgannwg (Edward Williams). A circle of stones was formed, surrounding the *Maen Gorsedd*, an altar stone, on which lay a sword. Iolo Morgannwg was an inspired mystic whose contributions to Druidism cannot be underestimated. The romantic interpretations of ancient Druidism are no more or less valid than the equivalent mythologies of other hagiographies. Materialist critics of Druidism who criticise Iolo fail to apply the same criteria of criticism to the prophets of other religions, all of whom have worked in more or less similar ways.

During the second half of the eighteenth century, and the beginning of the nineteenth, several significant books were published on Druidism. They include William Cooke's *An Enquiry into the Druidical and Patriarchal Religion* (1754); Edward Davies' *Celtic Researches* (1804), and *The Mythology and Rites of the British Druids* (1809); Jacques Cambry's *Monuments Celtiques* (1805); and Samuel Rush Meyrick and Charles Hamilton Smith's *Costume of the Original Inhabitants of the British Islands* (1815). Druidism found its way into opera, too: Bellini's *Norma*, produced in 1831 at La Scala, Milan, has a Druidic theme, the original set including a backdrop of Stonehenge. It was popular in England for the next few years, eclipsed eventually by a change in musical fashion rather than one in subject matter.

Legendary histories of esoteric movements like Wicca and Freemasonry often claim unbroken continuity from ancient times. Without the documentation, which remains secret or non-existent, it is impossible to verify or refute these claims. However, in 1979, Colin Murray of the Golden Section Order published a document containing research by Michel Raoult on the history of Druidry in the British Isles and France. According to Raoult, English Druids claim their descent from the Mount Haemus Grove of Oxford under the Bard Philip Bryddod, 1245. Whether or not this is genuine, later Druidry is intimately connected with the rise of Freemasonry. In 1670, John Aubrey set up a new Mount Haemus Grove. Later, John Toland, his successor, set up The Ancient Druid Order, which met first in 1717, the year that modern Freemasonry was formalised. In 1781, another group, The Ancient Order of Druids, was set up in London by Henry Hurle as an esoteric society patterned on Masonic lines. In 1833, a split between the mystics and those who wanted a friendly society led to the majority forming The United Ancient Order of Druids, which still flourishes today. The mystical side continued as the Albion Lodge of the Ancient Order of Druids of Oxford, claiming descent from the Mount Haemus Grove. In 1908, Winston Churchill was an initiate of this sect.

Welsh Bardism, from which another strand of Druidism can be traced, is documented from 1176, when the first historical Eisteddfod at Cardigan was attended by Lord Rhys ap Grufydd. In 1594, an unsuccessful Eisteddfod was called, but it was at the end of the eighteenth century that a significant revival occurred, in parallel with developments in England. In 1789, an Eisteddfod was held at Corwen; in 1790, at St Asaph; in 1791, at Llanwrst; and in 1792, at Denbigh. Also in 1792, and more significantly for later developments, Iolo Morgannwg held a Gorsedd of Welsh Bards in London at Primrose Hill on the autumnal equinox. Later Eisteddfodau were sporadic, but at Carmarthen in 1819, Iolo Morgannwg set up his Gorsedd stone circle, integrating his ideas with the traditional Eisteddfod. In 1838, H. de la Villemarque held an Eisteddfod at Abergavenny. The first official Welsh National Eisteddfod was held at Llangollen in 1860, and it has been a central part of Welsh culture since then. The Druids' robes were designed by Sir Hubert Herkomer, RA, and the regalia (sceptre, crown, sword and Hirlas Horn) by Sir Goscombe John. Welsh Druidism of this period was very eclectic, drawing from historical European Paganism, byways of gnosticism and non-European Paganism from the British Empire. At the Eisteddfod at Pontypridd in 1878, the archdruid offered prayers to the Hindu goddess, Kali. The Eisteddfod flourishes today in a rather secularised form. Continental Druidism was strongly influenced by Welsh practice. In 1869, Nicolas Dimmer instituted the United Ancient Order of Druids at Paris, reinstating French Druidism. Thirty years later, M. Le Fustec was invested as a Druid at the Welsh Eisteddfod. In 1900, he proclaimed himself to be the first Grand Druid of Brittany, founding an organisation which still exists.

For many centuries, cremation of the dead was illegal in Britain because it was a Pagan practice. But in 1873, Sir Henry Thompson brought the idea forward from a utilitarian point of view. He was strongly opposed by churchmen. The test-case which altered the legal status was that of the Druid Dr William Price of Llantrisant (1800–1893). He was tried at Cardiff Assizes for cremating his infant son, who died at the age of five months in 1884. He was acquitted and, when he died in 1893, he, too, was cremated in Pagan fashion.[23] Cremation has since become a normal practice in Britain, but it was a Druid who re-established it, on specifically religious grounds.

## ROMANTIC PAGANISM

Parallel with the restoration of Druidism, Classical Paganism underwent a new phase in northern Europe. It was through Thomas Taylor's translation of the *Orphic Hymn to Pan* (1787) that the Romantic poets rediscovered the soul of all things. The Romantic poets developed a nostalgia for lost ages, as in Schiller's *Götter Griechenlands*. In England, they had a mutually shared esteem for Paganism. After the death and destruction of the French Revolution and the Napoleonic Wars came the 'year without a summer' (1816), when famine swept Europe, accompanied by food riots. After the disintegration of the Old Order, the Romantic poets saw Paganism as the only remedy for the 'wrong turnings' of Christianity and industrialisation. In a letter to Thomas Jefferson Hogg (22 January, 1818), Leigh Hunt wrote:

> I hope you paid your devotions as usual to the Religio Loci, and hung up an evergreen. If you all go on so, there will be a hope some day . . . a voice will be heard along the water saying 'The Great God Pan is alive again', – upon which the villagers will leave off starving, and singing profane hymns, and fall to dancing again.[24]

In his letters, Thomas Love Peacock signed himself 'In the name of Pan, yours most sincerely'.[25] In October 1821, Percy Bysshe Shelley wrote to Thomas J. Hogg:

> I am glad to hear that you do not neglect the rites of the true religion.

*Plate 11.6* Woden depicted on a stained-glass window at Cardiff Castle, Wales, mid-nineteenth century. Nigel Pennick.

> Your letter awoke my sleeping devotions, and the same evening I ascended alone the high mountain behind my house, and suspended a garland, and raised a small turf-altar to the mountain-walking Pan.[26]

Later in the nineteenth century, Edward Carpenter (1844–1929) was influential in the Pagan movement. He was a member of several socialist groups, including William Morris' Socialist League and the Fellowship of the New Life, from which came the Fabian Society.[27] Giving up his Anglican ministry in 1874, he promoted neo-Paganism as a return to the essentials of life. In 1883, he set up a self-sufficient community at Millthorpe between Sheffield and Chesterfield. In *Civilisation: Its Cause and Cure* he wrote:

> The meanings of the old religions will come back . . . On the high tops once more gathering he will celebrate with naked dances the glory of the human form and the great processions of the stars, or greet the

bright horn of the young moon which now after a hundred centuries comes back laden with such wondrous associations – all the yearnings and the dreams and the wonderment of the generations of mankind – the worship of Astarte and of Diana, of Isis and the Virgin Mary; once more in sacred groves will he reunite the passion and the delight of human love with his deepest feelings of the sanctity and beauty of Nature; or in the open, standing uncovered to the Sun, will adore the emblem of the everlasting splendour which shines within.[28]

Oscar Wilde echoed the sentiments of Carpenter, when he wrote:

> O goat-foot god of Arcady!
> The modern world hath need of thee!

Other idealistic Nature movements such as the Social Credit Party (which held seats in the Canadian legislature until 1980), and its offshoot the Woodcraft Folk (a young people's movement which is still active today) have their origin in this time. In Germany the *Wandervögel* ('wanderers') expressed an equivalent initiative.

In his *Pagan Papers* (1904), Kenneth Grahame called himself one of the 'faithful pagans' continuing the Old Religion: 'one's blood danced to imagined pipings of Pan from happy fields far distant'. Chapter 7 of *The Wind in the Willows*, titled 'The Piper At the Gates of Dawn', describes a vision of the Great God Pan. Grahame's biographer, Peter Green, called this vision 'the supreme example of nineteenth-century neo-pagan mysticism',[29] possibly the result of an intense visionary experience by Grahame.[30] At this time in this intellectual milieu, there was a feeling that a New Religion was about to be created: 'A religion so splendid and all-embracing that the hierarchy to which it will give birth, uniting within itself the artist and the priest, will supplant and utterly destroy our present commercial age'.[31] This was none other than 'the creative Pagan acceptance of life' promoted by playwright Eugene O'Neill.[32]

During the nineteenth century, the Germanic legends were collected by the Grimm brothers, and crafted into a powerful mythos by Richard Wagner. As Wagner himself wrote in his essay, 'What is German?': 'In rugged forests, in the long winter, in the warmth of the fire upon the hearth of his castle-chamber towering aloft into the air, he indulges long in the memories of his forefathers, he transmutes his home-bred myths of the gods in legends manifold and inexhaustible.' Wagner's commitment to building a national identity for the Germans through native myth was sincere, and another constant theme in his art was the tension between the Christian asceticism which he inherited and the Pagan affirmation of life to which as an artist he was committed. The reconciliation between 'Parnassus and Paradise' in the concluding Prize Song of *The Mastersingers* is one of the happier moments in this search. Wagner's commitment to recreating the spiritual-emotional

*Plate 11.7* The Walhalla at Regensburg, Bavaria, Germany. A temple of national achievement, in the style of Classical Paganism. Modern 'halls of fame' are a direct continuation of the ancient worship of heroes. 1851 print. Nideck Picture Collection.

catharsis of Greek tragedy in his temple of music drama at Bayreuth was encouraged and partly shaped by his friend, the classicist Friedrich Nietzsche. Nietzsche split away from Wagner, however, when the latter also encompassed the Christian mythos in his final music drama, *Parsifal.*

Antiquarian study of the runes, especially in German-speaking countries, led to a reawakening of runic use, including their spiritual dimension. The runic inscription carved by William Kermode, the Manx antiquarian, on the tombstone of his family dog, is part of the re-emerging awareness.[33] On a more mystical level, the pan-Germanic mystic Guido von List dedicated himself to the service of Wotan and in 1904 devised a new system of runes based on the scriptural authority of the rune-song in the Eddic lay, *Hávamál.* In Germany, mystical elements from the northern tradition were used in architecture, most notably by Bernhard Hoetger (1874–1949). Hoetger respected the *genius loci* of the places where he built. In 1925, he used north German Pagan elements in the Worpswede Café and at the Große Kunstschau held at Worpswede in 1927. His most important work was the Böttcherstrasse development in Bremen (1923–1931), patronised by Ludwig Roselius. Called the Haus Atlantis, it was a 'high-tech' building, the first to use rolled steel in its construction. One façade had a sculpture of Odin on the tree, amid a wheel of runes. Elsewhere were northern tradition trees of life, solar imagery and a Hall of Heaven, reflecting Valhalla. Sadly, although the street was reconstructed in the 1950s after war damage, the image of Odin was the only part left out of the restoration.

In Britain, James Frazer (1854–1941), a Fellow of Trinity College, Cambridge, embarked on a programme of demonstrating that the Christian myth of the dying and resurrected god was simply one example of a universal Pagan story: the dying and reborn Nature god as exemplified in the Babylonian myth of Tammuz. *The Golden Bough*, published in two editions between 1890 and 1915, was the massively influential result of this search. It was not, in fact, successful in its search for a universal dying-and-resurrected god, but it documented a wealth of surviving folklore practices which in Pagan times would have been sanctified by a deity, it provided a programme of interpretation, of looking for the hidden religious significance of such practices, and it inspired both a programme of research (the 'Cambridge School' of anthropology) and a popular following which treated the former's hypotheses as proven.

## NEO-PAGANISM

The term 'neo-Paganism' is often applied to all contemporary Pagan practitioners, especially by American commentators. But it was applied first, in a rather pejorative way, to the artists of the Pre-Raphaelite movement. Later, there was actually a group that called itself the Neo-Pagans. Founded in Cambridge in 1908, it included the artist Gwen Raverat and the poet Rupert Brooke. But the Neo-Pagans seem to have had no real spiritual direction. The members went on long country walks and slept under canvas, but they made no serious attempt to restore the Pagan religion. After 1911, Francis Cornford continued neo-Paganism in Cambridge, but, by the 1920s, it had faded away.

Cornford was, however, one of the 'Cambridge School', a disciple of Jane Ellen Harrison (1850–1928), whose programme of demonstrating the 'primitive' substrate of Olympian religion, the folk-practices underlying the sophisticated art and rationality of Greek civilisation, showed how an elaborate intellectual structure could develop out of vernacular practice. She described this process as 'purging religion of fear'. She had a particular interest in Orphic mysticism, which she saw as the purification and consummation of the earlier, bloodthirsty rites of Dionysos. The sacramental idea of the higher Mystery religions such as Orphism, whereby the worshipper for a short time became the deity as he or she was shamanistically possessed by the latter, was in her opinion an ennobling influence on the human race. Her original inspirer was Sir James Frazer, and some of her work (e.g. *Themis*) and that of her followers is vitiated by an insistence on the universality of the dying-and-resurrected god. Other parts of her work, however, demonstrate the actual path of development between extremely primitive rites and the extremely sophisticated philosophies of the Mystery religions.

The search for a Frazerian-style fertility religion, if possible with signs of an 'esoteric core', led not only to the 'Cambridge School' of anthropology, but also to other initiatives which flourished in the early twentieth century.

216

*Plate 11.8* Hermes, patron of trade. Stone carving and shrine by Hildo Krop, on the Wendingen-style Schipvaarthuis, Amsterdam, 1911. ©1968 Nigel Pennick.

The theory of the Egyptologist Margaret Murray has already been criticised. It was, however, accepted by many scholars outside the narrow field of Reformation studies until the 1970s. Hence the modern 'witches' who emerged in Britain after the repeal of the Witchcraft Act in 1951 were strongly influenced by it. They saw themselves as well-meaning rustic Pagans, following the inner Mysteries of a simple Nature religion which had been cruelly distorted by the black propaganda of the Church. In 1921 Jessie Weston, a specialist in Romance literature at the University of Paris, published an influential study of the Grail romances, claiming that they recorded a higher Mystery initiation which used the symbolism of the old Celtic fertility religion as it was still dimly remembered in Europe at the time. Weston relied heavily on inside information about ritual and the esoteric interpretation of ancient mythology from modern ceremonial magic (the Order of the Golden Dawn, of which her informant was a member, had been founded in 1888), also on the Orphic and Gnostic fragments which were just then being collated by scholars. Clearly, at that point in the twentieth century, some civilised westerners were looking for an esoteric religion which would both exalt them spiritually and ground them in vernacular peasant practice. One of the schools which fulfilled those criteria was Wicca.

Wicca, which emerged in 1951 after the repeal of the last Witchcraft Act

217

in Britain, took its early self-image from Margaret Murray's interpretation of the north European medieval tradition as rendered by the religion's founder, Gerald Gardner, in his second novel *High Magic's Aid* (1948). It was leavened by an admixture of Classical Greek religion, particularly in the importance it placed on the Goddess, the female principle of divinity, who was modelled initially on the Greek goddess Aphrodite as described in Gardner's first novel, *A Goddess Arrives* (1941). This interpretation was perhaps derived from the description of the goddess Isis as given in Apuleius' *Golden Ass*, and was apparently influenced by a visionary experience of Gardner's own.[34] Later hands added more Classical touches. Part of an ode by Pindar is quoted to reveal the hidden nature of humanity, which initiation reveals. A Hellenised version of Ishtar's descent to the Underworld is a regular part of some later initiation rites; and a Sumerian hymn is used to pray for the return of the crops in spring. The hidden hand of Sir James Frazer has shaped this modern reinterpretation of ancient myth.

## REAFFIRMATION OF THE GERMANIC DEITIES

It is often written that Hitler's regime in Germany (1933–1945) was Pagan in inspiration, but this is untrue. Hitler's rise to power came when the Catholic party supported the Nazis in the Reichstag in 1933, enabling Nazi seizure of power. Many churchmen of both Protestant and Catholic persuasion were committed supporters of the Nazi regime. The belief that it was Pagan in outlook comes from propaganda during the Second World War. As anti-German propaganda, the occultist Lewis Spence wrote:

> The ancient faith of Germany and Scandinavia, popularly known as 'the religion of Odin and Thor', has been the subject of many a literary encomium. To myself, as a student of Folklore and Mythology, it makes an appeal no more gracious or stimulating than any other religion of the lower cultus, and very much less so than those even of Polynesia or old Peru.
>
> It is, indeed, only the fact that it is being resuscitated by extreme Nazi fanatics which makes it important at all, and, even so, it is worthy of notice only in a temporary sense, for with the downfall of Hitler and his caucus it will go the way of all artificially revived heterodoxies.[35]

Himmler and Hess, two 'extreme Nazi fanatics', seem to have been active followers of an Ariosophical mysticism, promoting the future rule of the super-race. But Hitler himself said, in 1941: 'It seems to me that nothing would be more foolish than to re-establish the worship of Wotan. Our old mythology ceased to be viable when Christianity implanted itself.'[36]

Spence wrongly connected National Socialist ritual, derived from Prussian and Austrian military custom, with Paganism, as 'The Nazi Pagan Church'. Recent research by John Yeowell[37] has shown that, far from being influential in Nazi Germany, Pagans were persecuted. Leading Pagans were harassed or arrested by the Nazi regime. For example, in 1936, the noted runemaster Friedrich Bernhard Marby was arrested and spent the next nine years in concentration camps. He was not alone. In 1941, on orders from Heinrich Himmler, many Pagan and esoteric groups were banned (including the followers of Rudolf Steiner, the Ariosophists and followers of the religion of Wotan). Like other victims of Hitlerism, many Pagans subsequently died in concentration camps.

Around 1930, one of the earliest Odinist books in the English language, *The Call of Our Ancient Nordic Religion*, by the Australian Tasman Forth (A.R. Mills), was published in the United States by the League of Cultural Dynamics.[38] In Iceland the indigenous religion, or rather, that imported to the uninhabited land by Norse settlers in the tenth century, has always been known from literature. The sagas have always been read as part of the Icelandic literary heritage. In 1973, Ásatrú ('allegiance to the Æsir') was officially recognised as an established religion with the right to conduct, for example, legally binding weddings and child namings. Its members include high-ranking business people and diplomats, unusually for a religion which had been revived by enthusiasts only a few years before.[39] In Great Britain the Odinist Committee was founded in 1973, becoming the Odinic Rite in 1980. In 1988, it was registered as a religious charity with the British Charity Commissioners. Previous to this registration, it was considered generally by legal opinion that British law allowed only monotheistic beliefs to gain charitable status under the rubric of promotion of religion. Thus the Odinic Rite became, in its own words, 'the first heathen polytheistic body to be accorded recognition'.[40] It was followed in 1989 by the Odinshof, another Ásatrú organisation.

## THE PRESENT DAY

At the end of the twentieth century, then, the indigenous religions of Europe, Nature-venerating, polytheistic and recognising deities of both genders, have re-emerged and are being reintegrated into the modern world. Some rely directly on surviving folk-practice, as in the Baltic countries; further west, the Germanic religions seek to adapt the myths recorded in the Viking Age for modern use. Celtic Druidry was influenced from the time of its re-emergence by Pythagorean (Masonic) and later Tibetan (Theosophical) traditions from oriental Paganism; and the latest form of resurgent Paganism, Wicca, derives its philosophy from the programme of the Cambridge School of anthropology as well as from the Goddess-venerating inspiration of its founder. A more broadly based, forward-looking Paganism has sprung from Wicca, dedicated to reaffirming what are seen as feminine values, embodied in the figure of an (often unnamed) Great Goddess, and the sanctity of the Earth, which is seen as being destroyed by unbridled technology. A nature-god, an image of unspoiled masculinity, is usually taken as the partner of the goddess in this more loosely defined pantheon, and both of these figures are seen as presiding over the surviving folk-rituals which we have described in the earlier chapters. Other goddesses and gods are seen as 'aspects' of these two. Their interaction is seen as offering an image of equal and complementary polarity rather than one of hierarchy and domination. This kind of Paganism looks ahead, offering a new philosophy, more strongly than it looks to its roots in the past.

It remains to be seen whether the various branches of re-emergent Paganism become a significant religious influence in the world of the future. Paganism is a possible religious philosophy for a pluralistic, multicultural society, but we are not concerned to debate its usefulness here. What we have attempted to do in the present volume is to show the extent of the modern resurgence's continuity with the Paganism of earlier ages. A new growth needs roots as well as blossoms, and we hope to have cut away some of the undergrowth which has entangled the current rejuvenation of an old and honourable stock.

# NOTES

## 1 INTRODUCTION: PAGANISM OLD AND NEW

1 Chuvin (1990), p. 17.
2 D. H. Lawrence, letter to Frederick Carter, 1 October 1929, from the *Collected Letters of D. H. Lawrence*, intro. and edited by Harry Moore, London: Heinemann (1962), p. 1205. © 1962 by Angelo Ravagli and C. Montague Weekley, Executors of the Estate of Frieda Lawrence Ravagli.
3 Mookerjee (1988), pp. 47, 71.

## 2 THE GREEKS AND THE EASTERN MEDITERRANEAN

1 There are accounts in several ancient sources, including *Odyssey* XIX.172 ff.; *Iliad* XVIII.591; Ovid, *Metamorphoses* VII.159.
2 See Burkert (1985), Introduction.
3 Patai (1967), ch. 1.
4 Burkert (1985), p. 89.
5 Ibid., pp. 25–26.
6 See, e.g., *Cambridge Ancient History*, 3rd edn, vol. II, pt 2 (1975), p. 161.
7 Burkert (1985), p. 15.
8 Ibid., pp. 136–139.
9 Harrison (1906), ch. 2.
10 See *Cambridge Ancient History*, 3rd edn, vol. II, pt 2 (1975), ch. xxii, a, iii(a), p. 172.
11 Burkert (1985), pp. 63–64.
12 Athenaeus IX.78.
13 Details of practices in Rajasthan can be found in Kothari (1982). See also Harrison (1903), chs 1 and 2, and Burkert (1985), pt II, on Olympian altars, earth-god escharas and underworld megaras.
14 Harrison (1903), pp. 16ff.
15 Porphyry, *De Abst.* II.56.
16 Burkert (1985), p. 73.
17 See the extensive investigation of this claim in Lane Fox (1986).
18 Herodotus II.54–58.
19 Pausanius X.12.10; Strabo VII.329; Aristeides, *Or.* XLV.11.
20 Plato, cited without source in W.R. Lethaby (1969, 1892), p. 79.
21 Bötticher (1856), p. 486.
22 Rutkowski (1986), p. 101.
23 Bötticher (1856), p. 14.
24 Hersey (1988).
25 Ibid.

26 Burkert (1979), p. 40.
27 Kothari (1982).
28 Boardman *et al.* (1991), p. 336.

## 3 ROME AND THE WESTERN MEDITERRANEAN

1 Accounts of Etruscan society can be found in Scullard (1967), Keller (1975) and Ogilvie (1976).
2 Zosimus, *Historia Nova* V.41.
3 Cicero, *De Divinatione*, XXIII.50.
4 Scullard (1967), p. 228.
5 Accounts are given in Santillana and Dechend (1969, 1977), Jones (1989).
6 *De Lingua Latina*, V.46.
7 *De Die Natali*, paraphrasing a lost work of Varro.
8 *Life of Romulus* XI.
9 Boardman *et al.* (1991), p. 400.
10 Warde-Fowler (1911), lecture VI, pp. 118ff.
11 Laing (1931), p. 16.
12 Trede (1901), vol. II, p. 210.
13 *Harusp. Resp.* 19.
14 Warde-Fowler (1911), p. 237.
15 *De agri cultura* 137.
16 See Palmer (1974), ch. 1.
17 C. Bailey in *Cambridge Ancient History*, 2nd edn, vol. VIII, ch. xiv (1970), p. 446.
18 Rose (1948), p. 77.
19 *De Russorum, Muscovitorum et Tartarorum Religione, Sacrificiis, Nuptiarum, Funerum ritu* (1582).
20 The translation is essentially Frazer's (Loeb, 1931). We have modified a few words.
21 Rose (1948), p. 51.
22 Lydus, *De Mensibus* III.22.
23 Cf. the *Fasti* of Fulvius Nobilior, *c.*189 BCE.
24 See Warde-Fowler (1911), ch. XII.
25 Accounts of the expansion of Rome can be found in the *Cambridge Ancient History*, 2nd edn, vols VII (1969) and VIII (1970), and in condensed form in Boardman *et al.* (1991), chs 16–18.
26 Rose (1948), pp. 120–121.
27 *Tusc. Disp.* I.16.36ff.

## 4 THE ROMAN EMPIRE

1 A detailed account of Octavian's influence can be found in Syme (1939, 1971).
2 Wissowa (1912), App. II.
3 Warde-Fowler (1911), pp. 439–447.
4 Baring and Cashford (1993), p. 270.
5 Rose (1948), pp. 134–135; Wissowa (1912), p. 356.
6 Wissowa (1912), p. 353.
7 See Wissowa (1912), § 59; Cumont (1910).
8 These six points are taken from the Introduction to Lane Fox (1986).
9 See Lane Fox (1986) for a detailed account of their persistence.

10 Aurelian, *Historia Augusta* 25.
11 Cyprian, *De Lapsis*, 7–9.
12 *Codex Gregorianus*, XV.13.1, quoted in Smith (1976), p. 26.
13 Ibid.
14 Lactantius, *De Mortibus Persecutorum* 46.
15 Quoted in Smith (1976), p. 48. The details of how accounts of Constantine's conversion developed are taken from Holland Smith's version, as are many details in what follows.
16 Frend (1984), p. 554.
17 Smith (1976), p. 99, citing Socrates, *Ecclesiastical History*, II.47.
18 Gregory of Nazianus, *Invective against Julian* I.58.61.
19 Sozomen, *Ecclesiastical History*, VII.15, quoted in Trombley (1993), pp. 126–127.
20 E.g. Eunapius, *Lives of the Philosophers*, pp. 475–476, Claudius Claudianus, *De Bello Gothico*, pp. 173ff., *De Raptu Proserpine* I.1ff., quoted in Smith (1976), pp. 189–190.
21 Smith (1976), p. 229.
22 Ibid, pp. 321–323.
23 Laing (1931), p. 217.
24 Ibid, p. 93.
25 Duchesne (1904), p. 288.
26 E.g. Council of Autun, ch. ix; Statutes of Boniface, xxi.
27 Nelli (1963), pp. 29–30.
28 Tille (1899), p. 120.
29 Wallace-Hadrill (1952), p. 41.
30 Petrie (1912), p. 112.
31 Salway (1981), p. 736.
32 J.C. Robertson (1874–1875), vol. IV, p. 118.

## 5 THE CELTIC WORLD

1 See any general account of Celtic history, such as Cunliffe (1992).
2 Strabo, IV.4.1–2.
3 Lucan, I.453–454; H. Usener, *Scholia in Lucanem*, Leipzig, 1869, p. 33.
4 Dio Cassius LXII.6.7.
5 Strabo, XII.5.1.
6 Tacitus, *Annales* XIV.30.
7 *Revue Archéologique*, vol. 2, 1959, p. 55.
8 *De Bello Gallico* VI.16.
9 Strabo IV.4.5.
10 Suetonius, *Divus Claudius* XXV.5; Pliny, *N.H.* XXX.4.
11 E.g. Tacitus, *Annales* XIV.30.
12 Strabo IV.4.6.
13 Ross (1974), p. 267.
14 Scholl (1929).
15 M. Green (1986), pp.78–79.
16 Herodian VIII.3.8.
17 *De Bello Gallico* VII.18.
18 M. Green (1986), p. 79.
19 M. Green (1991), pp. 126–128.
20 Campbell (1890), vol. 2, p. 373.
21 Kaul *et al.* (1991), *passim*.
22 Reinach, Salomon, *Cultes, Mythes et Religion*, quoted in Anwyl (1906), pp. 24–25.

23 Powell (1980), p. 148.
24 Kinsella, Thomas (ed.), *The Tain*, London, Oxford Paperbacks, 1970, p. 27.
25 Binchy (1959).
26 Kendrick (1927), pp. 116–119.
27 Dinan, W., *Monumenta Historica Celtica*, London, David Nutt, 1911.
28 Strabo, III.1.4.
29 Ibid. II.15.
30 Quoted in Smith (1976), p. 242.
31 *Agricola* 21.
32 Ibid. 16.
33 Dio Cassius LXXII.2.
34 Tacitus, *Hist.* IV. 54.
35 Ross (1986a), p. 116.
36 *Logoi* VIII.8.

# 6   THE LATER CELTS

1 Salway (1981), chs 10, 11.
2 *Inscriptions from Roman Britain*, London Association of Classical Teachers Original Records no. 4, ed. M.C. Greenstock, London, LACT Publications, 1972, 1987, p. 129.
3 Canon Mahé, 'Essai', pp. 333–334, quotation from *Histoire du Maine* I.17, cited in Evans-Wentz (1911), p. 435.
4 Nance (1935), pp. 190–211.
5 Gildas (1938), p. 152.
6 Wallace-Hadrill (1967), p. 69.
7 McCrickard (1986), p. 27.
8 Jocelin MS ch. 23, p. 227, in Pinkerton, *Lives of the Scottish Saints*, vol. ii, 1889, pp. 1–96.
9 Skene (1876), p. 156.
10 Nennius, *Genealogy* X.
11 Four Books of Wales II.455.
12 Baring-Gould and Fisher (1907–1914), vol. II, p. 237.
13 Dr Ellis Prys, Thomas Cromwell's Commissary-General for the Diocese of St Asaph, letter dated 6 April, 1538, in Baring-Gould and Fisher (1907–1914), vol. I, p. 333.
14 Leland, *Collecteana*, cited in Baring-Gould and Fisher (1907–1914), vol. I, p. 217.
15 Wedeck (1975), p. 157.
16 The Reverend T.M. Morgan, cited in Evans-Wentz (1911), p. 390.
17 Baring-Gould and Fisher (1907–1914), vol. I, p. 164.
18 Ibid., p. 165.
19 Ibid., vol. III, p. 169.
20 Dixon (1886), App. F.
21 Hadingham (1976), p. 183.
22 Walker (1883), p. 186.
23 Kermode and Herdmans (1914).
24 Reverend F.J. Lynch, cited in Evans-Wentz (1911), p. 79.
25 Mitchell (1862), pp. 6, 14.
26 Reeves (1861).
27 Mitchell (1862), p. 253.
28 Dixon (1886), p. 411.

29 *A Tour in Scotland and Voyage to the Hebrides, 1772–4*, pt II, p. 330.
30 Dixon (1886), p. 157.
31 Rodd (1892), pp. 165, 176, cited in E.S. Hartland, 'Pin wells and rag bushes', *Folk-Lore*, vol. 4, 1893, pp. 457–458.
32 Hartland, 'Pin wells and rag bushes', p. 458.
33 Ibid., p. 452.
34 Ibid.
35 Bord and Bord (1985), p. 66.
36 Baring-Gould and Fisher (1907–1914), vol. II, p. 440.
37 Rhys, J., 'Holy wells in Wales', *Folk Lore*, vol. 4, 1893, p. 74.
38 Walker (1883), p. 207.
39 Bord and Bord, p. 119.
40 O'Connor, *Ordnance Survey Letters*, p. 368, cited in Bord and Bord (1985), p. 39.
41 Evans-Wentz (1911), p. 118.
42 Ibid., pp. 92–93; authors' personal observation.
43 Henderson (1910), p. 101.
44 Evans-Wentz (1911), p. 200.
45 Ibid., p. 93.
46 MacNeill (1962), pp. 223–224.
47 Ibid., p. 68.
48 Ibid.

# 7  THE GERMANIC PEOPLES

1 E.g. Davidson (1987).
2 Schutz (1983), pp. 135–136, and *Cambridge Ancient History*, vol. IX (1966), ch. III, *Cambridge Medieval History*, vol. I (1967), ch. vii.
3 See Tacitus, *Germania* 6, for the simple weaponry of the early Germans.
4 Thompson (1966), p. 29.
5 Tacitus, *Germania* 40, and n. 5 in Loeb edition.
6 Ibid. 10.1–3.
7 Ibid. 7.2.
8 Statius, *Silvae* I.iv.89.
9 Rosenberg (1988), p. 51.
10 '*notae*': *Germania* 10.1–3.
11 '*ut minor et potestatem numinis prae se ferens*': *Germania* 39.3.
12 *Historiae Contra Paganos* V.16.4.
13 *De Bello Gallico* VI.
14 Ammianus Marcellinus XXXI.2, quoted in Diesner (1978), p. 71.
15 *Landnámabók* 2.12.
16 Magnússon (1901), pp. 348ff.
17 Buck, *Cartularium Saxonicum* 603.
18 Gamell, David, 'Rösaring and the Viking Age cult road', *Archaeology and Environment*, vol. 4, 1985, pp.171–185, University of Umea, Sweden.
19 Marstrander, C., 'Thor en Irlande', *Revue Celtique*, vol. 36, 1915–1916, p. 241.
20 Wilson and Klindt-Jensen (1966), pp. 135–136.
21 Tille (1899), p. 2; see also Chaney (1970), pp. 57ff. Translations of Bede and the *Heimskringla* in what follows are from Tille.
22 Tille (1899), p. 45.
23 Walter of Henley, *Husbandry*, ed. E. Lamond, London, 1890, p. 97.
24 Cf. Council of Cloveshou, 747, can. xvi.

25 Authors' personal observation.
26 Tille (1899), p. 194.
27 Bede, *De Mensibus Anglorum.*
28 Jamieson, J., *An Etymological Dictionary of the Scottish Language*, Yule, no. VII, 1879, Paisley, Gardner.
29 Goulstone (1985), p. 7.
30 J.C. Robertson (1874–1875), vol. III, p. 112.
31 Boretius, *Capitularia Regum Francorum* I.59.
32 J.C. Robertson (1874–1875), vol. III, p. 114.
33 Chaney (1970).
34 Ibid., pp. 25–28.
35 Wolfram (1988), p. 210.
36 St Bernard, *Vita Sancti Malachiae* 8.16, quoted in Bartlett (1993), p. 22.
37 Bede, *Hist. Eccl.* II.15.
38 J.C. Robertson (1874–1875), vol. III, p. 64.
39 Ibid., vol. III, p. 66.
40 *Conc. Germ*, I, c. 5; *Conc. Liptin*, c. 4; *Conc. Suession*, c. 6, cited in J.C. Robertson (1874–1875), vol. III, p. 72.
41 Zach., Ep. 10, col. 940, cited in J.C. Robertson (1874–1875), vol. III, p. 80.
42 G.R. Owen (1981), p.165.
43 J.C. Robertson (1874–1875), 330–331.
44 *Landnámabók* 95, 97.
45 Brent (1975), p. 63.
46 Stenton (1971), p. 586.
47 *Saga of Håkon the Good*, ch. 19.
48 Ibid., ch. 32.
49 *Saga of Olaf Tryggvason*, ch. 59; *Saga of St Olaf, Heimskringla*, ch. 113ff.
50 Strömbäck (1975), pp. 15, 31.
51 Quoted by Adolf Schück, *Den äldre medertiden*, Sveriges historia genom tiderna, vol. I, p. 169.
52 Reuter (1987), p. 8.

## 8   LATE GERMANIC RELIGION

1 Quoted in G.R. Owen (1981), p. 101.
2 Keysler (1720), p. 339.
3 Johnson (1912), p. 437.
4 Ibid., p. 438.
5 Ibid.
6 Ibid., p. 435.
7 Sepp (1890), p. 267.
8 Schwebel (1887), p. 117.
9 Bächtold-Stäubli (1927–1942), vol. VI, p. 1672.
10 Ibid., vol. V, p. 1673.
11 Kemble (1876), vol. II, p. 429.
12 Bächtold-Stäubli (1927–1942), vol. V, p. 1673.
13 *Notes & Queries*, 1st ser., vol. V, p. 274.
14 Ibid., 6th ser., vol. I, p. 424.
15 Gomme (1883), pp. 34–37.
16 Evans (1966), p. 198.
17 Cited in Porter (1969), p. 181.
18 Sepp (1890), pp. 165–166; Bächtold-Stäubli (1927–1942), vol. VI, p. 1672.

19 Evans (1966), p. 200.
20 G.R. Owen (1981), pp. 43–45.
21 Johannessen (1974), p. 130.
22 Anwyl (1906), p. 34.
23 Megaw and Megaw (1989), p. 33.
24 Tacitus, *Germania* 3.
25 Davidson (1964), pp. 79, 86–89.
26 Reuter (1934), vol. II, ch. v, p. 1.
27 H.M. Chadwick (1900), pp. 268–300.
28 *Grágás*, K 84. See Johannessen (1974), p. 59, for commentary.
29 Morris and Magnússon (1891), pp. xxviii–xlii.
30 *Landnámabók* 110.
31 The following quotations are taken from the translation by Hermann Pálsson and Paul Edwards, London, Hogarth Press, 1978.
32 Picardt (1660).
33 *Landnámabók* 289.
34 Tacitus, *Germania* 3.
35 Tacitus, *Annales* XIV.30.
36 Quoted in Wallace-Hadrill (1967), p. 57.
37 Brent (1975), p. 38.
38 *Flateyjarbók*, 1.63.
39 *Atlamál*, 91, 96.
40 Hallowell (1926), p. 2.
41 For example, see Nioradze (1925), p. 40, and Hallowell (1926), p. 2.
42 Danielli (1945).
43 Davidson (1964), p. 99.
44 Cramp (1957).
45 Beck (1965).
46 Text in Thorpe (1840), vol. II, pp. 32–33.
47 Text in Thorpe (1840), vol. II, p. 190.
48 Text and translation in Thorpe (1840), vol. II, p. 249.
49 Text and translation in Thorpe (1840), vol. I, p. 379.
50 Borchardt (1971), p. 282.
51 Herrmann (1929), p. 66.
52 *Thuringian Chronicle*, quoted by Baring-Gould (1967), p. 211.
53 Thonger (1966), pp. 15–18.
54 Information from Abbots Bromley Horn Dancers, 1987.
55 Grimm (1880–1888), vol. III, p. 2.
56 Brewster, Sir David, *Edinburgh Encyclopedia*, vol. XVI, Edinburgh, n.d., p. 5.
57 Hadingham (1976), p. 183.
58 Ibid.
59 C.G. Jung (1963), pp. 344–345.
60 Reuter (1934), p. 80.
61 Rochholz (1870), pp. 16, 18, 100.
62 Stober (1892), vol. II, p. 283.
63 Lohmeyer (1920), p. 21.
64 Heyl (1897), Nr. 52, p. 236; Graber (1912), Nr. 58, p. 50.
65 Montelius, Oscar, 'The Sun-god's axe and Thor's hammer', *Folk-Lore*, vol. XXI, 1910, pp. 60–78.
66 Hamkens, Freerk Haye, 'Heidnische Bilder im Dome zu Schleswig', *Germanien*, June, 1938, pp. 177–181.
67 Rancken, A.W., 'Kalkmåningarna i Sibbo gamla kyrka', *Finskt Museum*, vol. 42, 1935, p. 29.

68 Cavallius (1863), vol. 1, p. 230.
69 Laing (1931), pp. 247–248, citing Leroy-Brühl, *La Religion dans l'Empire des Tsars*, p. 113.
70 Borchardt (1971), p. 117.
71 *Landnámabók* 3.12.
72 Kålund (1907); Flowers (1989), p. 34.
73 Moltke (1984), p. 493.
74 Grimm (1880–1888), vol. II, p. 653; Bächtold-Stäubli (1927–1942), vol. III, p. 1653.
75 Bächtold-Stäubli (1927–1942), vol. III, p. 1654.

## 9   THE BALTIC LANDS

1 Ptolemy, *Geography* III.5.
2 Noonan, Thomas S., in Ziedonis *et al.* (1974), pp. 13–21.
3 Johannes Magnus IV.4.
4 Ibid. IV.5.
5 Ibid. V.2.
6 Ibid. VI.22.
7 *Gesta Hammaburgensis* II.30.
8 Saks (1981), p.41.
9 *Heimskringla* I.6.
10 Henry of Livonia 7.1; 14.1–5; Saxo Grammaticus XIV.40.3.
11 Bartlett (1993), pp. 303–304.
12 Quoted in Fisher (1936), pp. 203–205.
13 J.C. Robertson (1874–1875), vol. IV, p. 90.
14 Tacitus, *Germania* 39.
15 Saxo Grammaticus, 484–485.
16 Schuchhardt (1926), *passim.*
17 Christiansen (1980), p. 31.
18 Albrecht (1928), pp. 45–56, fig. 6.
19 Accounts of the Wends are included in: Saxo Grammaticus; Vyncke (1968), vol. I, pp. 321ff.; Davidson (1981), p. 123; and Pettazzoni (1954), pp. 151–163.
20 Christiansen (1980), p. 32.
21 Neal Ascherson in the *Independent on Sunday*, 19 September, 1993.
22 Cf. Saks (1981).
23 E.g. Adam of Bremen, *Gesta Hammaburgensis* IV.23: 'the land which is called Semland, touching Russia and Polanis, but inhabited by the Sembi or Pruzzi'; Chronicle of Nestor translated by A.L.V. Schlözer, 1802, p. 55, cited in Saks (1981), pp. 25–26: 'Prus – this nation for a long time known under the name Aesty, struck dead holy Adalbert'.
24 Ptolemy, *Geography* III. 5.21.
25 Saks (1981), ch. 1, *passim.*
26 Carston (1954), p. 5.
27 Prutz, H. *Preußische Geschichte*, vol. I, Berlin, 1900, p. 40.
28 Bartlett (1993), p. 296.
29 Ibid., p. 312; Christiansen (1980), p. 136.
30 Quoted in Christiansen (1980), p. 137.
31 Zaprudnik, J., in Ziedonis *et al.* (1974).
32 Jurgela (1948), p. 41.
33 See Wright, Caroline, 'Pagans in Lithuania', *The Wiccan*, no. 101; 'A Special Correspondent', 'Old Lithuanian Faith revived', *The Wiccan*, no. 109; also authors' personal communications from Lithuania.

34 Jurgela (1948), pp. 40–41.
35 E.g. Christiansen (1980); Bartlett (1993).
36 Budreckis, A.M. (ed.), *Eastern Lithuania: A collection of historical and ethno-graphic studies*, Lithuanian Association of the Vilnius Region, 1980, 1985, p. v.
37 Janis (1987).
38 Rutkis (1967), p. 501.
39 Velius (1989).
40 McCrickard (1990).
41 Rutkis (1967), p. 501.
42 Janis (1987).
43 Baltic Paganism is described in: Enthoven (1937), pp. 182–186; Jurgela (1948); Gimbutas (1963); Dunduliene (1989); and Searle (1992), pp. 15–17.
44 Wixman (1993), p. 427.
45 Schefferus (1704).
46 Manker (1968), p. 39.
47 Rabane, Peter, 'The Jüriöö Mäss Rebellion of 1343', in Ziedonis *et al.* (1974), pp. 35–48; Christiansen (1980), pp. 204–205.
48 Saks (1981), p. 12.
49 *Saga of Olaf Tryggvason* 78, 79.
50 *Gesta Hammaburgensis* IV.16.
51 Pliny IV.90.
52 Diodorus Siculus II.47.
53 Orosius, *Life of Alfred the Great*, ed. R. Pauli, London, 1893, pp. 253–257.
54 Henry of Livonia 24.8.
55 Moora and Viires (1964), p. 239.
56 McCrickard (1990), ch. 13.
57 Manker (1968), p. 36.
58 Raudonikas (1930), p. 78.

## 10  RUSSIA AND THE BALKANS

1 Descriptions of the Scythians can be found in Herodotus and in Pliny.
2 Details from Fisher (1936).
3 Fisher (1936), p. 383.
4 The Lithuanian word *balta* means 'white', hence Baltic Russia's translation into 'White' Russia: Russian *belo*.
5 *De Russorum, Moscovitorum et Tartarorum Religione, Sacrificiis, Nuptiarum, Funerum ritu* (1582).
6 Fisher (1936); *Cambridge Medieval History*, vol. IV (1966–1967).
7 What follows is taken from McCrickard (1990), ch. 9.
8 Accounts of Russian Paganism are scattered among various works on shaman-ism, totemism, etc. Some details can be found in J.C. Robertson (1874–1875), vol. V, ch. 7.
9 Oddo (1960).
10 Gunda (1968), pp.41–51.
11 Herodotus IV.33.
12 Leicht (1925), p. 249.
13 Beza (1920), *passim*.
14 Trombley (1993), ch. 1, *passim*.
15 Ibid., pp. 98–99, 147–168.
16 *Cambridge Medieval History*, vol. IV (1966–1967), p. 44.
17 *Bibliotheca*, codex 239.

18 Rodd (1892), p. 58, translation unattributed.
19 Ibid., p. 141, but see comments in Trombley (1993), p. 98, n. 4.
20 Rodd (1892), pp. 148–149.
21 Ibid., p. 139.
22 Ibid., pp. 138–140.
23 Ibid., p. 116.
24 Chuvin (1990), pp. 1–2.

## 11   PAGANISM REAFFIRMED

1 Bartlett (1993), p. 236.
2 Vesey-Fitzgerald (1973), p. 7.
3 Ibid., pp. 30–31.
4 Ibid., p. 207.
5 Liégeois (1986), *passim.*
6 Pizan (1489).
7 Borsi (1989), p. 96.
8 Valturio, Roberto, *De Re Militari*, vol. XII, Paris, 1532, p. 13.
9 Ricci (1925), pp. 166–199.
10 Authors' personal information, and cf. Hutton (1991), n. 37, p. 370.
11 Scarre (1987), p. 19.
12 E.g. Levack (1987), p. 21, with 60,000 deaths over the two centuries, and Hutton (1991), n. 37, p. 370, arguing for a mere 40,000.
13 Quoted in Scarre (1987), p. 20.
14 Levack (1987), p. 12; Scarre (1987), pp. 27–28, 53.
15 Arntz (1935), p. 268.
16 Flowers (1989), *passim.*
17 See Cohn (1975), chs 9 and 10, for the transformation of magic into witchcraft.
18 Cohn (1975), pp. 232–233.
19 Runeberg (1947), p. 239.
20 Cohn (1975), pp. 161–162.
21 Scarre (1987), p. 22, table 1, p. 25.
22 Anthony, John, 'A guide to tokens and allied "coins"', *Coin Year Book*, Brentwood, Numismatic Publishing Company, 1992, pp. 70–72.
23 Piggott (1968), pp. 178–179.
24 Cited in Scott, W.S., *The Athenians*, London, Golden Cockerel Press, 1943, pp. 43–44.
25 Scott, W.S., ed., *Shelley at Oxford*, London, 1944, p. 61.
26 Merivale (1969), p. 64.
27 Walter (1981), p. 9.
28 Carpenter (1906), pp. 46–47.
29 P. Green (1959), p. 252.
30 Ibid., pp. 139–147.
31 Eric Gill to William Rothenstein, 5 December, 1910, Clark Library, University of California, Los Angeles.
32 Clark (1947).
33 Hayhurst, Yvonne, 'A recent find of a horse skull in a house at Ballaugh, Isle of Man', *Folk-Lore*, vol. 100, no. 1, 1989, p. 105.
34 Bracelin (1960), pp. 153–154.
35 Spence (n.d., *c.*1941), p. 43.
36 *Hitler's Secret Conversations, 1941–1944*, eds N. Cameron and R.H. Steven, London, 1953, p. 51, cited by Yeowell (1993), p. 10.

37 Yeowell (1993).
38 *Odinic Religion Bulletin*, no. 40, November, 1984, p. 8.
39 Information from John Yeowell and Ralph Harrison of the Odinic Rite, Dr Ronald Hutton of the University of Bristol.
40 *The Moot Horn*, no. 1, September, 1992, p. 2.

# BIBLIOGRAPHY

(We have not given details of ancient texts, which are available in many editions, or of some of the articles in journals which are mentioned only once per chapter, especially in chapters 5–10. Details of these appear in the notes to the relevant chapter.)

Agrell, Sigurd (1934) *Lapptrumor och Runmagi*, Lund: C.W.K. Glerup.
Albrecht, C. (1928) 'Slawische Bildwerke', *Mainzer Zeitschrift*, vol. XXIII, pp. 46–53.
Anderson, J. (1868) *Scotland in Pagan Times*, Edinburgh: David Douglas.
Anwyl, Edward (1906) *Celtic Religion*, London: Archibald Constable.
Arntz, H. (1935) *Handbuch der Runenkunde*, Halle: Niemeyer.
Ayres, James (1977) *British Folk Art*, London: Barrie & Jenkins.
Bächtold-Stäubli, Hanns (ed.) (1927–1942) *Handworterbuch des deutschen Aberglaubens*, 9 vols, Berlin: Walter De Gruyter.
Backhouse, Edward and Tylor, Charles (1892) *Early Church History to the Death of Constantine*, London: Simpkin, Marshall, Hamilton, Kent & Co.
Baker, Margaret (1974) *Folklore and Customs in Rural England*, Newton Abbot: David & Charles.
Bannard, H.E. (1945) 'Some English sites of ancient heathen worship', *Hibbert Journal*, vol. XLIV, pp. 76–79.
Baring, A. and Cashford, J. (1993) *The Myth of the Goddess*, London: Book Club Associates.
Baring-Gould, S. (1967), *Some Curious Myths of the Middle Ages*, New York: University Books.
Baring-Gould, S. and Fisher, John (1907–1914) *The Lives of the British Saints*, 4 vols, London: Charles J. Clark.
Bartlett, R. (ed.) (1989) *Medieval Frontier Societies*, Oxford: Clarendon Press.
—— (1993) *The Expansion of Europe: Conquest, colonisation and cultural change 950–1350*, London: Book Club Associates.
Beck, H. (1965) *Das Ebersignum im Germanischen. Quellen und Forschungen zur Sprach- und Kulturgeschichte der Germ. Völker*, Berlin: De Gruyter.
Bernheimer, Richard (1952) *Wild Men in the Middle Ages*, Cambridge, Mass.: Harvard University Press.
Bettelheim, Bruno (1976) *The Uses of Enchantment. The Meaning and Importance of Fairy Tales*, London: Thames & Hudson.
Beza, M. (1920) *Paganism in Roumanian Folklore*, London and Toronto: J.M. Dent.
Binchy, D.A. (1959) 'The fair of Táiltiu and the feast of Tara', *Eriu*, vol. 18, 1958, pp. 113–138.
Bloch, Raymond (1958) *The Etruscans*, London: Thames & Hudson.

—— (1960) *The Origins of Rome*, London: Thames & Hudson.

Boardman, J., Griffin, J. and Murray, O. (1986, 1991) *The Oxford History of the Classical World*, Oxford: Oxford University Press.

Bonser, W. (1932) 'Survivals of Paganism in Anglo-Saxon England', *Transactions of the Birmingham Archaeological Society*, vol. LVI, pp. 37–71.

Borchardt, Frank (1971) *German Antiquity in Renaissance Myth*, Baltimore: Johns Hopkins University Press.

Bord, Janet and Bord, Colin (1985) *Sacred Waters*, London: Granada.

Borsi, Franco (1989) *Leon Battista Alberti, The Complete Works*, New York: Electa/Rizzoli.

Bötticher, Carl (1856) *Der Baumkultus der Hellenen*, Berlin: n.p.

Bracelin, Jack (1960) *Gerald Gardner, Witch*, London: Octagon.

Branston, Brian (1955) *Gods of the North*, London: Thames & Hudson.

—— (1957) *The Lost Gods of England*, London: Thames & Hudson.

Brent, P. (1975) *The Viking Saga*, London: Book Club Associates.

Bromwich, R. (1979) *Trioedd Ynys Prydein*, Cardiff: Cardiff University Press.

Brøndsted, J. (1964) *The Vikings*, Harmondsworth: Penguin.

Brown, A. (ed.) (1963) *Early English and Old Norse Studies*, London: Methuen.

Bucknell, Peter A. (1979) *Entertainment and Ritual, 600 to 1600*, London: Stainer & Bell.

Burkert, W. (1979) *Structure and History in Greek Mythology and Ritual*, Berkeley: University of California Press.

—— (1985) *Greek Religion, Archaic and Classical*, Oxford: Blackwell.

Byrne, Patrick F. (1967) *Witchcraft in Ireland*, Cork: The Mercier Press.

Cacquot, A. and Leibovici, M. (1968) *La Divination*, Paris.

*Cambridge Ancient History*, 3rd edn, vol. I, pt 1 (1970), vol. I, pt 2 (1971), eds I.E.S. Edwards, C.J. Gadd and N.G.L. Hammond; vol. II, pt 1 (1973), vol. II, pt 2 (1975), ed. I.E.S. Edwards, C.J. Gadd, N.G.L. Hammond and E. Sollberger, Cambridge: Cambridge University Press.

—— 2nd edn (1951–), vol. III (1970), vol. IV (1969), vol. V (1979), vol. VI (1969), ed. J.B. Bury, S.A. Cook and F.E. Adcock; vol. VII (1969), vol. VIII (1970), vol. IX (1966), vol. X (1971), vol. XI (1969), ed. S.A. Cook, F.E. Adcock and M.P. Charlesworth; vol. XII (1965), ed. S.A. Cook, F.E. Adcock, M.P. Charlesworth and N.H. Baynes, Cambridge: Cambridge University Press.

*Cambridge Medieval History* (1964–1967), vol. I. (1967), vol. II (1964), ed. H.M.G. Watkin and J.P. Whitney; vol. III (1964), ed. H.M.G. Watkin, J.P. Whitney, J.R. Tanner and C.W. Previté-Orton; vol. IV, pt 1 (1966), vol. IV, pt 2 (1967), ed. J.M. Hussey; vols V–VIII (1964), ed. J.R. Tanner, C.W. Previté-Orton and Z.N. Brooke, Cambridge: Cambridge University Press.

Campbell, J.F. (1860, 1890) *Popular Tales of the Western Highlands*, 4 vols, Edinburgh (1860), Paisley (1890).

Carpenter, Edward (1906) *Civilisation: Its Cause and Cure*, London: Swan Sonnenschein.

Carston, F.L. (1954) *The Origin of Prussia*, Oxford: Oxford University Press.

Cavallius (1863) *Hyltén: Wärend och Widerne*, Stockholm.

Chadwick, H. Munro (1899) *The Cult of Othin*, London: Cambridge University Press.

—— (1900) 'Teutonic priesthood', *Folk-Lore*, vol. XI, pp. 268–300.

Chadwick, N.K. (ed.) (1954) *Studies in Early British History*, Cambridge: Cambridge University Press.

Chaney, W. (1960) 'Paganism to Christianity in Anglo-Saxon England', *Harvard Theological Review*, vol. LIII, pp. 197–217.

233

—— (1970) *The Cult of Kingship in Anglo-Saxon England*, Manchester: Manchester University Press.

Christiansen, E. (1980) *The Northern Crusades*, London: Macmillan.

Chuvin, Pierre (1990) *Chronique des Derniers Païens*, Paris: Belles Lettres/Fayard.

Clark, Barrett O. (1947) *Eugene O'Neill: The Man and his Plays*, New York.

Clemen, Carl (1916) *Die Reste der primitiven Religion im ältesten Christentum*, Giessen.

Cockayne, T.O. (1864–1866) *Leechdoms, Wortcunning and Starcraft in Early England*, 3 vols, London: Rolls Series.

Cohn, N. (1975) *Europe's Inner Demons*, London: Heinemann.

Constantine, J. (1948) *History of the Lithuanian Nation*, New York: Lithuanian Cultural Institute Historical Research Section.

Cramp, R. (1957) 'Beowulf and archaeology', *Medieval Archaeology*, vol. I, pp. 60ff.

Crawford, O.G.S. (1957) *The Eye Goddess*, London: Phoenix House.

Cumont, F. (1910) *The Mysteries of Mithras*, London.

—— (1929) *Les religions orientales dans le paganisme romain*, Paris.

Cunliffe, B. (1992) *The Celtic World*, London: Constable.

Curtin, Jeremiah (1894) *Hero-Tales of Ireland*, London: Macmillan.

Danielli, M. (1945) 'Initiation ceremonial from Norse Literature', *Folk-Lore*, vol. 56, pp. 229–245.

Davidson, H.R.E. (1964) *Gods and Myths of Northern Europe*, Harmondsworth: Penguin.

—— (1969) *Scandinavian Mythology*, London: Paul Hamlyn.

—— (1981) 'The Germanic World', in M. Loewe and C. Blacker (eds), *Divination and Oracles*, London: George Allen & Unwin.

—— (1987) *Myths and Symbols in Pagan Europe*, Manchester: Manchester University Press.

Davies, Glenys (ed.) (1989) 'Polytheistic systems', *Cosmos Yearbook No. 5*, Edinburgh: The Traditional Cosmology Society.

Day, J. Wentworth (1963) 'Witches and wizards of the Fens', *Country Life*, 28 March.

Dennis, A., Foote, P. and Perkins, R. (trans.) (1980) *Grágás: Laws of Early Iceland*, Winnipeg: University of Manitoba Press.

De Vries, Jan (1961) *Keltische Religion*, Stuttgart: Kohlhammer.

Dickins, B. (1915) *Runic and Heroic Poems of the Old Teutonic Peoples*, Cambridge: Cambridge University Press.

Diesner, H.-J. (1978) *The Great Migration*, trans. C.S.V. Salt, London: George Prior.

Dillon, Myles and Chadwick, Nora K. (1973) *The Celtic Realms*, London: Cardinal.

Diószegi, V. (1968) *Popular Beliefs in Siberia*, Bloomington: Indiana University Press.

Dixon, J.A. (1886) *Gairloch*, Edinburgh.

Dodds, E.R. (1951) *The Greeks and the Irrational*, Berkeley: University of California Press.

Drake-Carnell, F.J. (1938) *Old English Customs and Ceremonies*, London: Batsford.

Duchesne, I. (1904) *Christian Worship, its Origin and Evolution*, trans. M.L. McLure, London, SPCK.

Dumezil, G. (ed) (1973) *The Gods of the Ancient Northmen*, trans. E. Haugen, Berkeley: University of California Press.

Dunduliene, P. (1989) *Pagonybe Lietuvoje: moteriskios dievybes*, Vilnius: Mintis.

Durdin-Robertson, Lawrence (1982) *Juno Covella*, Enniscorthy: Cesara Publications.

Durmeyer, Johann (1883) *Reste altgermanischen Heidentums in Unsern Tagen*, Nuremberg.

Elliott, D. and Elliott, J. (1982) *Gods of the Byways*, Oxford: Museum of Modern Art.

Ellis, Hilda R. (1943) *The Road to Hel*, Cambridge: Cambridge University Press.

Ellis, Peter Berresford (1990) *The Celtic Empire*, London: Constable.

Enthoven, R.E. (1937) 'The Latvians and their folk-songs', in *Folk-Lore*, vol. XLVIII, pp. 183–186.

Evans, George Ewart (1966) *The Pattern Under the Plough*, London: Faber & Faber.

Evans-Wentz, W.Y. (1911) *The Fairy Faith in Celtic Countries*, Oxford: Oxford University Press.

Ewen, C. L'Estrange (1938) *Some Witchcraft Criticisms*, London: privately published.

Fillipetti, Hervé and Trotereau, Janine (1978) *Symboles et pratiques rituelles dans la maison paysanne traditionelle*, Paris: Editions Berger Lerrault.

Firmicus Maternus (1952) *De Errore Profanorum Religionum*, Munich: Hüber.

Fisher, H.A.L. (1936) *A History of Europe*, London: Arnold.

Flowers, Stephen E. (1981) 'Revival of Germanic religion in contemporary Anglo-American culture', *Mankind Quarterly*, vol. 21, no. 3, pp. 279–294.

—— (1989) *The Galdrabók, an Icelandic Grimoire*, York Beach: Samuel Weiser.

Fol, A. and Marazov, I. (1978) *A la recherche des Thraces*, Paris.

Fowler, W. Warde (1911) *The Religious Experience of the Roman People*, London: Macmillan.

Frend, W.H.C. (1984) *The Rise of Christianity*, London: Dartin, Longman & Todd.

Gardner, Gerald (1941) *A Goddess Arrives*, London: Arthur Stockwell.

—— (1948) *High Magic's Aid*, London: Michael Houghton.

—— (1954) *Witchcraft Today*, London: Rider.

—— (1959) *The Meaning of Witchcraft*, London: Aquarian Press.

Garmonsway, G.N. (ed. and trans.) (1972) *The Anglo-Saxon Chronicle*, London: J.M. Dent.

Gelling, Peter and Davidson, Hilda Ellis (1969) *The Chariot of the Sun*, London: J.M. Dent.

Getty, Adele (1990) *Goddess, Mother of Living Nature*, London: Thames & Hudson.

Gildas (1938), *The Story of the Loss of Britain*, ed. and trans. A.W. Wade-Evans, London: SPCK.

Gimbutas, Marija (1963), *The Balts*, New York and London: Thames & Hudson.

—— (1982) *The Goddesses and Gods of Old Europe*, London: Thames & Hudson.

Glover, T.R. (1909) *The Conflict of Religions in the Early Roman Empire*, London: Methuen.

Godfrey, C.J. (1962) *The Church in Anglo-Saxon England*, Cambridge: Cambridge University Press.

Golther, Wolfgang (1895) *Handbuch der Germanisches Mythologie*, Leipzig: Köhler & Amelang.

Gomme, G.L. (1883) *Folklore Relics in Early Village Life*, London: n.p.

Goodison, L. (1990) *Moving Heaven and Earth*, London: The Women's Press.

Gorman, M. (1986) 'Nordic and Celtic religion in southern Scandinavia during the late Bronze Age and early Iron Age', in T. Ahlbäck (ed.), *Old Norse and Finnish Religions and Celtic Place-Names*, Stockholm: Almqvist & Wiksell International.

Goulstone, J. (1985) *The Summer Solstice Games*, Bexleyheath, Kent: privately published.

Graber, Georg (1912) *Sagen aus Kärnten*, Leipzig.

Graves, R. (1952) *The White Goddess*, London: Faber & Faber.

Green, M. (1986) *The Gods of the Celts*, Gloucester: Alan Sutton.

—— (1991) *The Sun-Gods of Ancient Europe*, London: Batsford.

Green, P. (1959) *Kenneth Grahame: A Biography*, London: John Murray.

Grimm, J.L. (1880–1888) *Teutonic Mythology*, 4 vols, ed. and trans. J.E. Stallybrass, London: Bell.

Grinsell, L. (1972) 'Witchcraft at barrows and other prehistoric sites', *Antiquity*, vol. 46, p. 58.

—— (1976) *Folklore of Prehistoric Sites in Britain*, Newton Abbot: David & Charles.

Grönbech, Vilhelm (1931) *The Culture of the Teutons*, London: Oxford University Press.

Guillaume, A. (1938) *Prophecy and Divination*, London.

Gunda, B. (1968) 'Survivals of totemism in the Hungarian táltos tradition', in V. Diószegi, (ed.), *Popular Beliefs in Siberia*, Bloomington: Indiana University Press.

Guyonvarc'h, Christian-J. (1980) *Textes Mythologiques Irlandais*, Rennes: Ogam-Celticum.

Hadingham, Evan (1976) *Circles and Standing Stones*, New York: Anchor/Doubleday.

Halifax, Joan (1968) *Shamanic Voices*, New York: Dutton.

Hall, Nor (1980) *The Moon and the Goddess*, London: The Women's Press.

Halliday, W.R. (1925) *The Pagan Background to Early Christianity*, London: Hodder & Stoughton.

Hallowell, A. Irving (1926) 'Bear ceremonialism in the northern hemisphere', *American Anthropologist*, N.S., p. 28.

Harding, M. Esther (1955, 1971) *Womens' Mysteries, Ancient and Modern*, London: Rider.

Harrison, Jane Ellen (1903) *Prolegomena to the Study of Greek Religion*, Cambridge: Cambridge University Press.

—— (1906) *Primitive Athens as Described by Thucydides*, Cambridge: Cambridge University Press.

—— (1924) *Mythology, our Debt to the Greeks and Romans*, London.

Haseleoff, Günther (1979) *Kunststile des Frühen Mittelalters*, Stuttgart: Württembergisches Landesmuseum.

Henderson, George (1910) *The Norse Influence on Celtic Scotland*, Glasgow: James Maclehose & Sons.

Henig, M. (1984) *Religion in Roman Britain*, London: Batsford.

Herold, Basilius Johannes (1554) *Heydenweldt und irer Götter*, Basle.

Herrmann, P. (1929) *Das altgermanische Priesterwesen*, Jena: Diederichs.

Hersey, G. (1988) *The Lost Meaning of Classical Architecture*, Cambridge, Mass.: MIT Press.

Heyl, Johann Adolf, (1897) 'Volkssagen, Bräuche und Meinungen aus Tirol', Brixen, Nr. 52.

Hibbert, S. (1831) 'Memoir on the Things of Orkney and Shetland', *Archaeologia Scotica*, vol. 3, pp. 103–211.

Hopf, Ludwig (1888) *Thierorakel und Orakelthiere in alter und neuer Zeit*, Stuttgart.

Hutton, R. (1991) *The Pagan Religions of the Ancient British Isles*, Oxford: Blackwell.

Huxley, F. (1974) *The Way of the Sacred*, London: Aldus.

Jahn, Ulrich (1886) *Hexenwesen und Zauberei in Pommern*, Breslau.

James, E.O. (1955) *The Nature and Function of Priesthood*, London: Thames & Hudson.

Janis, T. (1987) *The Ancient Latvian Religion*, Chicago: Dievturiba Lituanis.

Jeanmaire, H. (1951) *Le Culte de Dionysus*, Paris.

Johannessen (1974) *A History of the Old Icelandic Commonwealth*, Winnipeg: University of Manitoba Press.

Johnson, Walter (1912) *Byways in British Archaeology*, Cambridge: Cambridge University Press.

Jones, Prudence (1982a) *Eight and Nine: Sacred Numbers of Sun and Moon in the Pagan North*, Bar Hill: Fenris-Wolf.

—— (1982b) *Sundial and Compass Rose: Eight-fold Time Division in Northern Europe*, Bar Hill: Fenris-Wolf.

—— (1989) 'Celestial and terrestrial orientation', in Annabella Kitson (ed.), *History and Astrology*, London: Unwin Hyman.

—— (1990) 'The Grail quest as initiation: Jessie Weston and the vegetation theory', in John Matthews (ed.), *The Household of the Grail*, Wellingborough: Aquarian Press.

—— (1991) *Northern Myths of the Constellations*, Cambridge: Fenris-Wolf.

Jones, Prudence and Matthews, Caitlín (eds) (1990) *Voices from the Circle. The Heritage of Western Paganism*, Wellingborough: Aquarian Press.

Jung, C.G. (1963) *Memories, Dreams, Reflections*, Glasgow: Collins.

Jung, Erich (1939) *Germanische Götter und Helden in Christlicher Zeit*, Munich and Berlin: J.F. Lehmanns Verlag.

Jurgela, C. (1948) *A History of the Lithuanian Nation*, New York: Lithuanian National Institute Cultural Research Section.

Kålund, Kristian (ed.) (1907) *Den islandske Lægebog*, Copenhagen: Luno.

Kaul, Flemming, Marazov, Ivan, Best, Jan and De Vries, Nanny (1991) *Thracian Tales on the Gundestrup Cauldron*, publications of the Holland Travelling University, vol. 1, Amsterdam: Najade Press.

Keller, W.J. (1975) *The Etruscans*, London: Cape.

Kemble, J.M. (1876) *The Saxons in England*, London.

Kendrick, T.D. (1927, 1966), *The Druids*, London: Frank Cass.

Kermode, P.M.C. and Herdmans, W.A. (1914) *Manks Antiquities*, Liverpool: University of Liverpool Press.

Keysler, J.G. (1720), *Antiquitates Selectae Septentrionales et Celticae*, Hanover.

Kothari, K. (1982) unnamed chapter in Elliott, D. and Elliot J., *Gods of the Byways*, Oxford: Museum of Modern Art.

Kraft, John (1985) *The Goddess in the Labyrinth*, Åbo: Åbo Academy Press.

Laing, G.J. (1931) *Survivals of Roman Religion*, London: Harrap.

Lane Fox, R.L. (1986) *Pagans and Christians*, London: Oxford University Press.

Lasicius (Bishop Ján Lasicki) (1580, 1615) *De Diis Sarmagitarum*, Basle.

—— (1582) *Religio Borussorum*, Basle.

—— (1582) *De Russorum, Moscovitorum et Tartarorum Religione, Sacrificiis, Nuptiarum, Funerum ritu*, Basle.

Legge, E. (1915) *Forerunners and Rivals of Christianity*, 2 vols, Cambridge: Cambridge University Press.

Leicht, P.S. (1925) *Tracce de paganesmo fra gli Slavi dell'Isonzo*.

Leland, Charles G. (1899, 1974) *Aradia, The Gospel of the Witches*, London: C.W. Daniel.

Le Roux, Françoise and Guyonvarc'h, Christian-J. (1978) *Les druides*, Rennes: Ogam-Celticum.

Lethaby, W.R. (1969, 1892) *Architecture, Mysticism and Myth*, London: n.p.

Levack, B.P. (1987) *The Witch Hunt in Early Modern Europe*, London: Longman.

Lewis, Don (1975) *Religious Superstition through the Ages*, Oxford: Mowbray.

Lewis, I.M. (1971) *Ecstatic Religion*, Harmondsworth: Penguin.

Lewis, M.J.T. (1966) *Temples in Roman Britain*, Cambridge: Cambridge University Press.

Liebeschütz, J.H.W.G. (1979) *Continuity and Change in Roman Religion*, Oxford: Clarendon Press.

Liégeois, Jean-Pierre (1986) *Gypsies: An Illustrated History*, London: Al-Saqi Books.

Lindenschmit, L. (1874–1877) *Die Altherthümer unserer heidnischen Vorzeit*, Mainz.

Loewe, M. & Blacker, C. (eds) (1981) *Divination and Oracles*, London: Allen & Unwin.

Lohmeyer, Karl (1920) *Die Sagen des Saarbrücker und Birkenfelder Landes*, Leipzig.

Lommel, A. (1967) *Shamanism*, New York: McGraw-Hill.

Lönnrot, Elias, (1963), *The Kalevala*, trans. Francis Peabody Magoun, Cambridge, Mass.: Harvard University Press.

Lundkvist, Sune (1967) 'Uppsala hedna-tempel och första Katedral', *Norrdisk Tidskrift*, pp. 236–242.

McCrickard, J. (1986) (as Sínead Sula Grián) *The Sun Goddesses of Europe*, Glastonbury: Gothic Image.

——— (1990) *Eclipse of the Sun: An Investigation into Sun and Moon myths*, Glastonbury: Gothic Image.

MacFarlane, Alan (1970) *Witchcraft in Tudor and Stuart England*, London: Routledge & Kegan Paul.

McLean, Adam (1983) *The Triple Goddess*, Edinburgh: Hermetic Research.

MacMullen, Ramsay (1981) *Paganism in the Roman Empire*, Princeton: Yale University Press.

MacNeill, Maire (1962) *The Festival of Lughnasa*, Oxford: Oxford University Press.

Magnússon, E. (1901) *The Conversion of Iceland to Christianity, A.D. 1000*, Saga Book of the Viking Club, 2.

Manker, E. (1968) '*Seite*, cult and drum magic of the Lapps', in V. Diószegi (ed.), *Popular Beliefs in Siberia*, Bloomington: Indiana University Press.

Mannhardt, Wilhelm (1860) *Die Götter der deutschen und nordischen Völker*, Berlin.

Maringer, J. (1977) 'Priests and priestesses in prehistoric Europe', *History of Religions*, vol. 17, no. 2, pp. 101–120.

Matthews, Caitlín (1989) *The Elements of the Goddess*, Shaftesbury: Element Books.

Mauny, Raymond (1978) 'The exhibition on "The World of Souterrains" at Vezelay (Burgundy, France) (1977)', *Subterranea Britannica Bulletin*, no. 7.

Mayer, Elard Hugo (1891) *Germanische Mythologie*, Berlin: Mayer & Müller.

Mayr-Harting, H. (1972) *The Coming of Christianity to Anglo-Saxon England*, London: B.T. Batsford.

Megaw, Ruth and Megaw, Vincent (1989) *Celtic Art, From its Beginnings to the Book of Kells*, London: Thames & Hudson.

Merivale, Patricia (1969) *Pan the Goat-God: His Myth in Modern Times*, Cambridge, Mass.: Harvard University Press.

Merrifield, Ralph (1987) *The Archaeology of Ritual and Magic*, London: Guild.

Meyrick, Samuel Rush and Smith, Charles Hamilton (1815) *Costume of the Original Inhabitants of the British Islands*, London.

Michels, A.K. (1967) *The Calendar of the Roman Republic*, Princeton: Yale University Press.

Mitchell, Sir A. (1862) 'The various superstitions in the N.W. Highlands and Islands of Scotland', *Proceedings of the Antiquarian Society of Scotland*, vol. IV, Edinburgh.

Mogk, E. (1927) *Germanische Religionsgeschichte und Mythologie*, Berlin: Schikowski.

Moltke, Erik (1984) *Runes and Their Origin: Denmark and Elsewhere*, National Museum of Denmark: Copenhagen.

Mookerjee, A. (1988) *Kali, the Feminine Force*, London: Thames & Hudson.

Moora H. and Viires, A. (1964) *Abriss der Estnischen Volkskunde*, Tallinn: Estnischer Staatsverlag.

Morris, William and Magnússon, Eiríkr (1891) *The Saga Library Vol. I*, London: Bernard Quaritch.

Morrison, Arthur (1900) *Cunning Murrell*, London: Methuen.

Müller, W. (1961) Die Heilige Stadt, Roma Quadrata, himmliches Jerusalem und die Mythe vom Weltnabel, Stuttgart.

Murray, M.A. (1921) *The Witch Cult in Western Europe*, Oxford: Clarendon Press.
—— (1954) *The Divine King in England*, London: Faber & Faber.
—— (1963) *The Genesis of Religion*, London: Routledge & Kegan Paul.
Myres, J.N.L. (1986) *The English Settlements*, Oxford: Clarendon Press.
Nance, R.M. (1935) 'The Plen an Gwary', *Journal of the Royal Institute of Cornwall*, vol. 24, pp. 190–211.
Nelli, R. (1963) *L'Erotique des Troubadours*, Toulouse: Privat.
Nennius (1938), *History of the Britons*, ed. and trans. A.W. Wade-Evans, London: SPCK.
Neumann, Erich (1963) *The Great Mother*, Princeton: Princeton University Press.
Nioradze, Georg (1925) *Der Schamanismus bei den sibirischen Völkern*, Stuttgart: Strecker & Schröder.
Norman, E.R. and St Joseph, J.K.S. (1969) *The Early Development of Irish Society*, Cambridge: Cambridge University Press.
Oddo, Gilbert L. (1960) *Slovakia and Its Peoples*, New York: Robert Speller & Sons.
Ogilvie, R.H. (1976) *Early Rome and the Etruscans*, London: Oxford University Press.
Olsen, M. (1928) *Farms and Fanes of Ancient Norway*, Oslo: Bokcentralen.
O'Rahilly, T.F. (1946) *Early Irish History and Mythology*, Dublin: Institute for Advanced Studies.
Owen, G.R. (1981) *Rites and Religions of the Anglo-Saxons*, Newton Abbot: David & Charles.
Owen, Trefor M. (1987) *Welsh Folk Customs*, Llandysul: Gomer Press.
Paget, Robert F. (1967) *In the Footsteps of Orpheus: The Discovery of the Ancient Greek Underworld*, London: Robert Hale.
Paglia, C. (1990) *Sexual Personae, Art and Decadence from Nefertiti to Emily Dickinson*, New Haven: Yale University Press.
Palmer, R.E.A. (1974) *Roman Religion and the Roman Empire*, Philadelphia: University of Pennsylvania Press.
Pálsson, H. and Edwards, P. (trans.) (1978) *Orkneyinga Saga: The History of the Earls of Orkney*, London: Hogarth Press.
—— (trans.) (1980) *Landnámabók: The Book of Settlements*, Winnipeg: University of Manitoba Press.
Parke, H.W. (1939) *A History of the Delphic Oracle*, Oxford: Blackwell.
—— (1967) *The Oracles of Zeus: Dodona, Olympia, Ammon*, Oxford: Blackwell.
Patai, R. (1967) *The Hebrew Goddess*, New York: Ktav.
Pennant, Thomas (1774) *A Tour in Scotland and Voyage to the Hebrides*, London.
Pennick, N.C. (1981) *The Subterranean Kingdom: A Survey of Man-Made Structures Beneath the Earth*, Wellingborough: Turnstone.
—— (1990) *Mazes and Labyrinths*, London: Robert Hale.
—— (1992a) *Secret Games of the Gods*, New York Beach: Samuel Weiser.
—— (1992b) *The Pagan Book of Days. A Guide to the Festivals, Traditions and Sacred Days of the Year*, Rochester, Vermont: Destiny Books.
—— (in preparation) *Celtic Sacred Landscapes*.
Petrie, W. Flinders (1912) *The Revolutions of Civilisation*, London: Harper & Row.
Pettazzoni, R. (1954) 'West Slav Paganism', in *Essays on the History of Religion*, trans. H.J. Rose, Leiden: E.J. Brill.
Philippson, E.A. (1929) *Germanisches Heidentum bei den Angelsachsen*, Leipzig: Tauchnitz.
Phillips, Guy Ragland (1987) *The Unpolluted God*, Pocklington: Northern Lights.
Picardt, Johan (1660) *Korte Beschrijvinge van eenige verborgene antiquiteten*, Amsterdam.

Piggott, Stuart (1965) *Ancient Europe*, Edinburgh: Edinburgh University Press.
—— (1968) *The Druids*, London: Thames & Hudson.
Pizan, Christine de, trans. William Caxton (1489) *The Book of Fayttes of Armes and Chyvalrye*, ed. A.T.P. Byles, London, 1932.
Pomey, Antoine (1694) *The Pantheon, Representing the Fabulous Histories of the Heathen Gods and Most Illustrious Heroes*, London.
Porter, Enid (1969) *Cambridgeshire Customs and Folklore*, London: Routledge & Kegan Paul.
Powell, T.G.E. (1980) *The Celts*, London: Thames & Hudson.
Praetorius, M. (1780, 1871) *Delictae Prussicae oder Preussische Schaubühne*, Berlin: Duncker.
Raoult, Michel (1980) *Genealogical Tree of Occidental Bards, Gorsedds, Eisteddfods and Groves, 1100 AD to 1979 AD*, London: The Golden Section Order.
Raudonikas, W.J. (1930) *Die Nordmannen der Wikingerzeit und das Ladogagebiet*, Stockholm.
Rees, Alwyn and Rees, Brinley (1961) *Celtic Heritage*, London: Thames & Hudson.
Reeves, Dr (1861) 'Saint Maelrubha: his history and churches', *Proceedings of the Society of Antiquaries of Scotland*, vol. III, pt 2.
Reuter, Otto Sigfrid (1934) *Germanische Himmelskunde*, Leipzig: J.F. Lehmann.
—— (1987) *Skylore of the North*, trans. Michael Behrend, Bar Hill: Runestaff.
Rhys, John (1888) *The Hibbert Lectures on the Growth of Religion as Illustrated by Celtic Heathendom*, London: Williams & Norgate.
—— (1901) *Celtic Folklore*, Oxford: Clarendon Press.
Ricci, C. (1925) *Il tempietto Malatestiano*, Milan.
Riehl, Hans (1976) *Die Völkerwanderung*, Pfaffenhofen: Ilm.
Robertson, J.C. (1874–1875) *A History of the Christian Church*, 8 vols, London: John Murray.
Robertson, Olivia (1975) *The Call of Isis*, Enniscorthy: Cesara Publications.
Rochholz, E.L. (1862) *Naturmythen. Neue Schweizersagen gesammelt und erläutert*, Leipzig.
—— (1867) *Deutscher Glaube und Brauch im Spiegel der heidnischen Vorzeit*, 2 vols, Berlin.
—— (1870) *Drei Gaugöttinen, Walburg, Verena und Gertrud als deutsche Kirchenheilige*, Leipzig.
Rodd, R. (1892) *The Customs and Lore of Modern Greece*, London: David Stott.
Rose, H.J. (1948) *Ancient Roman Religion*, London: Hutchinson.
—— (ed.) (1954) *Essays on the History of Religion*, Leiden: Brill.
Rosenberg, Alfons (1988) *Die Frau als Seherin und Prophetin*, Munich: Kösel Verlag.
Ross, A. (1967, 1974) *Pagan Celtic Britain*, London: Cardinal.
—— (1970, 1986a) *The Pagan Celts*, London: Batsford.
—— (1986b) *Druids, Gods and Heroes of Celtic Mythology*, London: Routledge & Kegan Paul.
Runeberg, A. (1947) *Witches, Demons and Fertility Magic*, Helsingfors: Societas Scientiarum Fennica.
Rutkis, J. (ed.) (1967) *Latvia, Country and People*, Stockholm: Latvian National Foundation.
Rutkowski, B. (1986) *The Cult Places of the Aegean*, New Haven: Yale University Press.
Saks, E.V. (1981) *The Estonian Vikings*, Cardiff: Boreas.
Salway, P. (1981) *Roman Britain*, Oxford: Clarendon Press.
Santillana, G. de and Dechend, H. von (1969, 1977) *Hamlet's Mill*, Boston: Godine.
Scarre, G. (1987) *Witchcraft and Magic in Sixteenth- and Seventeenth-century Europe*, London: Macmillan.

Schefferus, J. (1704) *Lapponia, id est, Regionis Lapponum,* 1673, trans. T. Newborough, London.

Scholl, H.-C. (1929) *Die Drei Ewigen,* Jena: Diederich.

Schröder, Franz Rolf (1924) *Germanentum und Hellenismus,* Heidelberg: Carl Winter.

Schuchhardt, C. (1926) *Arkona, Rethra, Vineta,* Berlin.

Schütte, Godmund (1923) *Dänisches Heidentum,* 2 vols, Heidelberg.

Schutz, H. (1983) *The Prehistory of Germanic Europe,* London: Yale University Press.

Schwarzfischer, Karl (1975) 'Study of Erdställe in the Danubian area of Germany', *Subterranea Britannica Bulletin,* no. 2.

Schwebel, Oskar (1887) *Tod und Ewiges Leben in deutschen Volksglauben,* Minden.

Scott, George Riley (n.d.) *Phallic Worship,* Westport, Conn.: Associated Bookseller.

Scullard, H.H. (1967) *The Etruscan Cities and Rome,* London: Thames & Hudson.

Scully, Vincent (1962) *The Earth, The Temple and the Gods,* Yale: Yale University Press.

Searle, M. (1992) 'Romuva, the revival of Lithuanian heathenism', *Odinism Today,* vol. 5, London: Odinic Rite.

Sébillot, Paul (1904–1907) *Folk-lore de France,* 4 vols, Paris.

—— (1908) *Le Paganisme contemporain,* Paris.

Sepp (1890) *Die Religion der alten Deutschen und ihr Fortbestand in Volkssagen, Aufzügen und Festgebräuchen,* Munich.

Shippey, T.A. (1976) *Poems of Wisdom and Learning in Old English,* Cambridge: Cambridge University Press.

Simpson, J. (1967) 'Some Scandinavian sacrifices', *Folk-Lore,* vol. LXXVIII, pp. 190–202.

Skene, W.F. (1876) *Celtic Scotland,* Edinburgh.

Smith, J.H. (1976) *The Death of Classical Paganism,* London: Chapman.

Solmsen, F. (1979) *Isis among the Greeks and Romans,* Cambridge, Mass.: Harvard University Press.

Spence, Lewis (n.d., *c.*1941) *The Occult Causes of the Present War,* London: Rider.

—— (1971) *The History and Origins of Druidism,* London: Aquarian Press.

Stanley, E.G. (1975) *The Search for Anglo-Saxon Paganism,* Cambridge: D.S. Brewer.

Stenton, Sir F. (1971) *Anglo-Saxon England,* 3rd edn, Oxford: Clarendon Press.

Stober, August (1892), *Die Sagen des Elsasses,* 2 vols, Strasbourg.

Stokes, W. (1862) *Three Irish Glossaries,* London.

Storms, G. (1948) *Anglo-Saxon Magic,* The Hague: Nijhoff.

Strömbäck, Dag (1935) *Sejd,* Stockholm: Geber.

—— (1975) *The Conversion of Iceland,* trans. Peter Foote, London: Viking Society for Northern Research.

Strutynski, U. (1975) 'Germanic divinities in weekday names', *Journal of Indo-European Studies,* vol. 3, pp. 363–384.

Sturluson, Snorri (1964) *Heimskringla: History of the Kings of Norway,* trans. L.M. Hollander, Austin: University of Texas Press.

Syme, Ronald (1939, 1971) *The Roman Revolution,* Oxford: Oxford University Press.

Szabó, Miklós (1971) *The Celtic Heritage in Hungary,* trans. Paul Aston, Budapest: Corvina Press.

Temple, Robert K.G. (1984) *Conversations with Eternity: Ancient Man's Attempts to Know the Future,* London: Rider.

Thompson, E.A. (1966) *The Visigoths in the Time of Ulfila,* Oxford: Clarendon Press.

Thonger, Richard (1966) *A Calendar of German Customs*, London: Oswald Wolff.

Thorpe, B. (1840) *Ancient Laws and Institutes of England*, 2 vols, London.

Tille, A. (1899) *Yule and Christmas, their Place in the Germanic Year*, London: David Nutt.

Trede, T. (1901) *Das Heidentum in der römischen Kirche*, 4 vols, Gotha.

Trombley, F.R. (1993) *Hellenic Religion and Christianization, c. 370–529*, Leiden: E.J. Brill.

Turville-Petre, E.O.G. (1964) *Myth and Religion of the North*, London: Weidenfeld & Nicolson.

Velius, N. (1981, 1989), *The World Outlook of the Ancient Balts*, Vilnius: Mintis.

Vernaliken, Theodor (1858) *Völksüberlieferungen aus der Schweiz*, Vienna.

Vesey-Fitzgerald, Brian (1973) *Gypsies of Britain*, Newton Abbot: David & Charles.

Vyncke, F. (1968) 'La divination chez les Slaves', in A. Caquot and M. Leibovici (eds), *La Divination*, Paris.

Wacher, John (1974) *The Towns of Roman Britain*, London: Batsford.

Walker, J.R. (1883) '"Holy Wells" in Scotland', *Proceedings of the Society of Antiquaries of Scotland*, Edinburgh.

Wallace-Hadrill, J.M. (1952, 1967) *The Barbarian West, 400–1000*, London: Hutchinson.

Walter, Nicolas (1981) 'Edward Carpenter', *Freedom Anarchist Review*, vol. 42, no. 4.

Warburg, A. (1920) *Heidnisch-Antike Weissagung in Wort und Bild zu Luthers Zeiten*, Heidelberg: Carl Winter Verlag.

Warde-Fowler, W. (1911) *The Religious Experience of the Roman People*, London: Macmillan.

Wedeck, Harry E. (1975) *Treasury of Witchcraft*, Secaucus: Citadel Press.

Wesche, Heinrich (1940) *Der althochdeutsche Wortschatz im Gebiete des Zaubers und der Weissagung*, Haale a.d. Saale: Niemeyer.

Wheatley, Paul (1971) *The Pivot of the Four Quarters*, Edinburgh: Edinburgh University Press.

Wilson, D.M. and Klindt-Jensen, O. (1966) *Viking Art*, London: George Allen & Unwin.

Wilson, Steve (1993) *Robin Hood. The Spirit of the Forest*, London: Neptune Press.

Wirth, Hermann (1932–1936) *Die Heilige Urschrift der Menschheit*, Leipzig: Köhler & Amelang.

Wissowa, G. (1912) *Religion und Kultus der Römer*, 2nd edn, Munich: Beck.

Wixman, R. (1993) 'The Middle Volga: ethnic archipelago in a Russian sea', in I. Bremner and R. Taras (eds), *Nations and Politics in the Soviet Successor States*, Cambridge: Cambridge University Press.

Wolfram, H. (1988) *The History of the Goths*, Berkeley: University of California Press.

Wood-Martin, W.G. (1902) *Traces of the Elder Faiths of Ireland*, London.

Yeowell, John (1993) *Odinism and Christianity Under the Third Reich*, London: The Odinic Rite.

Zaborsky, Oskar von (1936) *Urväter-Erbe in deutscher Volkskunst*, Leipzig: Köhler & Amelang.

Ziedonis Jr, A., Winter, William L. and Valgemäe, M. (eds) (1974) *Baltic History*, Columbus, Ohio: Association for the Advancement of Baltic Studies.

Zosimus (1967) *Historia Nova*, trans. J. Buchanan, San Antonio: Trinity University Press.

# INDEX